MEDIEVAL TEXTS

GENERAL EDITORS

V. H. Galbraith and R. A. B. Mynors

VITA EDWARDI SECUNDI

THE LIFE OF
EDWARD THE SECOND

Vita Edwardi Secundi

Monachi Cuiusdam Malmesberiensis

Thomas Nelson and Sons Ltd

London Edinburgh Paris Melbourne Toronto and New York

The Life of
Edward the Second

by the
So-called Monk of Malmesbury

Translated from the Latin with Introduction
and Notes by

N. Denholm-Young, M.A., D.Litt.

*Sometime Fellow of Magdalen College, Oxford;
now Senior Lecturer in History, University College of
North Wales, Bangor*

Thomas Nelson and Sons Ltd
London Edinburgh Paris Melbourne Toronto and New York

THOMAS NELSON AND SONS LTD
Parkside Works Edinburgh 9
36 Park Street London W1
312 Flinders Street Melbourne C1
302–304 Barclays Bank Building
Commissioner and Kruis Streets
Johannesburg

THOMAS NELSON AND SONS (CANADA) LTD
91–93 Wellington Street West   Toronto 1

THOMAS NELSON AND SONS
19 East 47th Street New York 17

SOCIÉTÉ FRANÇAISE D'EDITIONS NELSON
25 rue Henri Barbusse Paris V^e

————

First published 1957

CONTENTS

v

ABBREVIATIONS

Ann. Lond.	*Annales Londonienses* in *Chronicles of the Reigns of Edward I and II*, vol. I (Rolls Series) 1882
Ann. Paul.	*Annales Paulini (ibid.)*
Bridl.	*Auctore Bridlingtoniensi (ibid.* vol. II)
Cal. Chanc. Warr.	*Calendar of Chancery Warrants* (P.R.O.) 1927
C.Cl.R.	*Calendar of Close Rolls* (P.R.O.)
Cal.I.P.M.	*Calendar of Inquisitions post Mortem* (P.R.O.)
Chapters	*See* Tout
Cod.	The *Codex* of Justinian, in Mommsen's edition
Cont. Trivet	*Nicholai Triveti Annales*, ed. Hall (English Historical Society) 1845
C.P.R.	*Calendar of Patent Rolls* (P.R.O.)
Decr.	The canonical *Decretales*, in Friedburg's edition
Dig.	The *Digest* of Justinian
E.H.R.	*English Historical Review*
Foed.	Rymer's *Foedera* (Record Commission) 1816
Geoff. Mon.	Geoffrey of Monmouth's *Historia Britonum* (Rolls Series)
Instit.	The *Institutes* of Justinian
Migne, *P.L.*	Migne's *Patrologia Latina*
Misc. Inq.	*Calendar of Miscellaneous Inquisitions* (P.R.O.)
Murimuth	*Chronicle of Adam Murimuth with the Chronicle of Robert of Avesbury* (Rolls Series)
Parl. Writs	*Parliamentary Writs and Writs of Military Summons* (Record Commission) 1827
P.L.	*See* Migne
P.R.O.	Public Record Office
Ramsay	*The Genesis of Lancaster* by Sir James Ramsay of Bamff, 1913
Rot. Parl.	*Rotuli Parliamentorum* (Record Commission) vol. I, 1873
R.S.	Rolls Series
Tout, *Chapters*	*Chapters in the Administrative History of Mediaeval England* by T. F. Tout, 6 vols. 1920-1933
Tout, *Edward II*	*The Place of Edward II in English History* 2nd ed. 1936
Trivet	See *Cont. Trivet*
V.C.H.	*Victoria County History*
Wilkins, *Conc.*	*Concilia Magnae Britanniae et Hiberniae* ed. D. Wilkins, 1737

vii

INTRODUCTION

I

THE REIGN

EDWARD II sat down to the game of kingship with a remarkably poor hand, and he played it very badly. His father Edward I had left him with enormous commitments in Scotland and Gascony, and had unwittingly, by subduing Wales, strengthened the Marcher lords. The finances were in extraordinary confusion. There had been mounting opposition to prerogative rule for the last decade. What was worse, when Edward of Carnarvon came to the throne in July 1307, though neither stupid nor criminal, he was not 'a man of business', but an aimless man, without poise or sense of values. He had not been trained to rule: he had never really been 'off the leash'.[1] His laziness, incapacity, and lack of sympathy with his greater subjects gave opportunity to the baronial opposition—the successors of his father's opponents of 1297—to air their grievances and seek time-honoured remedies. This period of baronial resurgence (1297-1330), in its cruelty and utter faithlessness, with its bitter private feuds, swollen households, and economic dislocation, anticipates in some essentials the age of Warwick the Kingmaker.

The author of the *Vita*, an exceedingly well-informed person, has made it his business to portray this period of

[1] For his life before 1307 see the admirable account by Professor Hilda Johnstone, *Edward of Carnarvon*, Manchester, 1946.

sworn confederations, local disorder, famine, and at last civil war, in terms of a shrewd assessment of personal relationships, tempered by sighs and groans and proverbial wisdom. His memoir (for it is much more than a chronicle) is the best, and often unique, source for the character and doings of the protagonists—Piers Gaveston, the upstart Gascon favourite; the two Despensers, father and son, less easy to attack because firmly rooted in baronial history for some generations; and the earls, who appear almost as a separate estate, not led, but harassed and to some extent dominated by Thomas of Lancaster, with his five earldoms, who appears until his execution in 1322 as vindictive, sulky, and a traitor (see p. 123ff. below). Gaveston occupies a perhaps disproportionate amount of space (pp. 1-32 below). Our author suggests that if only he had been a little more circumspect all would have been well (p. 40). But clearly he was unsuited to the climate of English politics, and the earls could not forgive his waspish tongue (p. 8), his superiority in the tourney, or his inequality of birth. The Despensers are not treated so vividly nor in so connected a manner. Most of the other earls and not a few prelates are characterised from time to time (p. 28 below), but there is no indication of what the author thought of Edward's passionate queen, Isabella, the 'she-wolf of France'. Of purely constitutional or administrative matters there is almost nothing; parliaments are mentioned as they occur, but parliamentary representation not at all; the only political forces recognised are the king and his court confronted by the barons, especially the earls. Our author tries desperately to be impartial, but cannot wholly conceal his pro-baronial sympathies. The great importance of his clear and accurate account of the middle years of the reign—the

struggle for the Ordinances[1]—is attested by the fact that there is hardly a sentence that has not been cited by modern historians.[2]

Readers of the *Vita* may well think that so far as the Ordainers were concerned it was a question of men, not measures. They wanted, among other things, to be rid of Gaveston, the Beaumonts, the Frescobaldi, and the *familia superflua regi et terrae nimis onerosa* (p. 59), as indeed (except for the Beaumonts) they did by 1315. They wanted also a strict audit, through the Exchequer, of all moneys received by the king's household. They wanted to control the appointment of public officials. But they were not attacking a *system* of government, and unlike the barons of 1258 they did not set up a Baronial Council to engulf and supersede the royal council. That happened only in 1316 and 1318, on each occasion with far less success than in Simon de Montfort's day. They lacked any moral purpose: no Adam Marsh or Grosseteste had helped to mould their ideas, and reforming bishops were at a discount. 'With the system of administration the Ordainers had no quarrel: their real grievance was that it was not being properly worked.'[3] This is not to say that there was no baronial or, as it was to become, Lancastrian view of government. From 1258 the barons, who still regard themselves as the Community, assert their right as well as their duty to counsel the king and also to share in the control of the administration, in opposition to the 'curialist' view that the king

[1] The Lords Ordainers were appointed to reform the realm and the King's household on 20 March 1310 to hold office until Michaelmas 1311, and their Ordinances were published on 27 September of that year, only to be revoked by the Statute of York in 1322.

[2] The best account of the reign, and the one most coloured by the *Vita* is in T. F. Tout's *Political History of England* (1216-1379) chs. XII-XIV.

[3] B. Wilkinson, *Constitutional Studies in the History of the 13th and 14th Centuries*, Manchester, 1937, p. 244

may and should appoint his own council and ministers. The issue is far broader than that sometimes envisaged of a struggle between departments of the household and so-called departments of state.

Neither Simon de Montfort nor Thomas of Lancaster could evolve a way of imposing permanent restrictions upon the Crown: that was to come much later, and by another route. At this time the only solution for either side lay in war or judicial murder.

The proscriptions after Boroughbridge and the Statute of York (missing from our text) made nonsense of the various baronial attempts to control the king's household or council. In this the barons were every whit as guilty as the king, for they had wanted to control the government, but throughout the Middle Ages they lacked the continuity of application that was always essential to their task.

The political history of this disastrous reign falls easily into four periods: first, the rise and fall of Gaveston 1307-1312. Next, the efforts of Lancaster to render the king powerless by forcing him to observe the Ordinances; these Edward continued to evade until his defeat by the Scots at Bannockburn in 1314 left him at the mercy of his barons. But baronial control of the government was stultified by the sloth of Earl Thomas and by the pan-European famine of 1315-1316. The rise of a Middle Party, under Pembroke and Hereford, led to a temporary reconciliation between the extremists by the Treaty of Leake in August 1318 (see p. 88 below), but the king fell more and more into the hands of the Despensers. Any constitutional ideas or political sagacity that these two may have had was vitiated by their inordinate greed and ambition. The partition of the Gloucester earldom in 1317 was the most important territorial upheaval of

the reign, with the widest repercussions. It left the younger Despenser as lord of Glamorgan, but he coveted the whole inheritance and his seizure of Gower from John Mowbray, nominally on behalf of the king, set the southern March in a blaze. The whole baronage took sides and the Despensers were exiled. A lucky success in taking Leeds Castle in Kent prompted Edward to march swiftly into the West, where, catching the Marchers 'on the wrong foot'—for they received nothing of the promised support from Lancaster (see p. 97)—he accepted their surrender and recalled the Despensers. The years from the exile of these men until the culmination of the king's counter-attack at Boroughbridge and the subsequent great proscriptions of Lancastrians we may regard as the third period (1321-1322).

Lastly, the years 1322-1326 set the seal upon the loss of Scotland by the thirteen years' truce (confirmed in 1328 by the better known Treaty of Northampton), and upon the confiscation of Gascony after the affair of the newly-built *bastide* of Saint Sardos, which was claimed by both sides. The loss of Edward's wisest counsellor by the death of Pembroke in 1324 allowed the king to give free play to all his most fatuous instincts. The Despensers quarrelled with the Queen, and the escape of her paramour[1] from the Tower in August 1323 really sealed their fate as surely as that of their unhappy master. Homage had been due to France for Gascony, but not done, in 1322 on the accession of Charles le Bel, and relations had by the summer of 1324 deteriorated into open war. The Queen, now almost a prisoner in her own house, proposed, and was allowed, to go to France

[1] The liaison between Isabella and Roger Mortimer of Wigmore probably dates from the autumn of 1321. Edward II's youngest child, Jeanne, was born on 5 July of that year.

to seek peace (March 1325), and a few months later (September 1325) young Edward [III] was sent to join her in his father's stead. By the end of the year Isabella had refused to come home, and here our author stops abruptly. For an account of the invasion of the Queen in September 1326 and the final tragedy at Berkeley Castle on 21 September 1327 the reader must turn to other sources.

II

SOURCES AND DATE

We do not know how far our author depended upon written sources, such as news-letters, or his own memoranda. What is certain is that he is nowhere dependent upon any extant historical narrative. There is no connection at all between his account and the well-known chronicles of London, St Pauls, Bridlington (for the North and Scotland) Lanercost priory, Geoffrey le Baker (valuable chiefly for the murder and deposition) or Ralph Higden (for the classical passage on Edward II's character), though some of these sources are dependent upon one another. Our author is writing a memoir: he reveals no sources and leaves no traces.

The *Vita* exists only in a transcript made by Thomas Hearne, the famous Oxford antiquary, in 1729 from a manuscript lent to him by Mr James West M.A., of Balliol.[1] Most, if not all, of Mr West's MSS. were burnt

[1] The story of the discovery of the manuscript by Hearne, its undoubted connection with Malmesbury, and its almost certain destruction by fire has been admirably told by Stubbs, in his edition of the *Vita* in *Chronicles* . . . *Ed. I and II*, vol. ii, pp. xxxi-xliii (Rolls Series 1883). The *Vita* was preceded by a list of Abbots of Malmesbury down to Nicholas of St Albans DD. (? late 12th cent.) and followed by a charter of Abbot Robert to Wybert, son of William, of 3½ virgates and half a hide of land in Charlton by Malmesbury and elsewhere. These are printed by Stubbs.

on 4 January 1737 in the Temple, and as this work has never been seen since it is thought to have perished with them. The lost manuscript may have been a composite one consisting of two parts bound up together for Sir Gervase Holles, but it is clear that the second part, containing the *Vita* (foll. 92-165), came from the Benedictine Abbey of Malmesbury. There is, however, no indication at all that the *Vita* copied at Malmesbury was composed there, or that the author was ever a monk at Malmesbury or anywhere else.

Thomas Hearne's original transcript of James West's lost manuscript, which served as printer's copy for his edition in *Johannis de Trokelowe Annales Eduardi II* (Oxford 1729) 93-250, survives in the Bodleian Library, Oxford, as part of MS. Rawlinson B.180, and is the source of this new edition as far as *exuta veste* (page 143 below). Pages 65 and 66 of the transcript being lost, the remainder depends on Hearne's printed text. Hearne's work was very careful, and he records well over 200 places where the MS. reading needs to be mended by the alteration, addition or removal of a single letter. These minutiae, nearly all of which are noted by Stubbs, are tacitly accepted in this edition, and as a rule only changes affecting more than one letter are recorded in the critical notes; words and syllables not in the MS., the addition of which seems necessary, are marked by square brackets. Apart from the loss of nine leaves in West's MS., the text appears to be reasonably well preserved; where defect is to be suspected, it can hardly be identified or cured without the discovery of another manuscript.

We have the evidence of Hearne, a competent judge, that the lost manuscript was fourteenth century, and both parts of the Gervase Holles volume contain chron-

icles which have been continued in 1346 and 1348 respectively. The second part, containing the *Vita*, not
only breaks off abruptly at 1325/6 but contains passages
showing that it had not undergone an author's final
revision. One passage in particular (p. 53 below) is
suggestive. It is a section of twelve lines which is written
twice, being reduced by omissions, on its second occur-
rence, to six lines. The passage in question might well
have been taken from a news-letter.[1]

A second and minor (but equally conclusive) clue to
the nature of the Malmesbury manuscript from which
Hearne copied is on page 23 where the barons moved
from place to place until they reached York and *about
sunset* the Earl of Lancaster set out on his way, to capture
Gaveston if possible. But we are not told on what day,
week, month, or even year this sunset occurred. Here
again, the author is editing some detailed account.

The work is not couched in the form of a chronicle.
There is none of the usual 'hoc anno . . .', no yearly
summaries, no regular mention of A.D., though this is
skilfully indicated, and the narrative of events is sub-
stantially in chronological order, though not obviously
so. The story flows on continuously, only checked from
time to time by a short sermon. Stubbs[2] tended towards
the view that the author wrote not much later than 1325,
but with his usual caution envisaged too the possibility
that it might be fifty years later. In this he may have
been influenced by the diatribe against the venality of
the papal court at Avignon (p. 45 below), and, though
he does not say so, by the similarity between a passage

---

[1] For this kind of material and its use see the account of the degradation
and death of Pope Boniface VIII in 1303, written by one of his partisans
from Rome. This is inserted in full by one St Albans chronicler, but com-
pressed and edited by another (*Wil. Rishanger Chronica et Annales* ed. H. T.
Riley (Rolls Series, 1865) pp. 483-491 and 216-221).   [2] *Op. cit.* p. xliv.

cited as from a 'certain well known Regular' (p. 75 below) and the *Speculum Regis*. When Stubbs wrote, the *Speculum* was attributed to Archbishop Simon Islip (1349-66), though it is now known to date from 1330-1333, and is probably by Simon Meopham, Archbishop of Canterbury, 1328-33.[1] This passage on the evils of purveyance and kindred abuses our author inserts under 1316: an ordinance on the subject had been issued 11 June 1315.[2] It is less explicit, more condensed than the *Speculum*, and might be a summary from a recension earlier than the two now extant: but it is so vague that there is no need to postulate any connection at all. The rest of the *Vita* is so carefully put together that there is no reason to suppose that the author is not accurate in the date ascribed by him to this petition.

The author's continual use of the 'historic present', and his deliberate method of summing up his narrative, but never going a step beyond the year he is writing about, make it extremely difficult to pin him down to any particular year. One passage points clearly to an early date. In his diatribe against the Papacy he tells us, with reference to the death of Clement V in 1314 that we may never have another one 'so much a neighbour' (*tam vicinus*), presumably because he was a Gascon.[3] But in 1334 Benedict XII, also a Gascon, was elected. The remark would be fatuous, even as a literary device, if written after 1334. Again, in speaking of Robert Bruce and the loss of Berwick in 1318, he suggests that fortune may once more smile upon the English and will bring Robert to a desolate end. Robert Bruce did not die until 1329, after he had secured the indepen-

[1] *E.H.R.* xvi. 110-115
[2] *Ann. Lond.* 234. Meopham was supported by Henry of Lancaster: his family came from Kent, but remarkably little is known about him.
[3] See p. 46 below.

B

dence of Scotland by the Treaty of Northampton in 1328. Fortune did not smile upon the English until the battle of Halidon Hill in 1333, but this was a barren victory. It seems most likely that the statement was written before 1328, as a pious aspiration. Thirdly, Bishop Stapledon's return to England late in 1325 receives this comment: 'Let him take care not to be seen again in France'— a pointless remark if written after September 1326 when Stapledon was murdered in London. Finally, no-one writing under Edward III would be at all likely to describe Edward I repeatedly as *rex senior*. These passages can scarcely have been inserted simply to create an illusion of contemporary writing: it is one thing to refuse to prophesy and hope for the best, but quite another to stultify oneself by falsifying history. Hence we may believe that the work which came to an abrupt end with the November parliament of 1325 was written before the landing of the Queen in September 1326. I imagine the author writing up his notes, very largely perhaps from an excellent memory, composing right up to his death in 1326. He certainly made no final revision.

Stubbs noted that the work becomes fuller as it proceeds, a judgment that is more striking if we remember that the equivalent of some twenty pages of printed text (as in the Rolls series edition) are missing for the period March 1322 to November 1324.[1] But he fails to note the slight change of pace and tone that some may detect towards the end. With his final verdict we wholly agree: 'I am inclined to think that, on the whole, the writer may have begun to write towards the close of the reign of Edward II. As he does not anticipate the revolution and murder of the king, and as his genuine work ends

[1] p. 127 ff. below

at the year 1325, we cannot infer that he wrote much later than that year.'[1]

III

AUTHORSHIP

That the author was a highly educated man is obvious from almost every sentence. His use of rhymed prose jars upon the modern ear, but was very much to contemporary taste. It is not so much that he is a learned man but that his learning is so thoroughly digested. His biblical quotations, particularly from the historical books of the Old Testament are apposite; his use of the Civil Law is not simply by way of *allegationes*, as the glossators understood them, but is the work of a man who is quoting for the logical substance rather than for the added authority of the text.[2] His references to English history suggest that we might have had a very interesting conversation with him. He was no monk; he was 'one of us'. Not a philosopher, nor a theologian, but a wise old man who must once have studied Civil Law. He is writing in order to be read: he refers us to other sources for the full text of the Ordinances, but gives in full (though not quite verbatim) a passage from the Decretals of Boniface VIII. We are expected to be able to come by a copy of the Statutes, but not of the Sext. But he is outspoken to a degree that would be madness in any rising man, and he is violently critical of 'the young men of today'. A close scrutiny of his

[1] p. xxviii below. The MS. is continued down to 1348 by extracts from the *Polychronicon* of Ranulf Higden.

[2] There are four quotations from the Code, five from the Digest, one from the Institutes, three references to the Decretals, and one to the Sext. Note also such words as *patrocinium, deportabit, concussio, mala mansio, pedanie iudices*, which are technical terms in Roman Law.

memoir makes it impossible to believe that it is other than the work of a man past middle age. He is established or retired, or both; so he can skate on thin ice, but he is no longer competing, he is skating *hors concours* and can please himself. So he is violently critical of corruption in the papal Curia, amongst the officials at court and on the bench, and, with pious reservations and hopes for the future, of the king himself. Towards the end of his story his attitude to the king seems to harden, and he ceases for the most part to call him *Dominus Rex*, as he almost invariably does up to 1324. In one of his invaluable *obiter dicta* he complains that Edward II always has plenty of money[1]; it appears that contemporaries even in high places were quite uninformed as to the state of the revenue.[2] Budgets or Estimates were not yet in vogue and the activities of Wardrobe and Chamber at this period might well make it impossible for a Treasurer to discover the true state of affairs. And there was one Treasurer named John Walwayn, who held office for only a few months. We shall hear of him again.

When the author wrote, the aristocracy was still the nation, and this is a chronicle of the aristocracy. If monks are included they are certainly not mentioned, and the 'people' appear only in elevated passages, as making harsh noises. The baronage, on the other hand, are explicitly spoken of as a chief constituent of monarchy.[3] They are led by the earls, who are still regarded almost as a separate estate. These he is sometimes prepared to judge. Guy de Beauchamp, Earl of Warwick,

---

[1] See p. 136 below.
[2] S. B. Chrimes, *Introduction to the Administrative History of Mediaeval England* (1952) p. 143, points out that the debts of the Wardrobe in 1307 totalled £60,000.
[3] See p. 28 below.

the 'cultivated, aristocratic ruffian',[1] is, as the brain behind the Ordinances, regarded as more of a hero than anyone else.[2] The 'brutal and disreputable' Warenne, Earl of Surrey,[3] is tacitly condemned[4]; his private war with Lancaster helped to weaken the baronial party. The early death of Gilbert de Clare, Earl of Gloucester, at Bannockburn, is lamented. The general thread of the narrative leaves no doubt as to the author's baronial, rather than royalist, sympathies, but he is clearly trying to seem impartial. He blames both the Despensers, as he had Gaveston, and, very reluctantly, Thomas of Lancaster; he praises Bishop Cobham for his learning, Melton for his integrity, Winchelsey for his defence of the church—though he does not even hint at his relations with the baronage[5]—and Henry of Lancaster for his sympathy with the oppressed. By implication he favours Orleton, the Bishop of Hereford who played so important a part in the deposition of the King. His own standpoint is scarcely visible: he believes in annual ministries; he quotes possibly with approval Lancaster's statement that parliaments should not be held *in cameris*. He is clearly embarrassed by the presence of Earl Thomas. Surely he is of the Middle party.

If he was a lawyer, the author was interested in the principles of jurisprudence rather than in points of constitutional law. Perhaps this is too flattering, for he is not even interested in the doctrine of capacities: his charges against the Despensers are purely feudal and primarily concerned with territorial aggrandisement. The new Coronation Oath is not mentioned. But it is

---

[1] Tout, *Place of Edward II*, p. 16   [2] See p. 62 below.
[3] Tout, *op. cit.*, p. 17   [4] See p. 87f. below.
[5] It is important to historians of the reign of Edward I that so well-informed a writer should go out of his way to recount Winchelsey's quarrel with the king without even hinting at this aspect of his pontificate.

very important to note the gap in the manuscript covering the period March to November 1322, so that there
is nothing of the Statute of York nor of the subsequent
proscription of the Lancastrian party. The omission of
a further leaf after Maurice de Berkeley has failed to
escape (January 1323) from Wallingford covers the rest
of 1323 (i.e. Mortimer's escape from the Tower in
August) and most of 1324.[1] We thus miss the elevation
and treachery of Harclay, the death of Pembroke in
June 1324, and the confiscation of the Queen's estates
in September. The narrative for 1325 is full and close
to the facts, but possibly written hastily. The author is
querulous about the King's meanness in not paying his
troops and his daily increasing harshness.

The author tells us that he is an Englishman,[2] though
he at once proceeds to speak just as objectively of the
English as he does of the Irish[3] or the Welsh.[4] He is
proud of English supremacy at sea,[5] and gives a detailed
account—though one that is chronologically difficult to
control—of the troubles at Bristol (1313-16).[6] He mentions Maurice de Berkeley, of Berkeley Castle near by,
five times, but makes no reference to any other member
of the family. This is not sufficient to localise the chronicle. Every *local* detail and name is suppressed in the
account of the riots, except among the attacking forces.
In spite of the author's interest in what happened, he is
viewing it from outside. But it is clear that apart from
the court, the bishops, and (a big reservation) Scotland,
the author's interests are in the south-west. A list of
persons of the second order of importance mentioned in
the *Vita* leaves no room for doubt that the author was

---

[1] See p. 127 below.
[2] See p. 63 below.
[3] See p. 61 below.
[4] See p. 61 below.
[5] See p. 60 below.
[6] See p. 70f. below.

a West Countryman.[1] He mentions Clifford of Clifford
and Tenbury, John Giffard of Brimpsfield (Glos), Henry
Tyes of Chilton (Wilts), Botetourt of Mendlesham
(Wilts), Wylington (Wilts), Montacute (Somerset and
Devon), Turbervile (Glamorgan), FitzWarin and Charlton (Salop), Segrave (Leics). He is very full on the
break-up of the Earldom of Gloucester and the subsequent troubles, which, of course, from a political point
of view are a large part of the reign after 1317. The
point is not the importance of these people or what they
did, but that for the author of this memoir no other
barons exist. Even when we go to Scotland, the men
captured at Bannockburn[2] are, with the exception of
Segrave (who is usually associated with the Marchers),
all barons of the southern Welsh March. Every other
passage where the author reveals special information falls
under this rule (e.g. the war against Llewelyn Bren).[3]

Apart from this all-pervading Marcher interest, the
Vita is unusually full (for a West Country chronicle) on
the Scottish campaigns, including the Bannockburn campaign, the siege of Berwick, Andrew Harclay's visit to
Edward II and the negotiations for a perpetual peace—
in describing which the author's zeal seems to have out-
run his capacity. Whatever value we set upon it, the
author's narrative shows an exceptional interest in Scottish affairs.

Within this range of interests we find a remarkable
treatment of Herefordshire material. For this reason,
in recalling Stubb's verdict, 'He might be a teacher
in a university or a retired civilian, but could scarcely
be a monk', we may add that we should probably

---

[1] The really inevitable people in any account of the reign—as Gaveston,
the Despensers, Thomas of Lancaster and Robert Bruce—are for the pur-
poses of localisation of no interest.
[2] See p. 55 below.   [3] See p. xxvii below.

look for a West Country lawyer, an authority on Scotland; one familiar with the court, though hating it; one who likes a good bishop, though not a young one, and who hates the papal Curia; hence one who is almost certainly not himself a bishop, though possibly a failed one.[1] The peak of his career should lie between 1315 and 1323, for this is the best part of the work before us, and he should have reason to break off, without revision, at 1326.

We must then look for some man in whom all the qualifications enumerated above are to be found, a man who well knows his way about the court '. . . and that not as an ignorant outsider',[2] and whose sympathies are with the Marchers. Since Stubbs wrote, a clue has been found among the careers of men who rose to positions in government service from smaller positions in baronial households.[3]

A Herefordshire lawyer, clerk to the Earl of Hereford, whose career was at its peak as a high government official 1315-23, an expert on Scotland, who had been demoted and also failed to obtain a bishopric, who retired in January 1324 and was dead in July 1326, has then some claim upon our attention. The legal qualification, the local qualification (including the essential link with Maurice de Berkeley), the court, Scotland, and the dates—all fit the career of Mr John Walwayn, D.C.L., who suffered in his lifetime from two major disappointments, and since his death has quite unfairly been labelled a turncoat, through confusion with a namesake.

[1] The chronicler seems to remember nothing about the year 1320 except the parliament of York, summoned for 20 January, the day that John Dalderby, Bishop of Lincoln, died. The story of the election to that See, with moralisings on young men being made bishops, takes up the whole of the rest of the year.

[2] Stubbs, *op. cit.*, Intro. p. xlvi

[3] See Conway Davies, *Baronial Opposition to Edward II* (1918), pp. 355-6 and N. Denholm-Young, *Seignorial Administration* (1937) *passim*.

If it was Walwayn who wrote this book, then Sir Edward Maunde Thompson's remark about Adam Murimuth, Walwayn's fellow Canon of Hereford and St Paul's, and also a D.C.L., will apply equally to Walwayn himself: 'We should naturally suppose that one, who had for many years led an active public life and had even had a share in some of the principal events of his day, would have been more communicative in his account of them.'[1] This may help to explain what many readers must have felt about the *Vita*, that the author speaks with the habit of authority and knows much more than he intends to say.   All the information in the book is explicable in the light of Mr Walwayn's career.[2]   What then of the Berkeley interest?   I suggest that this is a quite natural personal interest in a colourful contemporary and that no close connection or dependence is implied.

As has already been said, the author of the *Vita* refers to Maurice de Berkeley five times but ignores all the other members of the family.   He does not mention that the Berkeleys owned a large part of Bristol, nor that they had founded and cherished the Abbey of St Augustine in that town.   That no reference is made to Maurice's father is not surprising, for as he had fought at the Battle of Evesham he is unlikely to have been very active in the reign of Edward II.   Maurice did not inherit the family estates until 1321 and was in possession of them for only a few months.   Though he may well have been a hero to the author of the *Vita*, only the 'high spots' in Maurice's career are given: his capture at Bannockburn, his command of Berwick next year, his command at Bristol, the loss of all his estates, his imprisonment in 1322 and the attempt made to rescue him from Walling-

---

[1] *Ade Murimuth Continuatio chronicarum* (Rolls Series, 1889), p. xv
[2] See my article in *E.H.R.*, vol. lxxii (1956)

ford Castle in 1323 where he had been in prison for almost a year(*fere per unum annum detentus*). This attempt was more skilfully planned than Warin de Bassingbourne's effort to rescue the Lord Edward from the same prison in 1264, and was part of a larger plan to seize Wallingford, the Tower of London, Windsor and other of the King's castles. But this is all that we hear of Maurice de Berkeley in the *Vita*. Our author does not mention that Maurice was for a few months in 1316-7 Justice of South and West Wales, nor that in 1320 he was Seneschal of Gascony, nor that (according to *Flores* iii, 197) he attended Lancaster's 'parliament' at Sherburn in Elmet. The *Vita* ends abruptly at the end of 1325 or the beginning of 1326 while Maurice was still in captivity. He died on 31 May 1326.

The Berkeley interest shown in this chronicle does not amount to much. Maurice's two active commands on land and sea, at Berwick and Bristol respectively, are mentioned; but wherever possible similar comments are given on other barons—Botetourt, FitzWarin, Lewer, Montague, and Giffard. Maurice is twice, and inevitably, mentioned as a captive (1314) or confederate (1320) Marcher, and then the author relates the excellent story of his attempted escape. That is all. The significance of this is that this Maurice was not a great landed proprietor, except for a few months; his officials and executors, in so far as we know them, are not people of any standing, and neither he nor they moved in court circles. The Berkeleys at this time, even the head of the family, were only barons of the second rank. They dine with abbots and other barons, but their dependants are merely priests and chaplains. Maurice's household, at all material times, is unlikely to have contained a man of our author's calibre.

So the Berkeley interest may be deceptive. We are looking for a lawyer and a Marcher, but it may be that he was more interested in Herefordshire than in Gloucestershire. He is excessively discreet about local celebrities or notorieties, and the Earl of Hereford himself receives neither praise nor blame throughout. Yet his every move is recorded, almost automatically. After the pacification and feasting of October 1313 all the earls went home, *sed comes Herfordie remansit de familia regis*. He is captured at Bannockburn, but by an arrangement which is specified nowhere else he is released, *et sic comes noster rediit ad propria*. Why *noster*? Three times in the book the king is called *rex noster* and once James Douglas is *inimicus noster*, but *comes noster* is not a literary device like 'our hero'. At Bannockburn the Earl of Hereford had quarrelled with Gloucester: our chronicle is better than the *Flores* on this.[1] His commission to put down Llewelyn Bren, because he held the neighbouring stronghold of Brecon, is described. His change of sides is passed over without comment; his death recorded as a bare fact. All the blame for treasonable negotiations with the Scots is laid at Lancaster's door, though Hereford and the other Marchers were just as much to blame, and it may even be that Hereford was the prime mover as far back as 1311. It goes without saying that Hereford is mentioned on a number of other occasions, as, after Gloucester's death at Bannockburn, he was the leader of the Marchers. A 'temporiser', according to Professor Tout, like the author of the *Vita*.

When the king came to Hereford in 1321 he up-braided 'the bishop of the place', and later, in 1325,

---

[1] *Flores* iii, 158. The story here is that Edward II made Gloucester Constable for the occasion, which is surely rubbish, though J. E. Morris accepts it (*Bannockburn*, C.U.P., 1914, p. 67). The office of Constable *had been restored* to Hereford after his refusal to serve in 1310. Morris omitted that.

Herefordensis has a treasonable correspondence with Henry of Lancaster, which, if our author was writing only a year or so later, implies a special knowledge. But in this context it is the anonymity that is of interest. Again there is a graphic story about *quidam miles* of Hereford who had acted as sheriff wearing the livery of the barons, for which he was hanged in 1321. Yet the author can give an intimate and even disproportionate picture of Fulk FitzWarin and Robert Lewer who were in command of the royalist cavalry and infantry respectively this year, just as Montague and Giffard were in the war against Llewelyn Bren in 1315, Maurice de Berkeley at sea at Bristol, John Botetourt at sea at Berwick, or Robert Holland in command for Lancaster (though without details). He might have forgotten the sheriffs' name, five years later, but hardly that of Adam de Orleton, even in 1326: the letter he gives is proof (p. 144 below).

These facts suggest that the author knows more about *comes noster, episcopus loci,* and *quidam miles de Hereford* than he means to say. If the chronicle was written many years after 1326 the argument of course loses its validity, but if it is contemporary, then the career of the Earl of Hereford's agent (in Scotland, too), Mr John Walwayn, D.C.L., is important. If he wrote the book, his death shortly before 18 July 1326 would be sufficient explanation of its refusal to prophesy no less than its abrupt conclusion. He had left office as escheator on 10 January 1324, and the intervening period would be quite sufficient for the composition of the *Vita*.

LATIN TEXT
and
ENGLISH TRANSLATION

VITA EDWARDI SECUNDI

EDWARDUS post conquestum primus, anno regni sui xxxv°
in die Translationis Sancti Thome[1] nature debitum
soluens, suscepit regnum filius eius Edwardus secundus,
iuuenis et fortis robore, etatis sue annum agens circiter
uicesimum tertium. Hic propositum patris sui nondum
consummauit, sed in alia consilium mutauit. Petrum
de Gaueston, qui nuper precepto patris regis terram
Anglie abiurauerat, reuocauit. Fuerat autem dictus
Petrus, uiuente rege Edwardo sene, iuuenis Edwardi,
tunc principis Wallie, camerarius[2] familiarissimus et
ualde dilectus, quod manifeste satis apparuit non multo
post. Dominus enim rex iuuenis domino Petro, ab
exilio reuerso, de consilio et assensu quorundam magnatum terre, uidelicet Henrici de Lacy comitis Lincolnie
et aliorum, comitatum Cornubie contulit et donauit.[3]
Ipse etenim comes Henricus de Lacy, cum dubitaretur
an rex predictum comitatum a jure quod cum corona
habebat posset separare, proposuit regem posse, nam sic
et alii reges bis antea fecerant. Maior tamen pars
baronum terre non consensit, tum quia Petrus alienigena
erat a Vasconia oriundus, tum propter inuidiam. In-
uidebant enim ei magnates terre, quia ipse solus haberet
gratiam in oculis regis et quasi secundus rex dominare-/
F.156 tur, cui subessent omnes et par nullus. Inuidebat etiam
illi quasi tota terra, maior et minor et senex, et mala de
eo predicabant; unde et nomen eius ualde diffamatum
est. Nec tamen uoluntatem regis a Petro poterant separare, quin etiam quanto plura audiret rex que gratiam

---

[1] 7 July 1307
[2] *camerarius* is not used in its technical sense of Chamberlain.

I

LIFE OF EDWARD THE SECOND

On the day of the Translation of St Thomas in the thirty-fifth year of his reign,[1] died Edward the First after the Conquest, and his son Edward II began to reign, a robust young man in about his twenty-third year. He did not achieve the ambition that his father had set before himself, but directed his plans to other objects. He recalled Piers Gaveston, who had recently abjured the realm at his father's command. This Piers had been the most intimate[2] and highly-favoured member, as soon became abundantly clear, of the young Edward's household when the latter was Prince of Wales and the old king still alive. For the young lord king gave to Piers, on his return from exile, the earldom of Cornwall, with the approval of some of the magnates, namely Henry de Lacy, Earl of Lincoln, and others.[3] There was a doubt whether the king could lawfully alienate the said earldom, which he held with the crown, and Earl Henry had said that he could, as had been done twice before by other kings. The majority of the barons did not agree, as much because Piers was an alien of Gascon birth as through envy. For the magnates of the land hated him, because he alone found favour in the king's eyes and lorded it over them like a second king, to whom all were subject and none equal. Almost all the land hated him too, great and small, even the old, and foretold ill of him; whence his name was reviled far and wide. Nor could the king's affection be alienated from Piers, for

---

[3] *Foed.* II, 2 (Dumfries, 6 August 1307). On Gaveston's career up to this date see H. Johnstone, *Edward of Carnarvon* (1946), *passim*.

I

eius conarentur extinguere, tanto magis inualescebat amor et crescebat affectio regis erga Petrum. In tantum etiam ut ad partem Petri fortificandam et amicis stipandam, filiam sororis sue, que fuit filia quondam Gilberti comitis Gloucestrie,[1] dominus rex dicto Petro collocauit [in] matrimonium. Sane hec copulatio matrimonialis partem eius non modicum uallabat; fauorem namque amicorum sibi uehementer augebat et odium baronum refrenabat.

Interea conuocati sunt archiepiscopi, comites et ceteri terre magnates ad sepeliendum corpus regis nuper defuncti; et sepultus est dictus rex honorifice Londoniis apud Westmonasterium iuxta patrem suum Henricum tertium.[2] Post hec ad maiorem Petri famam augendam et nomen celebrandum, auxiliante et consulente domino rege, nomine domini Petri proclamatum est celebriter quoddam torneamentum in uilla uidelicet Walyngfordie, que est de dominico comitis Cornubie. Dies etiam prefigitur, dies scilicet sabbati proxima post festum Sancti Andree.[3] Hoc itaque torneamentum comites et barones in odium Petri magis excitabat. Adueniente igitur die prefixo ex una parte coniuncti sunt comites tres uel quatuor cum manu ualida, comes uidelicet Warennie, comes Herfordie, comes de Arundel, et barones non pauci; ex parte domini Petri comes nullus erat nominatus expressus, sed omnes fere milites iuniores et robustiores regni, qui prece uel pretio poterant conduci, partem domini Petri iuuabant. Vnde et in illo torneamento pars eius superiorem manum habebat, ac optata reportabat, quamuis campus / alteri parti remaneret. Nam ipsius ludi lex esse dinoscitur, quod qui plus perdit et qui sepius ab equo deicitur, probior et fortior iudicatur.

F.157

---

[1] 29 October. Margaret, daughter of Jeanne of Acre.

the more he was told, in attempts to damp his ardour, the greater grew his love and tenderness towards Piers. So much so that, to strengthen Piers and surround him with friends, he married him to his sister's daughter, that is to the daughter of the late Gilbert, Earl of Gloucester.[1] This marriage tie did indeed strengthen his position not a little; for it much increased the goodwill of his friends and restrained the hatred of the baronage.

Meanwhile archbishops, earls, and the other magnates forgathered to bury the body of the late king. He was buried honourably in London at Westminster, near his father Henry III.[2] Then, to enhance Piers' honour and glory, with the aid and counsel of the king, a tournament was ceremoniously proclaimed in Sir Piers' name, at Wallingford, a town on the Earl of Cornwall's demesne. A day was appointed, namely the Saturday next after the feast of St Andrew.[3] This tournament roused the earls and barons to still greater hatred of Piers. When the day came there were ranged on one side three or four earls with a strong troop, namely Earl Warenne, the Earl of Hereford, the Earl of Arundel, and not a few barons; Sir Piers' side could not raise an earl, but almost all the younger and more athletic knights of the kingdom, whom persuasion or hope of reward could bring together, assisted him. So it was that in this tournament his party had the upper hand and carried off the spoils, although the other side remained in possession of the field. For it is a recognised rule of this game that he who loses most and is most frequently unhorsed, is adjudged the more valiant and the stronger.

---

[2] 27 October 1307   [3] 2 December

C

Ex hiis et aliis indies crescebat odium; erat enim Petrus homo ualde elatus et superbus in gestu. Nam omnes quos sibi pares regni consuetudo esse dictabat, humiles et abiectos, nec ipsum in probitate quicquam attingere posse reputabat. Econtra comites et barones Anglie ipsum Petrum, quia alienigenam et humilem quondam armigerum, ad tantum decus et honorem prouectum, nec sui prioris status memorem, despiciebant. Vnde et apud omnes fere qui in regno erant pro ludibrio habebatur. Rex autem continuum amorem erga eum habebat, in tantum ut exiret a curia regis preceptum publicum ne quis eum nomine proprio uocaret, uidelicet dominum Petrum de Gauestone, sed comitem Cornubie nominaret.

Deinde eum rediissent nuntii qui ad dominum Philippum regem Francie missi fuerant pro matrimonio copulando inter filiam dicti regis Francie et regem Anglie, ac optata reportassent, dominus rex Anglie ad transfretandum se parauit et nauigio parato mare cum suis intrauit. Regnum autem in manu Petri in custodia deputatur. Mira res, qui nuper ab Anglia exul erat et eiectus, eiusdem terre iam factus est gubernator et custos. Celebratis itaque de more nuptiis, rex Anglie cum coniuge sua letus in Angliam est reversus.[1]

Post hec fiunt preparatoria coronationi regis. Vocantur archiepiscopi, episcopi, comites et barones. Venerunt igitur omnes, sed burgenses singularum civitatum aderant. Die Sancti Mathie apostoli[2] coronati et consecrati sunt rex et regina. Episcopus Wyntoniensis[3] coronam capiti regis apposuit, sed hoc de mandato et consensu archiepiscopi Cantuariensis,[4] cum ad eius digni-

---

[1] Edward sailed on 22 January and did homage on 24 January 1308 for Aquitaine and Ponthieu and married Isabella next day.

[2] 25 February

[3] Henry Woodlock (1305-1316)

From these and other incidents hatred mounted day by day, for Piers was very proud and haughty in bearing. All those whom the custom of the realm made equal to him, he regarded as lowly and abject, nor could anyone, he thought, equal him in valour. On the other hand the earls and barons of England looked down upon Piers because, as a foreigner and formerly a mere man-at-arms raised to such distinction and eminence, he was unmindful of his former rank. Thus he was an object of mockery to almost everyone in the kingdom. But the king had an unswerving affection for him, so much so that a public edict issued from the court that no one should call him by his own name, to wit Sir Piers Gaveston, but should style him Earl of Cornwall.

On the successful return of the embassy which had been sent to Philip King of France to contract the marriage between the said king's daughter and the king of England, the said lord king prepared to take ship and set sail with his retinue. The kingdom was left in the hands of Piers, as regent. An astonishing thing, that he who had lately been an exile and outcast from England should now be made ruler and guardian of the realm. When the marriage had been duly celebrated the king and his wife returned joyfully to England.[1]

After this, preparations were made for the king's coronation. Archbishops, bishops, earls and barons were summoned, and all attended, and burgesses from each city were present. The king and queen were crowned and consecrated on the feast of St Matthias the Apostle.[2] The Bishop of Winchester[3] placed the crown on the king's head, but this he did by command and assent of the Archbishop of Canterbury,[4] to whose dignity and

---

[4] Robert Winchelsey had been reinstated 22 January 1308.

tatem et ecclesie sue noscatur pertinere, factum est, ipso
archiepiscopo quominus adesset uel infirmitate / prepe-
dito uel nondum a transmarinis partibus in Angliam
reuerso. Finita igitur solempnitate et festiue celebrato
conuiuio rediit unusquisque ad propria.

Nunc primum insurrexerunt contra Petrum de
Gauestone omnes fere comites et barones Anglie, in-
uicemque iureiurando astricti sunt, a cœptis nunquam
desistere donec Petrus terram Anglie euacuaret, et comitatum Cornubie dimitteret; nullusque magnatum partem
Petri sustinuit excepto rege et Hugone le Despenser.
Comes autem Gloucestrie neutram partem promouit:
cum Petro non fuit ne pares suos offenderet; cum baronibus esse non potuit quia fratrem suum in lege expungnare non decuit. Sed et predictus Hugo Despenser
omnibus baronibus exosus factus est, eo quod ipsos pro
communi utilitate regni laborantes deseruerat et, magis
studio placendi et cupiditate lucrandi quam ex alia
iusta causa, parti Petri adheserat. Ille vero qui Petrum
prius fauore et amicitia pre ceteris excepto rege fouerat
et dilexerat, inter omnes barones maximus eius inimicus
factus est et persecutor. Hic erat Henricus de Lacy
comes Lyncolnie, et hec non ex vitio comitis sed ex
ingratitudine ipsius Petri noscitur accidisse.

Hec seditiosa dissensio inter dominum regem et barones orta per totam Angliam iam diuulgata est, sed et
tota terra pro tali tumultu ualde desolata est; omne enim
regnum in se diuisum desolabitur.[1] Homines mediocres
pacifici, pacis amatores, guerram et pacis exilium ualde
formidabant; predones uero qui predam captabant et ad
aliena manum extendere, bellum non pacem affectabant.

---

[1] Luke xi. 17

that of his church the privilege is known to pertain, the archbishop himself being prevented from being present by illness or continued absence abroad. At the conclusion of the ceremony and the wedding feast everyone went home.

It was only now that almost all of the earls and barons of England rose against Piers Gaveston, binding themselves by a mutual oath never to cease from what they had begun until Piers had left the land of England and given up the earldom of Cornwall; and none of the magnates took Piers' part except the king and Hugh le Despenser. The Earl of Gloucester favoured neither party; he could not side with Piers lest he offend his peers; nor could he go with the barons because it was unseemly to fight against his brother-in-law. Now the said Hugh Despenser was also hateful to all the barons, because he had deserted them as they worked for the common good of the realm and, more from a desire to please and a lust for gain than for any creditable reason, had become an adherent of Piers. But he who above all others except the king had cherished and made much of Piers by his grace and friendship, had now, of all the barons, become his greatest enemy and persecutor. This was Henry de Lacy, Earl of Lincoln, and this is known to have happened through no fault of the earl but through Piers' ingratitude.

Thus the seditious quarrel between the lord king and the barons spread far and wide through England, and the whole land was much desolated by such a tumult: for every kingdom divided against itself shall be brought to desolation.[1] Ordinary peaceful men, lovers of peace, greatly feared war and the destruction of peace; but robbers who hoped for booty and set their hands to the goods of others, desired war not peace. The king had

Rex uero ciuitates suas et castra muniri fecit et reparari,
sed magnates ex parte sua hoc idem fecerunt. Per totam
terram uero in comitatibus, hundredis, ciuitatibus, burgis
et uillis, conuocationes et inprouisiones facte sunt, et
quibus quilibet armis, necessitate inueniente, uteretur
ex debito prouisum est et ordinatum. Certissime enim
F.159 puta/batur dissensionem iam cœptam sine magna ruina
sedari non posse.

Post hec uidentes hii qui ex consilio regis erant, ex
tali discordia toti terre imminere discrimen, et pre-
cauentes in futurum, ne furor adhuc recens radices suas
ita extenderet, quod inueteratus de facili extingui non
possit, elaboratum est ab eisdem ut rex et barones sui in
amicitiam et concordiam reuocarentur. De communi
igitur consilio uocantur comites, barones et alii magnates
terre tractaturi[a] de pace,[1] conueniuntque Londoniis non
sine manu armata, proditionem metuentes; ubi rex eos
exspectabat. Igitur cum diu res ipsa uoluta et reuoluta
esset nec tamen finem acciperet (multi enim uolentes
utrique parti placere, uacillabant, ex quorum consilio et
discretione negotium dependebat), tandem post multos
et uarios circuitus, cum in aliud consentire non possent,
promissum est et concessum baronibus per regem quod
Petrus de Gauestone terram Anglie egrederetur.[2] Per
archiepiscopos etiam et episcopos sententia excommunicationis in Petrum lata est si ultra terminum statutum in
partibus Anglie moraretur. Terminus itaque positus est,
dies uidelicet Sancti Johannis Baptiste,[3] quo et eodem
festo per anni reuolutionem elapso idem Petrus eandem terram prius abiurauerat. Adueniente igitur die

---

[a] tractatus MS
[1] The council was summoned for 3 March, but postponed to 28 April;
the sentence against Gaveston was issued on 18 May.
[2] The writ is in *Ann. Lond.* 154, 18 May.
[3] 24 June

his towns and castles munitioned and repaired, and the magnates on their part did likewise. Throughout the land in shires, hundreds, cities, boroughs, and vills, gatherings and regulations were made, and it was duly provided and ordained what arms each should use in the coming emergency. For it was held for certain that the quarrel once begun could not be settled without great destruction.

At this, those who were of the king's council, seeing that by such discord the whole land could be put in peril, and taking thought for the future, lest the turmoil while still fresh should extend its roots, in such a way as to take hold and not be easily weeded out, formed a plan by which the king and his barons might once more be brought together in friendship and harmony. By common consent the earls, barons and other magnates of the land were summoned to treat of peace,[1] and they arrived at London with their men-at-arms, as they feared treachery; and there the king was awaiting them. Thus when the matter had been discussed and rediscussed for a long time without a settlement (for many, on whose advice and discretion the matter hung, wished to please each side and so wavered), after much circumlocution, since they could not agree to anything else, the king promised and granted[2] to the barons that Piers Gaveston should leave England. Sentence of excommunication was pronounced upon Piers by the archbishops and bishops if he should delay in England beyond the appointed term. The term was fixed thus, to wit St John the Baptist's day,[3] on which same feast a year before Piers had forsworn the same land. When the appointed day arrived, the lord king and Piers set out for Bristol with a great company; and there after a little while

prefixo, dominus rex et Petrus cum multo comitatu ad
portum Bristollie sunt profecti; ibidemque post modicum
a rege licentiatus Petrus cum multa familia in partes
Hibernie se transtulit et recepit, totaque terra ex precepto domini regis Anglie sue dominationi et potestati
subdita est.

Hiis itaque peractis nec adhuc uerus amor successit,
nec uera concordia.   Estimabant enim comites, in
F.160 om/nibus gestis adhuc se esse circumuentos, et priorem
laborem inanem et cassum; propositum namque eorum
exitum non sumpsit optatum.   Voluissent certe comites
quod Petrus Anglia recessisset, ita quod amplius in
familiaritate regis non permansisset, nec terra diutius
sumptibus suis sicut prius grauaretur; antecedebat enim
fere regem in expensis.   Defecit itaque propositum
comitum.   Nam Petrus in Hibernia iam moram faciens,
omnes redditus illius terre, qui ad regem Anglie per-
tinebant, ex uoluntate regis et precepto, in suos usus
sumpsit et consumpsit, sicque nouissimus error priore
factus est peior.

Interea[1] Gilbertus comes Gloucestrie, filius quondam
comitis Gilberti, filiam comitis de Holuestere duxit in
uxorem.   Ad nuptias conuenerunt multi magnates et
nobiles, preposuerantque rotundam tabulam ibidem
tenuisse; sed pauor circumuentionis, timorque proditionis, quosdam inuasit fecitque quominus cœpta
procederent.

Videns itaque rex barones suos quasi murum ex aduerso consistere, et propter hoc propositum suum non
posse procedere, conatus est fœdus eorum rumpere, et
potentiores ad se inclinare.   Igitur paterna et patria
fretus cautela, blandiuntur enim Anglici cum uires oneri
sufficere non uident, unum post alium donis, promissis
et blanditiis, ad suum nutum reduxit, in tantum ut uix

Piers took leave of the king and crossed with a large household to Ireland, where by command of the lord king of England the whole land was subjected to his authority and power.

Even when this was accomplished neither true love nor harmony resulted. The earls thought that they were still outwitted in all their doings, their former labour vain and futile, for their designs had not achieved the desired results. The earls undoubtedly wanted Piers to leave England, so that he should no longer remain intimate with the king, nor the country be burdened as hitherto with his expenses: he almost outdid the king in his extravagance. The earls' plan failed, for now that Piers was in Ireland, he converted to his own use and devoured, with the king's express consent, all the revenues of that land which pertained to the king of England. And so the last state was worse than the first.

Meanwhile,[1] Gilbert, Earl of Gloucester, son of the late Earl Gilbert, took to wife the Earl of Ulster's daughter. At the marriage many magnates and nobles congregated, and had planned to hold a Round Table there; but some of them were afraid of being beset, and dreaded treachery, so that their plans came to nought.

When the king saw that his barons stood against him like a wall, by reason of which he could not carry out his intentions, he tried to break up their confederacy and draw over the more powerful to his side. Therefore, relying on inherited and native caution—for the English flatter when they see their strength is insufficient for the task—he bent one after another to his will, with gifts, promises, and blandishments, with such success that

---

[1] The marriage took place at Michaelmas.

unus ex baronibus remaneret qui prius decreta et concessa defenderet. Solus autem comes de Warewyk flecti
non potuit. Dicebat enim sana conscientia se a placitis
recedere non posse. Sed cum omnes dissimularent ipse
solus stare non potuit. Nec tamen expresse consensit.
Interea multi tractatus et consilia habita sunt de defen-
F.161 sione terre Scotie et ex/pugnatione Roberti de Brutz;
cuius tamen effectus fuerunt, nec in palam uenit neque
de facto apparuit.

Dum hec ita agerentur et iam appropinquaret au-
tumpnus, uiderenturque barones cum rege unanimes,
Petrus de Gauestone clam propter insidias aduersario-
rium per partes Wallie ab Hibernia in Angliam reuersus
est. Sententia uero que contra eum lata erat, si amplius
in Anglia moraretur, procurante rege, auctoritate apostolica remissa est.

Rex itaque, sciens Petrum iam rediisse, obuiam illi
uenit ad Cestriam,[1] ibique de reditu suo letus gratanter
ualde eum tamquam fratrem suum honorifice suscepit.
Reuera fratrem suum semper appellauerat. Nullus
autem baronum ausus est amplius uel contra eum
manum extendere, uel de reditu suo querelam deponere;
claudicabat enim coetus eorum, et pars eorum, in se
diuisa, infirmata est. Sic igitur qui bis antea dampnatus
erat in exilium, iam exultat reuersus ad solium. Comes
autem Lincolnie, qui anno preterito inter omnes barones
exilium Petri maxime procurauerat, amicabilis com-
positor iam factus est et mediator; ad cuius preces
sollicitas et continuas comes de Warenna, qui, ab eo tempore quo torneamentum de Walyngford finem accepit,
hilarem uultum Petro nunquam exhibuit, necessarius

---

[1] Edward was at Chester, 27 June-1 July 1309. Gaveston seems to
have reached London on 11 July. *Ann. Lond.* 157.

scarcely a baron remained to defend what had already been decided upon and granted. The Earl of Warwick alone could not be prevailed upon. He said that he could not with a clean conscience go back upon what had been decided. When all practised deceit he could not stand alone: but he would not expressly give his consent. Meanwhile many colloquies and councils were held for the defence of the land of Scotland and the defeat of Robert Bruce, but the effects of these were not clear nor did they issue in action.

While these things were happening and autumn was approaching, and the barons seemed to be at one with the king, Piers Gaveston returned to England secretly (on account of the ambushes of his enemies) through Wales from Ireland. The sentence which had been pronounced against him, if he should delay any longer in England, was with papal authority and at the king's instance remitted.

The king, knowing that Piers had returned, came to meet him at Chester,[1] and there rejoicing at his return he very thankfully received him with honour as his brother. Indeed he had always called him his brother. None of the barons now dared to raise a finger against him, or to lay any complaint about his return. Their ranks wavered, and their party, divided against itself, broke up. So he who had twice been condemned to exile, returned exulting and in state. The Earl of Lincoln, who the year before had been the foremost of the barons in bringing about Piers' exile, now became a friendly go-between and mediator; at his repeated and anxious requests the Earl Warenne who, ever since the conclusion of the Wallingford tournament, had never shown Piers any welcome, became his inseparable friend and faithful helper. See how often and abruptly great

amicus iam factus est et fidelis adiutor. Ecce quam frequens et subita magnatum mutatio! Quibus sine fide*a* adhibemus in borea, contrarium reperimus in austro.*b* Amor magnatum quasi ludus in alea, et uota diuitum pennis simillima.

Petrus uero ad pristinum statum iam reuersus deterius se cœpit habere quam prius. Comites et barones despiciebat, et turpia cognomina[1] similiter addebat. Offi-

F.162 cia et potestates ab aliis auferebat, et suis famili/aribus pro libito conferebat. Unde magnates terre cœperunt hec pro malo habere, et precipue comes Lancastrie, quia unus ex familiaribus suis procurante Petro eiectus erat ab officio suo. Iccirco caue tibi, Petre, quia comes Lancastrie retribuet tibi simile.

Ipse igitur dominus rex de presentia Petri ualde gauisus est; quasi qui recepit amicum ex longa peregrinatione reuertentem, letos dies agitabat. Instante uero Natiuitate Domini, dominus rex et Petrus ad locum quem rex ipse ualde dilexit cum tota familia iter direxit. Locus autem ille Langeleye dicitur, qui iuxta uillam Sancti Albani situatur. In hoc igitur loco festa natalitia celebrarunt, cotidie colloquentes ac mutua conuersatione et diu affectata presentia priorem absentiam plene redimentes.

Transacto natali solatio conueniunt Londoniis[2] edicto regio barones uniuersi, qui cum ad locum consuetum parliamenti nostri uenire differrent, et rex inconsuete more causam requireret, nuntiis regis tale dederunt re-

---

a Hearne suggests 'sane fidem', Stubbs 'si fidem'; the text is uncertain.
b auster MS
[1] This is the earliest allusion to the *turpia cognomina*. The *Vita* later mentions in passing that Warwick was called a Dog (p. 25 below), but all the other evidence is much later. See a summary of the evidence in Tout, *Edward II* pp. 12-13. It seems always to have been assumed that it was Joan of Acre's *son* Gilbert de Clare (*b.* 1291) who was 'the bastard'. But Gilbert de Clare at first supported Gaveston (though with reservations) which he would hardly have done if Gaveston had been going about calling

men change their sides. Those whom we regard as
faithless in the North we find just the opposite in the
South. The love of magnates is as a game of dice, and
the desires of the rich like feathers.

Now that Piers had regained his former status his
behaviour was worse than before. The earls and barons
he despised, and gave them insulting nicknames.[1] From
others he took their offices and authority, granting these
at his pleasure to members of his household. This the
magnates of the land began to resent, and particularly
the Earl of Lancaster, because one of his household had
been thrown out of office at Piers' instance. Wherefore
look to yourself, Piers, for the Earl of Lancaster will pay
you like for like.

The lord king himself was overjoyed at Piers' presence, and, as one who receives a friend returning from
a long pilgrimage, passed pleasant days with him. At
Christmas the lord king and Piers with the whole household directed their steps to a place of which the king
was fond. The place is called Langley, situated near
the town of St Albans. There they passed the festive
season, fully making up for former absence by their long
wished-for sessions of daily and intimate conversation.

When the Christmas respite was over the barons met
at London by royal edict,[2] but they were unwilling to
come to the normal meeting place of our parliament,
and when the king enquired the reason for the unusual
delay, they answered the royal messengers thus, that it

---

him a bastard. Now there is a passage in *Ann. Lond.* 133 (A.D.1304),
saying that *Comes Gloucestrie J [for Le?] Bastard, qui dicitur, Radulfus Heanmer*
[i.e. Monthermer] . . . was present at Earl Warenne's funeral. Nothing is
known of Monthermer's extraction and it is well known that Edward was
furious at Joan's secret marriage to him in 1297 (Trivet, 258). It seems
likely, then, that it is Ralph, not Gilbert, Earl of Gloucester in right of his
wife from 1297 to 1307, to whom one of these unsavoury epithets should be
applied.   [2] This assembly met 8 February 1310 at Westminster.

sponsum, dicentes quod ad mandatum regis et domini
naturalis uenire tenebantur ex debito, sed dum capitalis
inimicus eorum, qui regnum turbauerat et ipsos, regio
lateret in thalamo, accessum eorum non fore securum,
ac hoc, nec in hoc regis precepto fore parendum, uno
ore protestabantur, addentes quod, si se regio conspectui
representare oporteret omnimodo, non inermes ut facere
solebant, sed armati copiam sui facere promiserunt.
Nec ob hoc offensam se regia maiestas sentiret aut lesam
dum unusquisque naturali uiam affectu tenetur eligere
tutiorem.

Tandem rex de suorum consilio Petrum ad satis tuta
loca profectum*a* dimisit ad tempus, ut cœptum negotium
F.163 uel finem caperet optatum, uel saltem mora / eius
non faceret imperfectum. Extunc conuenerunt comites
et barones,[1] causamque uocationis audituri, regem
adierunt; inter quos multa interlocutoria habita sunt,
que non in communem uenere notitiam. Sed cum per
multos dies protelatum esset consilium, hoc demum ex
parte baronum audiui fuisse petitum, scilicet quod cum
status regis et regni a tempore quo bone memorie
Edwardus rex senior diem clausit extremum ualde de-
clinasset in deuium, ac per hoc totum regnum lederetur
non modicum, petebant quod ex consensu et assensu
domini regis et suorum baronum eligerentur duodecim
uiri[2] discreti, bone opinionis et potentes, quorum arbitrio
et decreto status reformaretur et consolidaretur; et si
quid in regni grauamen redundaret, eorum ordinatio
destrueret; si uel in aliquo casu regno esset prospectum,[3]
eorum discretione plenarie foret consultum.

a prefectum MS
[1] Early in March 1310
[2] There were 21 not 12.
[3] *prospectum* seems (in view of the following clause) to have the force of
prospectatum.

was their bounden duty to come at the command of
their king and natural lord, but as long as their chief
enemy, who had set the baronage and the realm in an
uproar, was lurking in the king's chamber, their approach would be unsafe, and this they protested with
one accord, that in this the king's mandate would not
be obeyed; adding that if it was absolutely necessary
to present themselves before the king, they vowed
that they would make their appearance not unarmed as
they were wont to do, but armed. His royal majesty
should not on this account feel offended or injured, since
everyone is bound by natural feeling to choose the safer way.

At length by the advice of his friends the king sent
Piers away for a time to a very safe place, that the
business he had undertaken should reach the desired
end, or at least should not fail of accomplishment by his
delay. Thereupon the earls and barons met together[1]
and approached the king to hear the cause of the summons; they held many deliberations amongst themselves,
and these were not made public. But when the council
had dragged on for many days, this at length was, I
heard, asked for by the barons: that as the state of the
king and the kingdom had much deteriorated since the
elder king Edward of happy memory had died, and by
this the whole kingdom had been not a little injured,
they asked that with the agreement and consent of the
lord king and his barons, there should be elected twelve[2]
discreet and powerful men, of good reputation, by whose
judgment and decree conditions should be reformed and
ameliorated; and if anything should be found a burden
on the realm, their ordinance should destroy it; and if
in any emergency the realm should be threatened,[3] by
their discretion adequate and appropriate action should
be taken.

Rex igitur, super hiis habita deliberatione, quia uidebantur sibi in quibusdam suspecta, diutius differebat inexpedita; sed barones unanimes uiriliter instabant multa allegantes, plurima minantes, ac demum quasi uno ore in hiis residebant, dicentes quod, nisi rex petita concederet, iam non ipsum pro rege haberent, nec fidelitatem iuratam sibi seruarent, maxime cum ipse iusiurandum in sua coronatione prestitum [non] seruaret, cum in lege et naturali ratione caueatur, quod 'frangenti fidem fides frangatur eidem'. Hiis et aliis allegatis rex, artiori habito consilio, cum uideret rem iam in arto positam, nec sine discrimine uel scandalo necessitatem posse euitari, electiones, ordinationes et quicquid saluo honore regio pro communi utilitate regni crederent statuendum, expresse concessit, et scriptis sigillo suo roboratis confirmauit. /

F.164   Electi sunt[1] igitur ordinatores de potentioribus et discretioribus totius regni, et tempus*a* jurisdictionis siue ordinationis faciende et publicande limitatum est. Quibus sub tali forma concessis et consilio finito secessit unusquisque ad propria.

Post paucos dies dominus rex de consilio suo Robertum de Brutz expugnare disposuit. Fecit enim edicto regio per totum regnum proclamari, quod uidelicet omnes qui regi exercitum ducenti ad bellum certum patrocinium[2] ferre tenebantur, die Sancti Johannis Baptiste apud Berewyk super Twede[3] presto regi assisterent, debitum seruitium et auxilium ibidem impensuri. Vnde uiri ecclesiastici, episcopi, abbates et priores, qui pro baroniis quas de rege tenebant in capite, et pro

---

a tempus] episcopis MS (Hearne's copy)

[1] The ordainers were elected 20 March 1310; and the number was twenty-one, not twelve as mentioned above (*Parl. Writs* II.ii.26).

[2] For this use of *patrocinium* (a technical term in Roman Law), cf. p. 94 *infra*.

[3] For the details of this muster, which took place in September 1310, see Ramsay 31.

The king, when he had considered these proposals, was in no hurry to expedite them, as they seemed to him suspect in certain particulars; but the united barons held strongly to their plan, citing many instances, with many threats, and at length almost unanimously took their stand upon them, saying that unless the king granted their demands they would not have him for king, nor keep the fealty that they had sworn to him, especially since he himself had not kept the oath which he had taken at his coronation; since in law and common sense there is this reservation, that with the breaker of faith faith may be broken. When these and other matters had been ventilated, the king, having taken closer counsel, when he saw that the business was delicate, and that the necessity could not be avoided without danger or scandal, expressly granted and by his sealed writings confirmed the elections, ordinances, and whatever (saving the royal honour) they thought should be decreed for the common good of the realm.

Ordainers were therefore elected[1] from amongst the more powerful and discreet men of the whole realm and a term was set by which their decrees or Ordinances were to be made and published. When these concessions had been duly made and the council had come to an end, each man departed to his own estates.

A few days later the lord king of his own accord decided to attack Robert Bruce. He had a royal edict proclaimed throughout the kingdom that all who were bound to bring a certain quota[2] to the king when he led an army to battle, should attend the king in a state of readiness on St John the Baptist's day at Berwick-on-Tweed,[3] there to lend him their due service and aid. Ecclesiastics, bishops, abbots and priors, who in return

quibus ad diuersa seruitia domino regi ex fidelitate et
homagio prestitis tenebantur astricti, pro talibus oneribus
precipue*ᵃ* compensabant non modicum thesaurum, sed
prout quisque conuenire poterat cum thesauro, regis
infundentes erario.[1] Quidam autem comitum et baronum huic precepto regis minime obtemperarunt. Comes
enim Lincolnie custodiam terre a rege acceperat, iccirco
uenire non poterat; comes de Warewyk et alii barones,
circa ordinationes predictas occupati, quominus adessent
fuerant impediti; comes vero de Lancastre, comes de
Penbrok, et comes de Hereford, in odium Petri preceteris
inuecti regem in Scotiam non sunt secuti. Profectus est
igitur rex, a tribus comitibus tantum comitatus, comite
uidelicet Glouuernie, comite Warennie et comite Cor-
F.165 nubie, qui uocatur Petrus. Alii / tamen barones et
milites, et peditum turba copiosa Walensium et Angli-
corum, qui animum ad questum habebant intentum,
regem e uestigio sequebantur ad bellum. Reuera, ut
dicebatur, simulatum erat hoc regis opus et fictum; non
enim accessit rex finaliter in Scotiam ut Robertum de
Brutz expugnaret, sed ut mandatum regis Francie caute
declinaret. Mandauerat enim rex Francie regi Anglie,
ut pro terris quas in partibus transmarinis ab ipso tenebat, ueniret sibi ut domino suo fidelitatem facturus, et
pro eisdem terris debita et consueta seruitia similiter
impensurus. Sed timuit rex; coniciebat pro certo quod,
si ad mandatum regis Francie explendum accederet,
Petro suo in Anglia inter inimicos suos dimisso, mors,
carcer, uel si quid deterius est, forsan eueniret. Talia
predicabantur in populo; si uera uel falsa sint, Deus
scit, nescio.

ᵃ precipuum MS (Hearne's note)
[1] Here as on pp. 78, 108, 116 the writer seems to equate *erarium*
with Exchequer and *fiscus* with chamber. But he also uses the phrase *fiscali
erario* (p. 78).

for the baronies which they held from the king in chief,
for which they were bound to the lord king in various
services by the fealty and homage that they had performed, paid considerable sums in exchange for such
burdens, pouring their money into the royal treasury,[1]
each according to his agreement. Some of the earls and
barons disobeyed this royal command. The Earl of
Lincoln had been made keeper of the realm and therefore could not come; the Earl of Warwick and other
barons were busied about the said Ordinances and so
were prevented from being present; but the Earl of Lancaster, the Earl of Pembroke, and the Earl of Hereford
did not follow the king to Scotland because they hated
Piers more than the others. So the king set out accompanied by only three earls, the Earl of Gloucester, Earl
Warenne, and the Earl of Cornwall, called Piers. However, other barons and knights and a numerous crowd of
Welsh and English infantry, who were intent on gain,
followed in the king's footsteps to war. This indeed, it
was said, was a mere pretext on the king's part; he was
not going to Scotland with the express purpose of fighting Robert Bruce, but that he might shrewdly evade the
king of France's summons. For the king of France had
sent to the king of England that he should come and do
fealty to him, as to his lord, for the lands which he held
of him in foreign parts, and that for the same lands he
would also perform the due and accustomed services.
But the king was afraid; he was convinced that if he
obeyed the summons of the King of France and left
Piers in England in the midst of his enemies, death,
imprisonment, or worse would perhaps befall him. Such
things were openly spoken of; whether they are true or
false God knows: I do not.

Intrauit rex autem Scotiam cum exercitu suo,[1] nullusque ei rebellis inuentus est, qui uel regi manum
apponeret uel hominibus regis insidias pararet, nisi forsan contingeret aliquos de exercitu causa foragii uel
prede capiende longius abscedere. Tunc enim Robertus
de Brutz, qui in insidiis semper latebat, omne malum
quod poterat eis inferebat. Nam quadam die, dum sic
quidam Anglorum et Walensium, qui parati sunt ad
predam, causa depredationis exissent, necnon et equites
quamplurimi simul cum eis pro tutela ab exercitu dis-
cessissent, subito superuenerunt homines Roberti de
Brutz, qui in speluncis et locis nemorosis latuerant, ac
grauem insultum nostris hominibus dederunt. Videntes
autem equites nostri quod eis succurrere non possent,
horrendo clamore ad exercitum reuersi sunt; statimque
prosilierunt omnes ad arma et ad succurrendum suis,
inter hostes relictis, unanimiter properabant; sed sera
fuit defensio quam nostrorum precessit occisio. Nam
F.166 'sero seram ponis stabulo post / furta latronis'. Antequam enim milites nostri uenirent, trucidati sunt de
Walensibus et Anglicis usque ad trecentum animas,
hostesque reuersi sunt ad speluncas suas. Ex talibus
insidiis frequenter inuenerunt homines nostri multa mala.
Robertus enim de Brutz, sciens se tam ex uiribus quam
ex fortuna sua regis Anglie imparem, decreuit sibi magis
expedire contra regem nostrum arma latenter mouere
quam in bello campestri de iure suo contendere. Reuera
dominum Robertum de Brutz affectarem laudibus ex-
tollere nisi reatus homicidii et nota proditionis cogerent
me tacere; 'reatus autem excludit omnem honorem.'[2]

Verumtamen quo iure regnum Scotie ad se pertinere
contendit in breuibus apparebit. Post finem Alexandri
regis Scotie,[3] in dubium uenerat quis ei deberet succe-
dere, erantque duo uel tres quorum quilibet se uerum et

The king entered Scotland with his army,[1] but not a rebel was found to lay a hand upon him or to ambush his men, except that a few out foraging or on a plundering raid were cut off. At that time Robert Bruce, who lurked continually in hiding, did them all the injury that he could. One day, when some English and Welsh, always ready for plunder, had gone out on a raid, accompanied for protection by many horsemen from the army, Robert Bruce's men, who had been concealed in caves and in the woodlands, made a serious attack on our men. Our horsemen, seeing that they could not help the infantry, returned to the main force with a frightful uproar; all immediately leapt to arms and hastened with one accord to the help of those who had been left amongst the enemy; but assistance came too late to prevent the slaughter of our men. For it is no use locking the stable door after the theft has occurred. Before our knights arrived, up to three hundred Welsh and English had been slaughtered, and the enemy returned to their caves. From such ambushes our men often suffered heavy losses. For Robert Bruce, knowing himself unequal to the king of England in strength or fortune, decided that it would be better to resist our king by secret warfare rather than to dispute his right in open battle. Indeed I might be tempted to sound the praises of Sir Robert Bruce did not the guilt of homicide and the dark stain of treachery bid me keep silent; for a criminal conviction involves the loss of all honour.[2]

Nevertheless by what right he maintained that the kingdom of Scotland belonged to him will shortly appear. On the death of Alexander king of Scotland,[3] it was doubtful who should succeed him. And there were two

---

[1] 16 September 1310
[2] *Cod.* 3.24.1
[3] 19 March 1286

proximum heredem asseruit. Sed ex decreto magnatum
utriusque regni Johannes de Bailliol ut proximus heres
Alexandro successit,[1] quem rex Anglie, debita seruitia
negantem et fidem non seruantem, regno priuauit, re-
ceptisque fidelitatibus et homagiis a magnatibus illius
terre regnum in breui totum occupauit. Porro, Johanne
de Bailiol excluso, Robertus de Brutz comes de Carryk
ius succedendi ad se deuolutum uisus est uendicare, ac
diadema sibi imponens[2] contra regem et dominum suum
cui fidelitatem prestiterat ceruicem cœpit erigere, quem
rex Edwardus cum exercitu suo diu persecutus est. Sed
capto[3] Willelmo Waleys, Symone Frysel, Johanne de
Arseles et aliis quampluribus, hic solus euasit, et mediante probitate et industria sua, decreto regis nostri suo
tempore subici non potuit. Hic alter Eneas, a captivitate
Troiana solus effugiens,

> Laudibus Enee, nisi crimina nota necarent,
> Attolli meruit, sed eas mala tot macularunt.

F.167   Perhendinauit itaque rex in Scotia per totam hiemem,
et usque ad Nativitatem Sancti Johannis Baptiste,[4] et
castra sua ex omnibus necessariis muniri fecit et restau-
rari. Circuiuitque per ciuitates, uillas et castra, et
omnium optinuit munitiones. Robertus autem de Brutz
stetit a longe ut uideret finem.[5] Non enim in tali uicinio
uidebatur sibi locus esse securus, sed semper appropinquante exercitu tenebat loca montana inuia aquosa, ad
que non poterat talis exercitus faciliter peruenire. Et
certe quamuis rex Anglie tam breui manu per septen-
nium Scotiam obsideret, Robertum[a] de Brutz suo carceri
nequaquam manciparet. Verum occupatus erat rex

[a] Roberto MS
[1] 17 November 1292
[2] 27 March 1306
[3] In 1305-6
[4] Edward was at or near Berwick, 1 November 1310 to end of June 1311.
[5] Matt. xxvi. 58

or three, each of whom put himself forward as the true
and nearest heir. But by decree of the magnates of both
kingdoms John Balliol succeeded Alexander as nearest
heir.[1] He refused his due service and did not keep faith
with the king of England, who deprived him of his kingdom, received the fealty and homage of the magnates
of that realm and in a short time occupied the whole
of it. Further when John Balliol had been excluded,
Robert Bruce, Earl of Carrick, claimed that the right of
succession had devolved upon him, and placing the dia-
dem upon himself,[2] he waxed bold against the king and
lord to whom he had sworn fealty, and was for long
pursued by king Edward and his army. When William
Wallace, Simon Fraser, John de Athol, and many others
were captured,[3] he alone escaped, and aided by his valour
and diligence, could not be subdued by royal decree in
Edward I's time. Here was another Æneas fleeing alone
from the captivity of Troy:

> Whose fame, but for his crimes, he might have won;
> By evil deeds his honour was undone.

So the king stayed in Scotland throughout the winter
and until the following Midsummer,[4] and had his castles
munitioned and restocked. He went round about the
cities, towns and castles, and obtained supplies of all
things. But Robert Bruce stood afar off, to see the end.[5]
For in such a neighbourhood there seemed no safe place
for him, but always as the army approached he kept to
the trackless boggy mountain places, whither such an
army could not easily penetrate. And indeed although
the king of England shorthanded as he was, were to lay
siege to Scotland for seven years, he never would consign
Robert Bruce to his prison. For the king was really
occupied with two projects: one was with the defeat of

circa duo, unum circa expungnationem Roberti de
Brutz, in quo remissius agebat, pro eo quod maior pars
baronum Anglie ad istud negotium non ferebat auxilium;
aliud erat circa retentionem Petri de Gauestone, ad cuius
expulsionem et exilium omnes fere barones Anglie unanimiter laborabant.   In hiis duobus rex anxius et satis
afflictus unum ob aliud non est consecutus.   Nam*a*

> Qui binas lepores una sectabitur hora,
> Vno quandoque, quandoque carebit utroque.

Queret autem aliquis unde tantam indignationem
baronum meruerat Petrus; que causa odii, quid semi-
narium ire et inuidie extiterit, uehementer forsan ad-
mirabitur, cum in omnium fere magnatum domibus
optentum sit hodie ut unus aliquis de familia dominice
dilectionis gaudeat prerogatiua.   Sane ut reprobatio
unius alios instruat, et ruina reprobati ad aliorum cedat
documentum, causas odii et inuidie pro posse meo
curabo exprimere.

Hic Petrus a Wasconia oriundus filius fuit cuiusdam
militis regis Edwardi senioris quondam familiaris.   Dum
F.168 autem Edwardus iunior adhuc esset princeps / Wallie,
dictus Petrus armiger iuvenis in familiarem domus eius
assumptus est, et grata exhibitione obsequiorum apud
dominum suum summi fauoris apicem optinuit in breui.
Et, ut paucis uerbis multa concludam, rex noster, cum
mortuo patre suo regnum Anglie iam esset adeptus,
Petrum de Gauestone comitem fecit Cornubie.   Sed
Petrus iam comes Cornubie olim se fuisse Petrum et
humilem armigerum noluit intelligere.   Nullum suum
comitem, nullum suum parem reputabat Petrus nisi
solum regem.   Reuera uultus eius maiorem reuerentiam

---

a Before 'nam', MS inserts 'Versus'—presumably a marginal note in
the original.

Robert Bruce, in which he was very remiss, because the greater part of the English baronage brought him no help in this business; the other was with the retention at his side of Piers Gaveston, on whose expulsion and exile almost all the barons of England were determined. In these two matters the king, worried and sorely tried, could not attain one on account of the other. As has been well said:

> He who hunts two hares together,
> Will lose now one, or else the other.

But if anyone seeks to know how Piers had come to merit such baronial wrath, what was the cause of the hatred, what was the seed-bed of envy and dislike, perchance he will be very surprised, since in almost all noble houses today it happens that some one of the lord's household enjoys a prerogative of affection. Thus, that the chastisement of one may serve to instruct others, and the downfall of the victim become a warning to others, I shall endeavour to explain the causes of this envy and hatred as best I can. This Piers originated in Gascony, the son of a certain knight who had been of the household of the elder king Edward. While Edward the younger was still Prince of Wales, the said Piers was received into his household as a young esquire, and by a gratifying attention to his duties he quickly found the highest favour in his master's sight. And, to make a long story short, our king when he had obtained the kingdom on the death of his father, made Piers de Gaveston Earl of Cornwall. But Piers now Earl of Cornwall did not wish to remember that he had once been Piers the humble esquire. For Piers accounted no one his fellow, no one his peer, save the king alone. Indeed his countenance exacted greater deference than

exigebat quam regis. Erat igitur baronibus fastus eius
intollerabilis et prima causa odii simul et rancoris. Nam
uulgariter dicitur,

* Si tibi copia, si sapientia, formaque detur,
    Sola superbia destruit omnia si comitetur.[1]

Credo igitur et constanter teneo quia, si Petrus ab
initio prudenter et humiliter erga magnates terre se
gessisset, nunquam eorum aliquem sibi contrarium habuisset. Erat enim causa odii secundaria hec, quod
cum ab antiquo omnibus desiderabile exstiterit habere
gratiam in oculis regum, solus Petrus gratiam et uultum
hilarem regis habuit et fauorem, in tantum ut, si comes
uel baro colloquium habiturus cum rege cameram regis
intraret, in presentia Petri nulli rex uerba dirigebat,
nulli faciem hilarem ostendebat, nisi soli Petro. Et
reuera ex talibus frequenter oriri solet inuidia. Sane
non memini me audisse unum alterum ita dilexisse.
Jonathas dilexit Dauid, Achilles Patroclum amauit; sed
illi modum excessisse non leguntur. Modum autem
dilectionis rex noster habere non potuit, et propter eum
sui oblitus esse diceretur, et ob hoc Petrus malificus
putaretur esse.

Causa autem quare a comitatu Cornubie nitebantur
eum expellere fuit hec. Dominus Edwardus rex senior /
F.169 uni ex filiis suis Thome uel Edmundo comitatum Cornubie contulisse decreuerat; sed mors amara preueniens
factum quod erat conueniens fecit inperfectum. Unde
barones iunioris regis ingratitudinem uidentes, quia
ignotum noto, extraneum germano, et aduenam incole

---

[1] In J. Werner, *Lat. Sprichwörter und Sinnsprüche des Mittelalters* (Heidel-
berg 1912) p. 92; from a 14-15th cent. MS (Universitätsbibl. Basel A.XI, 67).

that of the king. His arrogance was intolerable to the barons and a prime cause of hatred and rancour. For it is commonly said,

> You may be rich and wise and handsome,
> But insolence could be your ruin.[1]

I therefore believe and firmly maintain that if Piers had from the outset borne himself prudently and humbly towards the magnates of the land, none of them would ever have opposed him. But there was a secondary cause of their hatred, namely that, though of old it has been desirable for all men to find favour in the eyes of kings, Piers alone received a gracious welcome from the king and enjoyed his favour to such an extent that if an earl or baron entered the king's chamber to speak with the king, in Piers' presence the king addressed no-one, and to none showed a friendly countenance save to Piers only. And in truth it is from such-like behaviour that envy frequently springs. Indeed I do not remember to have heard that one man so loved another. Jonathan cherished David, Achilles loved Patroclus. But we do not read that they were immoderate. Our king, however, was incapable of moderate favour, and on account of Piers was said to forget himself, and so Piers was accounted a sorcerer.

The reason why they strove to expel him from the earldom of Cornwall was this. The lord king Edward the elder had decided that the earldom of Cornwall should be conferred upon one of his sons Thomas or Edmund; but his sad death prevented what would have been appropriate from being consummated. Whence the barons, seeing the ingratitude of the young king, that he was trying to promote the unknown over the known, the stranger over his brother, and the foreigner

conabatur preferre, dominum illegitimum, comitem
superbum (uelle consilio preuium) nisi sunt mittere in
exterminium. Hiis maxime de causis excitata erat contra
Petrum indignatio baronum; et Petrus nihilominus
magnanimus, tumidus et elatus permansit. Sed vereor
ne superbia in ruinam et precipitium ipsum deuoluat;
scriptum est enim, ante ruinam exaltabitur cor[1]; ille qui
in altis habitat et humilia[2] respicit superbiam super
omnia detestatur. Hec Luciferum mire claritudinis
angelum[a] ad yma deiecit; hec reginam Vasti a solio
regni similiter abiecit[3]; nec mirum si in superbia sua nec
Deo nec homini foret acceptus. Nam in superbia et in
abusione sublimes oculos distorquens in fastum, quadam
pomposa et superciliosa facie despexit uniuersos, et
omnia quasi pro imperio agens, magnates terre, quibus
necessarius esse non potuit quin eorum auxilio magis
indigeret, uix aliquando et indignantissime respexit. Et
certe in filio regis satis esset intollerabile supercilium
quod pretendit. Publice tamen scitur quod non erat
filius regis nec regalem prosapiam quicquid attingens.

Imminente festiuitate Sancti Johannis Baptiste, conueniunt Londoniis ordinatores, quibus anno preterito
commissa fuit potestas ordinandi, corrigendi et ad meliorem statum reducendi, si quid contra leges regni uel in
commune dispendium fuisset attemptatum. Potestas
enim eorum limitem habuit proximum futurum festum
beati Michaelis. Vt ergo antequam exspiraret eorum
iuredictio, statuta et ordinata per eos in publicum
F.170 uenirent, uocauerunt dominum regem et alios / magnates
terre ut coram eis recitata uel infirmarentur uel appro-
barentur. 'Quod enim omnes tangit ab omnibus debet
approbari.'[4] Recessit igitur rex a Scotia, et uenit

---

[a] angelorum MS
[1] cf. Prov. xvi. 18   [2] cf. Ps. cxiii. 5, 6
[3] Esther i. 9-22   [4] *Cod.* 5.59.5

over the native, determined—the wish being father to
the thought—to destroy this illegitimate lord, this insolent earl. These were the principal causes which had
aroused the anger of the barons against Piers; and Piers
remained a man of big ideas, haughty and puffed-up.
I fear that his pride will bring about his ruin and head-
long fall; for it is written, the heart is exalted before
destruction.[1] He who dwells on high[2] and looks down
upon the lowly hates pride above all things. This it was
that hurled Lucifer, an angel of wonderful brightness,
down to the depths; this likewise cast queen Vashti from
the throne of her kingdom[3]; nor is it surprising if he in
his pride should be acceptable to neither God nor man.
For, scornfully rolling his upraised eyes in pride and in
abuse, he looked down upon all with pompous and super-
cilious countenance, and carrying everything on his own
authority, he scarcely ever condescended disdainfully to
notice the magnates of the land, to whom he could not
be necessary, but whose help he needed. And indeed
the superciliousness which he affected would have been
unbearable enough in a king's son. Yet it was generally
known that he was not a king's son, nor had he any claim
to royal blood.

As Midsummer approached the Ordainers came to
London. They had been given the year before the power
of ordaining, correcting and reforming anything attempted against the laws of the realm or to the common loss,
and the term set to their power was the feast of St Michael
next coming. In order that their decrees and ordinances
should be published before their jurisdiction expired,
they invited the lord king and the rest of the magnates
of the land to confirm or reject what was recited before
them. 'For what touches all should be approved
by all.'[4] So the king left Scotland and came to

Londonias,[1] et apud fratres Predicatores hospitio se recepit. Cum quidam autem procerum moram facerent,
sine quorum presentia res expediri non posset, dominus
rex sacra loca visitare Cantuariam proficiscitur, ac
demum circa finem mensis Augusti reuertitur.

Omnibus itaque quorum interesse uertebatur adunatis, profertur in medium labor annalis, et capitula
singillatim recitantur, et regis consiliariis copia porri-
gitur. Rex autem de consilio suo quedam sibi incommoda, quedam in odium suum adinuenta protestatur, et
se hiis assensum prebere non teneri arguit et causatur,
cum in commissione concessa regia magestas fuisset excepta. Sciebant tamen barones regis excusationes friuolas esse et fictas et ad exquirendas dilationes semper
intentas; unde et ipsi uiriliter instabant, et cum omnium
incommodo regis magis commodum compensabant. Fuit
autem inter ordinationes illas una quedam que magis
inter ceteras regem affligebat, uidelicet expulsio Petri de
Gauestone et eius exilium; sed rex ad hoc nullo sensu
inclinari potuit uel induci. Vt tamen baronibus satisfaceret hoc offerebat; quecunque, inquit, ordinata sunt,
quecunque statuta, quantumcunque in meum priuatum
incommodum redundent, ad petitionem uestram ualeant
atque perpetuo subsistant. Verum a persecutione fratris
mei Petri desistatis, et comitatum Cornubie habere per-
mittatis. Hoc sepe et sepius petebat sic rex, nunc illos
blanditiis palpans, nunc autem minas adiciens; sed barones uiriliter instabant, plurima allegantes ut fideles regis
regi consulentes, ac demum, quasi uno animo et una
uoce, hoc in calce sermonis adiciebant, quod aut[a] Petrus/
F.171 iuxta arbitrium ordinatorum exilium subiret, aut unus-

a autem MS
[1] 13 August 1311

London,[1] where he lodged with the Dominicans. When certain of the notables delayed, as the business could not proceed without them, the king set out to visit the shrines at Canterbury and at length returned towards the end of August.

When all those concerned had been gathered together, the year's work was produced and recited chapter by chapter, and a copy made available to the king's counsellors. But the king and his council protested that some things were disadvantageous to him, some fabricated out of spite, and he argued and pleaded that he was not bound to give his consent to these, since from their terms of reference all things touching the king's sovereignty had been excluded. The barons knew, however, that the king's excuses were frivolous pretexts for gaining time; they therefore held firmly to their purpose, setting the common good above the king's loss. But there was one of those Ordinances that more than the rest distressed the king, to wit the expulsion of Piers Gaveston and his exile. To this the king could in no way be brought to agree. But to satisfy the barons he offered these terms: whatever has been ordained or decided upon, he said, how much soever they may redound to my private disadvantage, shall be established at your request and remain in force for ever. But you shall stop persecuting my brother Piers, and allow him to have the earldom of Cornwall. The king sought this time and again, now coaxing them with flattery, now hurling threats; but the barons firmly held their ground with many arguments, as faithful subjects consulting the king's interests, and finally, at one in sentiment and speech, they concluded their reply by stating that either Piers should suffer exile according to the judgment of

quisque de capite proprio defendendo sibi consuleret.
Videntes igitur hii qui de consilio regis erant quod, si
dominus rex ordinatorum decretis et placitis non acqui-
esceret, turbaretur regnum et pacis sequeretur exilium;
scientes etiam quod ciuile bellum nunquam finem habuisset acceptum, de quo bellum de Lewes manifestum
reliquit exemplum et bellum de Euesham eternam ser-
uabat memoriam, in quo pro tempore iustitie nobilis ille
comes Leycestrie Symon occubuit; considerabant etiam
quam dura inter regem et barones suos et quam periculosa foret dissensio, quod totius terre sequeretur deso-
latio, quod inter dubios euentus uix euitaretur regis
captio, et, sicut Roboam qui consilium seniorum respuens
consilio iuuenum adhesit,[1] incaute solio forsan priuaretur
et regno; hec et hiis similia considerantes qui consulares
regis esse dicebantur, attentius instare cœperunt pro
regno, pro populo, pro semetipso regem interpellantes,
quatinus suorum dignaretur acceptare consilium, ineui-
tabile protestantes euenire periculum quod sibi et suis
perpetuum afferret obprobrium, nisi decretis baronum
assentiret, nisi ordinationes eorum sine fraude concederet.

Rex igitur, suorum monitis et precibus inductus,
ordinationes, prouisiones et statuta, quocunque nomine
censeantur, pro se et suis successoribus inuiolabiliter et
imperpetuum rata teneri consentit. Directa est igitur
copia ordinationum sub magno sigillo ad quemlibet
comitatum,[2] et ibidem publice proclamantur, et ab
omnibus proclamari precipiuntur. Quas hic ideo inter-
serere nolui, quia seriem huius materie rescinderem uel
fastidium legentibus afferrem: sed, si quis eas sibi dixerit
ignotas, inter alia statuta suo loco reperiet insertas.

---

[1] cf. 1 Kings xii. 8; 2 Chron. x. 8
[2] 11 October 1311.   *Rot. Parl.* I. 281-286; *Statutes of the Realm* I. 157.

the Ordainers, or each man would take steps to defend
his own life. The king's advisers seeing that if the lord
king would not agree to the decrees and resolutions of
the Ordainers, the kingdom would be in turmoil and
peace driven out of the land; knowing also that civil war
never yet had an acceptable end, of which the battle of
Lewes is a manifest example, and the battle of Evesham
an everlasting reminder, where that noble man Simon
Earl of Leicester laid down his life in the cause of justice;
considering also how ruthless and perilous would be the
struggle between the king and his barons, that the desolation of the whole land would ensue, that amidst the
varying fortunes of war the capture of the king could
hardly be avoided, and like Rehoboam who rejected the
counsel of the elders and followed the advice of the
young,[1] he might through imprudence be deprived of
his throne and of the kingdom; considering these things
and the like, those who were said to be the king's counsellors began to press the king more insistently, urging
him for the sake of the kingdom, the people, and himself
that he should deign to accept their advice, showing that
inescapable danger would arise, bringing everlasting disgrace upon him and his, unless he consented to the
decrees of the barons, and granted their Ordinances in
a straightforward manner.

So the king, moved by their warnings and entreaties,
agreed that the Ordinances, provisions and statutes, by
whatever name they may be called, should be held in-
violate and valid for evermore by him and his successors.
A copy of the Ordinances was therefore sent under the
great seal to every county,[2] and there publicly proclaimed, and commanded to be proclaimed by all. I do
not insert them here as it would break the flow of this
narrative and prove tedious to my readers: but if anyone

E

F.172 Verum quia ordinatio illa que Pe/trum de Gauestone eiecit ab Anglia pluribusque inter alias magis uidebatur accepta (inspicientes enim ordinationes statim ad illam recursum habebant, cum tamen in ordine prima non esset, sed decimum uel ulteriorem locum optineret), et ut ipsa ordinatione perlecta manifeste appareat ipsius exilii causa, iccirco in hac mee narrationis serie, quia multum concordat materie statutum illud, de uerbo ad uerbum, prout fuerat in audientia publicatum, interserui sub forma que sequitur:—

Quia notum est[1] et per examinationem prelatorum, comitum, baronum, militum et aliorum bonorum et legalium hominum regni repertum, quod Petrus de Gauestone dominum regem male duxit, domino regi male consuluit, et ipsum ad male faciendum deceptorie et multiformiter induxit, contractando sibi totum thesaurum regis, quem etiam extra regnum elongauit; attrahendo sibi homines qui secum morarentur contra omnes gentes, et per thesaurum regis quem sic adquisiuit, de die in diem dominando supra statum regis et corone in destructione regis et regni; specialiter elongando cor domini regis a suis legiis hominibus, consilia eorum despiciendo, bonos ministros legem facere non permittendo et bonos ministros amouendo; tales autem de sua familiaritate, tam alienigenas quam alios, constituendo, qui ad suum preceptum et uelle iustitiam offendunt [et] legem terre, acceptando terras et tenementa contra suum homagium de corona, nedum ante ordinationes ad profectum regis et regni ab ordinatoribus concessas sed etiam post, contra dictorum ordinatorum prouisiones et decreta.

Sustinet etiam predones et homicidas ipsisque cartas domini regis de pace adquirit, et sic aliis malefactoribus magis delinquendi prebet audaciam. Conduit regem in terram guerre sine communi consensu suorum baronum, in periculum regis et destructionem regni; albas cartas sub magno sigillo regis facit consignari in captio-
F.173 nem et exheredationem regis et corone; et callide false et prodi/torie fecit hec omnia predicta in magnum dedecus et dampnum regni, exheredationem corone, in destructionem populi multimode;

Insuper habentes respectum ad facta nobilissimi regis patris domini nostri regis qui nunc est, [cuius] edicto dictus Petrus regnum Anglie abiurauit et exulauit, qui et uoluit quod dominus noster rex filius suus pro omni tempore societatem illius abiurasset;

---

[1] *Quia notum est*: this is a Latin translation of the 20th Ordinance: see *Statutes of the Realm*, I 162.

shall say that he is unacquainted with them, he will find them in their proper place among the other Statutes. But because the ordinance which expelled Piers Gaveston from England was more welcome to many than the rest (for when people examined the Ordinances they at once turned to it, although it did not come at the head of the list, but was tenth or later), and in order that this ordinance may be read and the cause of banishment appear clearly, I have inserted it in my narrative as very relevant to my theme, word for word as it was given to the audience in the following form:—

Because it is well-known[1] and has been made clear by the examination of prelates, earls, barons, knights and other good and lawful men of the realm, that Piers Gaveston has led the lord king astray, counselled him badly and persuaded him deceitfully and in many ways to do evil, by gathering to himself all the king's treasure which he then exported from the country; by attracting to himself men who would dwell with him against all people, and by means of the king's treasure so acquired, dominating from day to day the state of the king and of the crown to the destruction of the king and kingdom; more especially by turning away the lord king's heart from his liege men, despising their counsel, not permitting good ministers to make law and removing good ministers; setting up such persons from the circle of his familiars, both foreigners and others, as at his command act unjustly and break the law of the land; by receiving lands and tenements against their homage to the crown, not only before the Ordinances made by the Ordainers for the profit of the king and the kingdom, but also afterwards, against the provisions and decrees of the said Ordainers.

Also he maintains robbers and homicides and obtains pardons for them from the king, and so encourages other evil-doers to greater boldness in crime. He persuades the king to make war without the common consent of his barons, to the danger of the king and the destruction of his realm; he has blank charters made under the great seal to the fraud and disherison of the king and the crown; and all the aforesaid he does cunningly, falsely, and treacherously to the great disgrace and loss of the realm, the disherison of the crown, and the manifold destruction of the people;

Moreover, having regard to the deeds of the most noble king father of the lord king who now is, by whose edict the said Piers abjured and was exiled from the realm of England, who wished,

Inspicientes etiam quod postea communi assensu totius regni pariter et regis prospectum erat, quod Petrus idem regnum euacuaret, et euacuauit, et quod per communem assensum non rediit, sed duntaxat per consensum aliquorum, qui sub conditione, si post regressum suum bene se gereret, ad hoc consentiebant; et nunc certissime repertus est male gesisse;—

Quamobrem et propter sua malefacta predicta, et propter alia que uerisimiliter domino regi et populo contingere possent, et ad bonam concordiam inter dominum regem et suos subditos nutriendam et multimodas discordias et pericula euitanda, nos ordinatores, ut ordinatores et uirtute dicte commissionis regie, concessimus quod Petrus de Gauestone, tanquam publicus hostis regis et regni, a regno penitus eiciatur et exuletur, nedum ab Anglia sed etiam Wallia, Scotia, Hibernia, Wasconia, et ab omni terra tam ultra mare quam citra mare dominationi regis Anglie subiecta, pro omni die et sine reditu. Et quod citra festum Omnium Sanctorum proxime futurum regnum Anglie et omne regis dominium*a* relinquat et penitus euacuet, et portum apud Douere sibi damus in forma predicta. Nec liceat sibi alibi terram exire uel in alio sinu maris portum arripere. Et si dictus Petrus in regno Anglie uel alibi in dominio regis nostri ultra statutum diem faciat moram, extunc fiat*b* de ipso tanquam de inimico regni, regis et populi. Et quicunque contra hanc ordinationem uenerit, ad tardationem dicti exilii, fiat de ipsis prout uisum fuerit expedire cum super hoc fuerint conuicti.

Et Petri quidem exilium ex decreto ordinatorum sic erat.

Post festum Omnium Sanctorum, quia rex ordinationibus baronum stare iurauerat, Petrum in exilium / F.174 ire disposuit, quia in breui satis competenter sibi prouidere proposuit. Antequam tamen Petrus terram Anglie egrederetur, de consilio quorundam qui parti sue adherebant, litteras regis bone conuersationis et fidelitatis testimoniales a rege impetrauit et optinuit; et hiis litteris rex sigillum suum apposuit, et multi magnates similiter fecerunt, qui magis reprehensione digni quam ex hoc facto laudandi fuerunt. Inter quos comes Gloucestrie Gilbertus, iuuenis et precibus regis inductus,

---

a regis dominium] regnum domū MS
b faciat MS

too, that our lord king his son should have abjured for all time the company of this person;

Bearing in mind, further, that afterwards by the common consent of the whole realm and of the king it was decided that the said Piers should leave the realm, and he left it, and that he did not return by common consent, but only by the consent of some, who consented to this on condition that after his return he should be of good behaviour; and now it is found of a certainty that he has behaved badly;—

Wherefore on account of his aforesaid misdeeds, and on account of other things which are likely to happen to the lord king and the people, and to encourage good harmony between the lord king and his subjects, and to avoid manifold discords and perils, we, the Ordainers, as Ordainers and by virtue of the said royal commission, have granted that Piers Gaveston, as a public enemy of the king and of the kingdom, shall be utterly cast out and exiled, not only from England, but from Wales, Scotland, Ireland, Gascony, and from every land as well beyond the sea as on this side of the sea subject to the lordship of the king of England, for ever and without return. And that before the feast of All Saints next coming he shall leave and utterly depart from the realm of England and every lordship of the king, and we assign him Dover harbour in the said form. Nor may he leave the land elsewhere nor from another harbour. And if the said Piers delays in the realm of England or elsewhere in the lordship of our king beyond the appointed day, he shall thereafter be treated as an enemy of the kingdom, the king, and the people. And whosoever shall contradict this Ordinance, to the delaying of the said exile, shall suffer as seems expedient when they shall be found guilty of it.

And this was the manner of Piers' banishment by decree of the Ordainers.

After the feast of All Saints, because the king had sworn to stand to the Ordinances of the barons, he arranged for Piers to go into exile, because he planned soon to provide for him very adequately himself. Before Piers left England, by the advice of some who clung to his side he asked for and obtained from the king letters testifying to his good character and loyalty; and to these letters the king affixed his seal, and many magnates more worthy of reproof than praise did likewise. Amongst whom Gilbert Earl of Gloucester, a young man moved

predictis litteris testimonium prebuit. Nam et illas
sigillo suo roborauit, sed postea saniori ductus consilio,
et pretextu minoris etatis excusatus, errorem suum reuocauit, et impressionem sigilli sui a litteris illis extorsit.

Petrus igitur tali testimonio munitus clam propter
aduersarios secessit in Flandriam,[1] omni fere populo
ignorante ad quas partes diuertisset. Post hec comites
iuxta ordinationes domini regis ulterius disponere uolentes, complices et fautores Petri a curia regis sub pœna
incarcerationis recedere decreuerunt, ne et ipsi animum
regis ad reuocandum Petrum de cetero instigarent. Ad
hec rex ultra modum commotus, quod nec unum familiarem iuxta proprium uotum retinere sibi liceret, sed
sicut prouidetur fatuo, totius domus sue ordinatio ex
alieno dependeret arbitrio, in odio comitum reuocauit
Petrum, per animam Dei iurans ex solito quod libere
proprio uteretur arbitrio.

Et Petrus quidem ad regis mandatum statim reuersus
est in Angliam, quia regem Francie suspectum habebat,
per Flandriam. Sed quamuis periculosa sibi foret Francia, periculosior futura sibi fuit Anglia. Euenit enim
sibi quod quidam ait,

> Incidit in Scillam cupiens uitare Caribdim.[2]

Reuersus[3] igitur Petrus caute ambulabat, et nunc in
camera regis, nunc apud Walyngford, nunc in castello
de Tyntagel latere putabatur. Cum autem appropinquaret Natale Domini dominus rex et Petrus ad partes
F.175 boriales sunt profecti, et apud Eboracum[4] festa*a* / natalitia celebrarunt. Et dominus rex studiose indies cum
omni consilio suo de statu Petri et pace tractabat; et

---

a facta MS

[1] Ramsay, *op. cit.* 42 note 3

[2] Dr R. A. Browne very kindly tells me that the Latin verse occurs in
Walter of Chatillon, *Alexandreis* v 301 (Migne, *Pat. lat. 209*) and is proverbial
after his time (J. E. Sandys, *Hermathena* xii (1902-3) 438).

by the king's entreaties, lent his testimony to these letters. For he confirmed them with his seal, but afterwards thought better of it and excusing himself on the ground of his minority, corrected his mistake by tearing the impression of his seal from the letters.

Thus fortified with his testimonial Piers secretly, on account of his enemies, departed to Flanders,[1] almost everyone being ignorant of his destination. After this, the earls wishing to make further dispositions according to the Ordinances declared that Piers' friends and partisans should leave the court under penalty of imprisonment, lest they should stir up the king to recall Piers once more. At this the king's anger knew no bounds, that he was not allowed to keep even one member of his household at his own wish, but, as is provided for an idiot, the ordering of his whole house should depend upon the will of another; so out of hatred for the earls he recalled Piers, swearing as he was wont on God's soul that he would freely use his own judgment.

So Piers immediately returned to England at the king's command, by way of Flanders, because he suspected the king of France. But though France might be dangerous for him, England was going to be more so. For it so turned out that, as is commonly said, 'He falls into Scylla in trying to avoid Charybdis'.[2] When he returned[3] Piers proceeded cautiously, and was thought to be lurking now in the king's apartments, now at Wallingford, now at Tintagel Castle. As Christmas approached the lord king and Piers set out for the North, and celebrated the feast at York.[4] The lord king zealously discussed day by day with his whole council the

---

[3] His estates were restored on 20 January 1312. *Foed.* II.i. 153-4.
[4] Edward was at York 18 January to 8 April, but *not* for Christmas.

quia non erat Petro tutus locus in Anglia, Hibernia,
Wallia, Wasconia nec Francia, de mora Petri tractare
disposuit in Scotia, donec impetus baronum cessaret, uel
Petro decentius et alibi prouideret; sed inane studium
uix habuit initium. Cum enim Robertus de Brutz de
fidelitate Petro seruanda et conditione pacis require-
[re]tur et invitaretur; cum etiam sibi multa offerrentur
ac demum ipsum regnum*a* Scotie tranquille et imperpetuo
domino Roberto promitteretur, hoc modo regis mandato
fertur respondisse, 'Quomodo rex Anglie pactum michi
seruaret, qui legiis suis hominibus, quorum fidelitatem
et homagia recepit, quibus etiam mutuo fidem seruare
tenetur, promissa etiam iuramento uallata non custodit?
Non est adhibenda fides homini tam uario: non me
decipiet sua promissio.' Sic cassata spes regia, sic
eluduntur regis promissa.

Audientes autem comites et pro certo iam scientes
quod rediisset Petrus, uidentes autem quod non procederet ordinatio quam statuerant circa eum, congregati
sunt cum primate suo Roberto Cantuariensi archiepiscopo. Et primas quidem,*b* sicut erat spiritu feruens
et pacem regni zelans, gladium suum arripuit et Petrum
anathemate percussit,[1] ut sic lata sententia euacuaretur
gratia; nam qui iuste ligatur raro efficaciter operatur.
Et barones ex parte sua non minus laborant ad queren-
dum remedia, fueruntque ad defensionem ordinationum
principaliter intenti et inuicem iureiurando similiter
astricti comites subscripti; Thomas comes Lancastrie,
Adolmarus comes Penbroke, Humfridus comes Herfordie, Edmundus comes Darundel, et Guydo comes

---

a regem MS
b quid MS
[1] *Foed. II,* 167

question of Piers' position and the peace of the realm; and because there was no place of safety for Piers in England, Ireland, Wales, Gascony or France, he tried to arrange for Piers' residence in Scotland, until the baronial attack should cease, or Piers be more fittingly provided for elsewhere; but this fatuous scheme was scarcely even set in motion. For when Robert Bruce was sounded about keeping faith with Piers and the terms of peace; when, too, many offers were made to him, and at length that the kingdom of Scotland itself should be allowed to Sir Robert freely and for ever, he is said to have replied to the king's message in this manner: 'How shall the king of England keep faith with me, since he does not observe the sworn promises made to his liege men, whose homage and fealty he has received, and with whom he is bound in reciprocity to keep faith? No trust can be put in such a fickle man: his promises will not deceive me.' Thus was the king's hope shattered, thus the royal promises made light of.

When the earls had heard and knew for certain that Piers had returned, realising that the ordinance which they had made concerning him would not be executed, they met together with their primate Robert [Winchelsea] Archbishop of Canterbury. And the primate, a passionate man having the peace of the realm much at heart, seized his sword and struck Piers with anathema,[1] so that as an excommunicate he should be excluded from grace; for he who is duly bound is seldom effective in action. And the barons on their part laboured no less to find a remedy. They were chiefly concerned with the defence of the Ordinances, and the following earls were likewise bound by a mutual oath: Thomas Earl of Lancaster, Aylmer Earl of Pembroke, Humphrey Earl of Hereford, Edmund Earl of Arundel, and Guy Earl of

F.176 Warewyke. Hii quinque / comites armis strenui, genere preclari, et copiosa armatorum multitudine uallati, circa captionem Petri unanimiter consultant. Quid autem in illo consilio fuerit decretum, uel quibus insidiis molirentur in Petrum, diu quidem latuit; sed quid ibidem actum fuerit ex post factis satis apparuit; et caute quidem et prouide actum, ut ita lateret eorum propositum, ne diuulgata intentio immunem prestaret in uitio.*a* Secesserunt igitur comites ab inuicem unusquisque in uiam suam, et comes Glouuernie, quamuis in hoc proposito socius non esset, ratum tamen habere promisit quicquid comites facerent, quicquid in hac expeditione disponerent. Comes autem Lancastrie ad partes boriales se transtulit, et ceteri comites, ne ex uisu armorum terreretur prouincia, fecerunt per diuersa loca proclamari torneamenta, ut sub tali pretextu colligerent quos sibi necessarios esse, et sic mouerunt se de loco ad locum donec transirent Eboracum, et comes Lancastrie circa solis occasum aggressus est iter suum.

> Sic Thomas de nocte uolat, sub luce moratur,
> Ut lateat, modicum cursum ne fama loquatur;

et hac cautela nisus ad Nouum Castrum[1] subito uenit et inprouisus, ubi*b* dextrarii et magni caballi ipsius Petri uel uerius domini regis morabantur. Erat etiam ibidem copiosa multitudo armorum, in quibus erat fiducia Petri defendendi et resistendi se. Sed hec omnia cepit comes, et custodibus eiectis suis hominibus et hec omnia custodienda mandauit, ut [que] regis erant, fideliter restituerentur et regi.

Accidit itaque modicum post hec ut dominus rex et

---

a in uitio] innicio MS
b ubi nisi MS
[1] 4 May 1312

Warwick. These five earls, good soldiers, of famous families, and surrounded by a strong contingent of men-at-arms, took counsel together about the capture of Piers. What was decreed in that council or what snares were constructed for Piers was long kept secret; but what had been done there later became apparent; and indeed it was shrewdly done and with foresight, that their plan should be so concealed, lest a knowledge of their intentions should keep him safe in his crime. So the earls separated from one another, each going his own way, and the Earl of Gloucester, although he was not a partner in this plan, promised that he would ratify whatever the earls did, whatever they should decide upon in this enterprise. The Earl of Lancaster betook himself to the North, and the other earls, lest the province should be terrified by the sight of arms, had tournaments proclaimed in different places, that under cover of these they might assemble those who were necessary to them; and thus they moved from place to place until they passed York, and about sunset the Earl of Lancaster set out on his way.

> Thus Thomas flies by night and hides by day
> And to check rumour slowly wends his way.

Relying on this cautious procedure he came suddenly and unexpectedly to Newcastle,[1] where the war-horses and great riding-horses of the said Piers, or rather of the lord king, were stabled. There was also a large supply of arms there, in which lay Piers' confidence that he could resist and defend himself. But all these the earl took, and having thrown out the guards ordered his own men to guard them, since they belonged to the king and should be faithfully restored to him.

It happened shortly after this that the lord king and Piers were separated from one another; the one staying

Petrus ab inuicem separarentur; unus apud Scarde-
burghe, alter apud Knaresbrugg morabatur. Quod cum
perpendisset comes Lancastrie, disposuit se in medio esse,
ne unus ad alterum posset habere regressum, et ceteri
F.177 comitum interim obsiderent Petrum. / Cum igitur
uideret Petrus obsidionem iam cœptam, auxilium regis
interceptum, castrum uictualibus destitutum et socios
minus sufficientes ad bellum, misit ad comitem Penbrokie
se reddere uolens sub conditione[1]; et erat conditio hec
uidelicet quod dictus comes Petrum usque ad gulam
Augusti seruaret illesum, et, si placeret ei quod interim
comites disponerent, bene quidem; sin autem, resti-
tueretur in pristinum statum, scilicet ad castrum unde
exierat et ad sororem quam prius reliquerat.

Comes autem de hac captione gauisus, sociis incon-
sultis, immo ex proprio capite sumpto consilio, cepit
Petrum, et placuit conditio, et ad Petrum seruandum
sub forma predicta obligauit regi terras et tenementa.
Nam et huius rex conscius erat, quia de consilio regis
res ipsa prodierat; sperauit enim ante predictum terminum sufficiens prestare Petro subsidium: quia si Petrus
exspectasset Augustum, ad libitum, ut dicitur, rediisset
arbitrium. Nam papa et rex Francie ordinassent remedium, quia rex Anglie donasset Wasconiam eis in feodum.

Comes igitur Adolmarus cum uinculato suo Petro
recessit a borea, ad Anglie tendens interiora, et cum
circiter quinque dietas uel amplius peregisset, tandem
in comitatum Northamtoniensem[2] deueniens, uocato
Petro dixit, 'Fatigatus es ex itinere, et opus esset tibi
recreatione; est autem hic iuxta uilla modica, locus
amenus et ampla edificia. Egouero [circa] quedam
negotia ad tempus recedem; ibidem morare donec

[1] 19 May, *Ann. Lond.* 204-6
[2] 9 June 1312

at Scarborough, the other at Knaresborough. When
the Earl of Lancaster realised this, he took up his position
in between them, so that the one should not fall back
upon the other, and meanwhile the other earls could
besiege Piers.

When Piers saw that the siege had begun, help from
the king cut off, the castle without food, and his supporters too few to give battle, he sent to the Earl of
Pembroke, wishing to surrender conditionally[1]; the condition was that the said earl should keep Piers unharmed
till the first of August, and if he agreed to what the earls
had in the meantime decided, well and good; if not he
should be restored to his former state, namely to the
castle whence he had gone out, and to the sister whom
he had left.

The earl was delighted by this capture and without
consulting his fellows, but on his own initiative, took
Piers, accepted the condition, and pledged his lands and
tenements to the king under the said form for Piers'
safety. Now the king knew of this, because the matter
had been put forward by his counsel. He hoped to give
Piers adequate support before the said term: because if
Piers could have waited until August, he would have recovered, it is said, his personal freedom. For the Pope
and the king of France would have appointed a remedy,
because the king of England would have given them
Gascony in fee.

Thus Earl Aylmer left the North, and with Piers in
bonds as his prisoner made for the heart of England,
and when he had gone about five days' journey or more,
coming at length to the county of Northampton,[2] he sent
for Piers and said, 'You are tired from the journey, and
need rest; there is a small village near here, a pleasant
place with ample lodgings. I am going off on certain

ueniam.' Et Petrus quod comes optulit gratanter
accepit; et misit cum ad dictam uillam cum custodia;
sed non uidit comes Petrum amplius in Anglia.[1]

Cum autem didicisset comes Warewykye omnia que
F.178 agebantur circa Petrum, accepta manu ualida, / accita
etiam tota patria, clam tendit ad locum ubi cognouit
esse Petrum, et ualde mane una sabbatorum[2] ueniens
ad uillam intrauit portam curie et circumdedit cameram.
Exclamauit autem comes uoce magna, 'Surge proditor,
captus es.' Et Petrus audiens comitem, uidens etiam
manum comitis superiorem et custodiam cui deputatur[a]
non resistentem, induens uestimenta sua descendit de
camera. Capitur igitur Petrus et non sicut comes, immo
sicut latro, producitur; et qui solebat palfridos ascendere
iam pedes cogitur ire.

Cum autem transissent a uilla ad modicum, iussit
comes preberi Petro iumentum ut eo uelocius maturaret
iter suum. Et[b] Petrum sequebantur cornua / tonantia,
populus clamans et uox horrida. Iam Petrus deposuit
cingulum militie, sicut fur et proditor tendit Warewykye,
et ibidem ueniens mittitur in carcerem. Modo suis
uinculis Petrum subiugauit quem canem Warewyk
Petrus appellauit.

Et Petrus quidem seruabatur in carcere,[3] oratio
autem fiebat sine dilatione ab Adolmaro comite ad
barones pro eo. Statim enim ut cognouit captum esse
Petrum, accessit ad comitem Glouernie plorans et orans
quatinus iniuriam sibi illatam uindicaret, et Petrum
omnimodo sibi restitueret. Addidit etiam quod, nisi
comes succurreret, obprobrium sempiternum subiret, et

[a] deputatus MS
[b] et et MS
[1] Pembroke went off to visit his wife at Brampton in Northamptonshire,
leaving Piers at Deddington, Oxon.
[2] cf. Mark xvi. 2. This was on 10 June.
[3] Acts xii. 5

business for a time; stay there till I come.' Piers grate-
fully accepted the earl's offer; and he sent him to this
village under guard; but the earl never saw Piers again
in England.[1]

When the Earl of Warwick learned all that was happening in this matter, he took a strong force, raised the
whole countryside and secretly approached the place
where he knew Piers to be. Coming to the village very
early one Saturday[2] he entered the gate of the courtyard
and surrounded the chamber. Then the earl called out
in a loud voice: 'Arise traitor, thou art taken.' When
Piers heard this, seeing that the earl was there with a
superior force and that his own guard did not resist, he
dressed himself and came down. In this fashion Piers
was taken and led forth not as an earl but as a thief;
and he who used to ride on a palfrey is now forced to
go on foot.

When they had left the village a little behind, the
earl ordered Piers to be given a nag that they might
proceed more quickly. Blaring trumpets followed Piers
and the horrid cry of the populace. They had taken off
his belt of knighthood, and as a thief and a traitor he
was taken to Warwick, and coming there was cast into
prison. He whom Piers called Warwick the Dog has
now bound Piers with chains.

Piers therefore was kept in prison,[3] but Earl Aylmer
without delay made intercession for him with the barons.
As soon as he knew that Piers had been captured he
approached the Earl of Gloucester, beseeching him with
tears to vindicate the wrong that had been done to him,
and at all costs to restore Piers to him. For, he added,
unless the earl would help, he would suffer eternal disgrace, and lose the lands which he had pledged. The
Earl of Gloucester is said to have replied thus: 'My lord

terras quas obligauerat amitteret. Et comes Glouernie
ita fertur respondisse, 'Domine comes, iniuria tibi illata
comiti Guydoni non est imputanda. Quod enim fecit,
consilio et auxilio nostro fecit; et si, ut tu dicis, terras
tuas obligasti, ipsas utique perdidisti. Nichil ergo
ulterioris restat consilii nisi ut discas alias cautius
negotiari.' Comes autem, ut uidit preces suas sic esse
repulsas, confusus abscessit et uenit apud Oxoniam: con-
gregate uniuersitati clericorum ostendit causam suam, et
F.179 transcriptum obliga/tionis legi fecit coram omnibus
clericis et burgensibus similiter adunatis, deposuit querelam suam coram eis, ut uel sic ad recuperandum Petrum
consilium communicarent et auxilium, uel ut iustitiam
suam ostenderet ne quis forsan de se aliter presumeret.
Habebatur enim apud quosdam suspectus, quasi in
captione Petri tam durum peccatum dolo confirmasset,
ut Petrum facilius morti traderet quem longa obsidione
forsan non cepisset. Sed nec clerici nec burgenses rem
ad se non pertinentem tractare uel attemptare curabant.

Altera autem die non longe post captionem Petri,
reliqui comites Warewykye conueniunt, et de morte
Petri tractantes sic tandem diffiniunt, quod propter
affinitatem comitis Glouernie nec ut fur suspenderetur
nec ut proditor protraheretur, sed sicut nobilis et ciuis
Romanus capitalem pœnam pateretur. Comes autem
Warewykye acutum nuntium emisit ad Petrum, mandans ei ut consuleret anime sue, quia hec foret dies
ultima quam uisurus esset in terra. Et nuntius accelerans
mandatum statim accessit ad Petrum: 'Consule,' inquit,
'tibi, domine, quia morte morieris hac die.' Et Petrus,
ubi nomen mortis audiuit, modicum suspirans ingemuit;
'O,' inquit, 'ubi sunt dona mea quibus tot familiares
amicos acquisieram, et quibus potestatem sufficientem
habuisse putaueram? Ubi sunt amici mei, in quibus

earl, the wrong done to you is not to be imputed to
Earl Guy. He did this with our aid and counsel; and
if, as you say, you have pledged your lands, you have
lost them anyhow. It only remains to advise you to
learn another time to negotiate more cautiously.' When
the earl saw that his prayers were thus rejected, he departed in confusion and came to Oxford. To the assembled university he explained his cause, and had a copy
of his pledge read to a joint meeting of clerks and
burgesses. He laid his plea before them, either that they
might lend their aid and counsel in recovering Piers, or
that they might show the justice of his cause in case
anyone should think otherwise. For he was suspected
by some of having guilefully countenanced so unfeeling
a crime, in order to hand over to death more easily one
whom perhaps he would not have captured by a lengthy
siege. But neither the clerks nor the burgesses cared to
take up or discuss a matter that did not concern them.

On a day not long after the capture of Piers, the
remaining earls met at Warwick, and after discussing
Piers' death they at length decided that on account of
his kinship with the Earl of Gloucester he should not be
hanged as a thief nor drawn as a traitor, but should suffer
the penalty of beheading as a nobleman and Roman
citizen. The Earl of Warwick sent a sharp-tongued messenger to Piers, telling him to look to his soul, because
this was the last day that he would see on earth. When
the messenger, hastening with his message, reached
Piers, he said: 'Look to yourself, my lord, for this day
you shall die the death.' And Piers when he heard the
word death sighed a little and groaned: 'Oh! Where
are the presents that bought me so many intimate friends,
and with which I had thought to have sufficient power?

erat fiducia mea, corporis tutela et tota salutis substantia;
quorum iuuentus ualida, probitas inuicta et uirtus ad
ardua semper accensa? qui etiam in bello pro me stare,
carcerem intrare, et mortem promiserant non uitare.
Certe superbia mea, elatio quam nutriuit eorum una
promissio, regis fauor et regis curia, duxerunt me in hec
tedia.   Non habeo subsidium, uacat omne remedium,
fiat uoluntas comitum.' /

F.180   Circa horam tertiam[1] educitur Petrus de carcere; et
comes de Warewyk Petrum uinculatum reliquit comiti
Lancastrie, et Petrus, ut comitem illum uidit, procidens
in terram orauit dicens, 'Generose comes, miserere mei.'
Et comes, 'Tolle,' inquit, 'tolle eum, per Deum per-
ducetur.'   Et qui uiderunt lacrimas continere non
potuerunt.   Quis enim continere se posset cum uideret
Petrum, nuper gloriose militantem, nunc autem misericordiam in tam flebili fine petentem?   Eductus Petrus de
castro properauit ad locum ubi passurus erat supplicium;
et ceteri comites sequebantur a longe ut uiderent finem,[2]
nisi quod comes Guydo remansit in castro suo.

Cum autem uenissent ad locum qui Blakelowe
dicitur, pertinens ad comitem Lancastrie, missus quidam
a comitis latere iussit Petrum in predicto loco remanere;
et statim iussu comitis traditus est Walensibus duobus,
de quibus transfodit hic corpus, amputauit ille[a] caput.
Et nuntiatum est comiti quod res sic se haberet.   Ille
autem non credidit donec caput ipse uideret; et post
rem sic consummatam reuersi sunt comites in uiam
suam.   Fratres autem Jacobini colligerunt Petrum, et

----

[a] illos MS
[1] 19 June 1312 *Cont. Trivet.* ed. Hall, p. 9
[2] cf. Matt. 26, 58

Where are my friends, in whom was my trust, the protection of my body, and my whole hope of safety; whose
lusty youth, unbeaten valour, and courage was always
aflame for hard tasks? They had promised to stand by
me in war, to suffer imprisonment, and not to shun
death. Indeed my pride, the arrogance that one single
promise of theirs has nourished, the king's favour and
the king's court, have brought me to this sorry plight.
I have no help, every remedy is vain, let the will of the
earls be done.'

About the third hour[1] Piers was led forth from prison;
and the Earl of Warwick handed him over bound to the
Earl of Lancaster, and Piers, when he saw the earl, cast
himself on the ground and besought him, saying, 'Noble
earl, have mercy on me.' And the earl said 'Lift him
up, Lift him up. In God's name let him be taken away.'
The onlookers could not restrain their tears. For who
could contain himself on seeing Piers, lately in his martial
glory, now seeking mercy in such lamentable straits.
Piers was led out from the castle and hastened to the
place where he was to suffer the last penalty; and the
other earls followed at a distance to see his end,[2] except
Count Guy who remained in his castle.

When they had come to a place called Blacklow,
which belonged to the Earl of Lancaster, an envoy from
the earl ordered that Piers should remain there; and
immediately by the earl's command he was handed over
to two Welshmen, one of whom ran him through the
body and the other cut off his head. It was announced
to the earl that thus it had been done, but he would not
believe it until he had seen the head. When the business
had been thus despatched the earls again went their
ways. The Dominican Friars gathered up Piers, and

caput corpori consuentes detulerunt illud Oxoniam; sed quia innodatus erat sententia, non sunt ausi sepelire corpus in ecclesia.

Exitus hic Petri qui, dum conscendit in altum,
Labitur in nichilum qui fuit ante nichil.

Ecce Petrus nuper in aula regis ceteris nobilior, nunc propter inportunitatem sui gestus iussu comitis Lancastrie iacet decolatus. Videant amodo curiales Anglici ne, de regio fauore confisi, barones despiciant. Sunt enim membrum regis principale, sine quo nil grande poterit rex aggredi uel consummare. Ergo qui / barones paruipendunt, regem utique contempnunt et lese magestatis se reos ostendunt.

Sed quare iussu comitis Lancastrie occiditur Petrus magis quam aliorum comitum, dubitabit aliquis in posterum. Sciat autem in occisione Petri comites Anglie arduum negotium assumpsisse, nec diebus nostris aliquando simile contigisse. Occiderunt enim magnum comitem quem rex adoptauerat in fratrem, quem rex dilexit ut filium, quem rex habuit in socium et amicum. Opus ergo erat ut ille magnus esset qui tale factum defenderet. Vnde Thomas comes Lancastrie, sicut omnibus generosior, ita et ceteris potentior, periculum huius rei in se assumpsit, et Petrum post tria exilia, quasi post tres monitiones legittimas, non obtemperantem, occidi mandauit.

Hic comes Thomas dominum regem in secundo gradu consanguinitatis contingebat, utpote qui ex duobus fratribus qui primum faciunt gradum descendebant, ex rege scilicet Edwardo seniore et fratre eius Edmundo comite Lancastrie. Mater eius erat regina Nauarie, et soror eius regina Francie, et filia sororis sue regina nunc est Anglie. Sic utroque parente regios habens natales

F.181

sewing the head to the body they carried it to Oxford; but because he was excommunicate they dared not bury the body in church.

> Such Peter's end, who, climbing up too high,
> Crashed into nothingness from whence he came.

See how Piers who had lately been more notable than the rest in the King's hall, now for his insolent behaviour lies beheaded by order of the Earl of Lancaster. Let English courtiers beware lest, trusting in the royal favour, they look down upon the barons. For they are a chief constituent of monarchy, and without them the king cannot attempt or accomplish anything of importance. Therefore those who vilify the barons assuredly despise the king and show themselves guilty of treason.

Posterity is sure to wonder why Piers was killed by order of the Earl of Lancaster rather than by that of the other earls. It must be remembered that in slaying Piers the earls of England had undertaken a difficult task, unlike anything that has happened in our time. For they put to death a great earl whom the king had adopted as brother, whom the king cherished as a son, whom the king regarded as friend and ally. Therefore it was necessary for him to be great who should defend such a deed. Hence Thomas, Earl of Lancaster, being of higher birth and more powerful than the rest, took upon himself the peril of the business, and ordered Piers, after three terms of exile, as one disobedient to three lawful warnings, to be put to death.

This Earl Thomas was related to the king in the second degree of kinship, for they were descended from two brothers in the first degree, to wit King Edward the elder, and his brother Edmund, Earl of Lancaster. His mother was Queen of Navarre, his sister Queen of France, and his sister's daughter now Queen of England. As

generosior apparet quam ceteri comites. Per uires patri-
monii potentiam eius attendere potes. Habebat enim
quinque comitatus in Anglia, uidelicet comitatum Lancastrie, Leycestrie, et comitatum de Ferers ex parte
patris; comitatum Lyncolnie et Saresburie ex parte
uxoris. Ecce dominatio tot comitatuum olim nobilium
redigitur in unum. Potest nunc solus Thomas quod
aliquando comes Edmundus, dominus de Longespeye,
dominus de Lacy, et dominus de Ferers singillatim
potuerunt. Nec credo ducem uel comitem, sub imperio
Romano militantem, de terrarum prouentibus tantum
facere posse quantum Thomas comes Lancastrie.

Post consummationem Petri, cum uox publica mortem eius auribus singulorum inculcasset, letata est /
F.182 terra, gauisi sunt omnes habitantes in ea. Confidenter
dicam mortem unius hominis, nisi grauasset rem publi-
cam, nunquam antea tot et tantis gratanter acceptam.
Gaudet terra, gaudent incole, Petro mortuo pacem
inuenisse: soli familiares eius, et maxime quos ipse pro-
mouerat, mortem domini sui egre ferebant. Nam multa
multis contulit, de stabulo ad cameram quosdam ascendere fecit, de quibus quidam militant qui nunquam
militasse decreuerant; et ut paucis multa concludam,

De causa Petri gaudent omnes inimici,
Atque dolent pauci nisi qui sunt eius amici.

Post tres pluresue dies conueniunt Wygornie predicti
comites, ut de predictis tractarent et aduersus futura
consulerent. Sciebant enim quod, cum res in regis
ueniret notitiam, tanquam ob illatam sibi iniuriam, si
liceret ei, procederet ad uindictam. Iccirco caute et
prouide inter eos prospectum est, quod, si processum
eorum iure tueri[a] non possent, saltem se et sua armorum

---

[a] teneri MS

each parent was of royal birth he was clearly of nobler
descent than the other earls. By the size of his patrimony
you may assess his influence. For he had five earldoms
in England, namely those of Lancaster, Leicester, and
Ferrers from his father, and the earldoms of Lincoln and
Salisbury from his wife. See how the lordship of so many
noble earldoms is now reduced to one. Thomas alone
can now achieve as much as formerly Earl Edmund, the
Lord Longespee, the Lord Lacy, and the Lord Ferrers,
four separate lords. Nor do I believe that any duke or
count under the Roman empire, received as much from
the profits of his lands as Thomas Earl of Lancaster.

When Piers had met his end, and the voice of the
people had dinned his death into the ears of all, the
country rejoiced, and all its inhabitants were glad. I may
assert with confidence that the death of one man, unless
he had been a burden upon the state, had never before
been acceptable to so many. The land rejoices, its inhabitants rejoice that they have found peace in Piers'
death: only his household, and particularly those whom
he had promoted, took the death of their lord to heart.
For many owed much to him, and some he had promoted from the stable to the chamber, of whom some
go about as knights who never thought to have been
knighted; and, to speak briefly,

> For Peter's fate his enemies rejoice,
> And few there are to grieve except his friends.

After three or more days the aforesaid earls met at
Worcester, to discuss what had happened and make
plans for the future. For they knew that when the
matter came to the king's notice, he would, if he could,
proceed to take vengeance as though for a wrong done
to himself. Therefore they cautiously and with foresight
took their bearings, so that if they could not bring their

suffragiis unanimiter defenderent. Nam uim ui repellere
lege permittitur, et quod quis ob tutelam sui fecerit, iure
fecisse uidetur.

Postquam notificatum est autem regi quod mortuus
est Petrus, contristatus ualde condoluit, et post modicum
astantibus dixit: 'Per animam Dei, ut fatuus egit. Nam
de consilio meo ad manus comitum nunquam peruenit.
Hoc est quod semper inhibui. Nam et que nunc facta
sunt prius quam fierent excogitaui. Quid sibi fuit de
comite de Warewyk, quem constat Petrum nunquam
dilexisse? Sciebam certe quod, si eum apprehenderet,
de manibus eius nunquam euaderet.' Hoc uerbum regis
leuiter prolatum, cum tandem deueniret in publicum,
plures excitauit [ad] risum. Sed certus sum regem ita
doluisse de Petro, sicut aliquando dolet pater de filio.
Nam quanto magis procedit dilectio, tanto magis dolet
F.183 infortunio. In / planctu Dauid super Jonatan amor osten-
ditur, quem dicitur super amorem mulierum dilexisse.[1]
Fatetur et sic rex noster; superaddit dum mortem Petri
uindicare disposuit. Nam accitis consiliariis suis querit
consilium quid super istis foret agendum, ratum tamen
habens propositum illos destruere qui occiderunt Petrum.
Et erat cum rege comes Penbrokye, cuius intererat
comites debellare, et dominus Hugo le[a] Despenser apud
regem latuit, qui plus quam Petrus forte demeruit.
Henricus de Beamount adhuc est in curia, qui iuxta
ordinationes recedere debuisset ab illa; Edmundus de
Maulee et alii milites qui nuper fuerant Petri familiares.
Hii siquidem regem instigabant ut ex fidelibus suis
exercitum colligeret, et aduersarios suos audacter im-
peteret. Nam triumphum secure reportaret ex quo pro

[1] 2 Sam. i. 26

proceedings within the law, they could at least entrust themselves and theirs to the arbitrament of arms. For it is permissible in law to meet force with force, and what anyone does for his own protection he is deemed to have done lawfully.

When the king was notified that Piers was dead, he was saddened and grieved very much and after a little said to the bystanders: 'By God's soul, he acted as a fool. If he had taken my advice he would never have fallen into the hands of the earls. This is what I always told him not to do. For I guessed that what has now happened would occur. What was he doing with the Earl of Warwick, who was known never to have liked him? I knew for certain that if the earl caught him, Piers would never escape from his hands.' When this light utterance of the king became public it moved many to derision. But I am certain the king grieved for Piers as a father grieves for his son. For the greater the love, the greater the sorrow. In the lament of David upon Jonathan, love is depicted which is said to have surpassed the love of women.[1] Our king also spoke thus; and further he planned to avenge the death of Piers. For, having summoned his counsellors, he enquired from them what should be done about these things, although he had already decided to destroy those who had killed Piers. With the king was the Earl of Pembroke, whose interest it was to vanquish the earls; and Sir Hugh le Despenser, who was perhaps even less deserving than Piers, lurked with the king. Henry de Beaumont was still at court, though according to the Ordinances he should have left it; Edmund de Mauley and other knights lately of Piers' household. These men urged the king to collect an army of loyalists and boldly attack his enemies. He would surely win the day because he was

iure suo legittime tractaret. Addunt etiam infideles uincere non posse, quos constat domino suo fidem non seruare; protestantes a seculo inauditum simile delictum in aliquem regem esse commissum, et cum pro quouis crimine minori*a* possit satisfieri, crimen lese magestatis non poterit purgari. Alii uero sanioris consilii, bene scientes futura metiri, nullo sensu prebebant assensum, ut rex cum baronibus iniret conflictum. Nam si rex caperetur hoc foret absurdum; nec regi proficeret destructio comitum, maxime cum Robertus de Brutz iam totam Scotiam occupauerat, et terram Northumbrorum ad tributum compulerit; plus expediret terram defendere quam terre defensores uelle destruere. Placuit tamen regi prius consilium, quia magis secessit ad uotum suum; quod enim iuxta uelle consulitur, frequenter apud homines magis acceptatur. Ad hoc etiam naturaliter regem inducebat indignatio quam contra comites pro morte Petri conceperat, magnanimitas in paucis ex/perta, et suggestio malorum hominum nimis assidua. Nam hii qui post mortem Petri ad regem confugerant, guerram magis quam pacem procurabant. Timebant enim quod, si rex placitis baronum adquiesceret, hoc in dampnum eorum forsan redundaret. Semper enim trepidat qui sibi conscius exstat.[1]

Certe adulatorum figmenta milites decipiunt et ad finem desperatum frequenter perducunt. Bene cum magnatibus ageretur, si uerum a falso discernerent, si simulationes a uero iudicio separarent. Sed nescio qua deprauatione nature aures diuitum delicate gratius acceptant mendacis lingue blandicias quam aperte testimonium ueritatis. Nam iuxta poetam,

F.184

---

a crimine minori] crimior MS
[1] An unidentified hexameter

lawfully striving for his rights. They add that faithless
men, known to have broken faith with their lord, cannot
triumph, protesting that for such a crime to be committed against any king was utterly unheard of, and
though satisfaction could be made for any lesser crime,
the crime of treason could not be purged. Others of
wiser counsel, well knowing how to estimate what would
happen, would have nothing to do with the proposal
that the king should engage in a struggle with the barons.
For if the king was taken it would be absurd; nor would
the destruction of the earls profit the king, particularly
since Robert Bruce had already occupied the whole of
Scotland, and forced all Northumbria to pay tribute; it
would be better to defend the land rather than to try to
destroy its defenders. The king however, preferred the
former counsel, because it was more in accord with his
desires; indeed it is frequently more acceptable to advise
a man to follow his bent. The indignation which the
king had conceived against the earls on account of
Piers' death naturally inclined him to this view. Few
people are magnanimous and the suggestions of evil men
are always with us. For those who on Piers' death had
fled to the king, were striving for war rather than peace.
They feared that if the king agreed to the baronial
decrees, this would perhaps redound to their loss. 'He
is always fearful who is thinking of himself.'[1]

Truly the imaginings of flatterers deceive soldiers
and frequently bring them to a desperate end. It would
be well for magnates if they could distinguish truth from
falsehood, if they could separate deceit from sound
judgment. But by some depravity of nature the delicate
ears of the rich more readily receive the blandishments
of the lying tongue than the candid testimony of truth.
As the poet says,

Cum quis adulator facilem placauerit*a* aurem,
Continuo cunctos superat cum uera loquentur.

Huius pestis detestanda frequentia hodie nimis regnat
in curia.

Rex igitur noster in ultionem Petri quosdam de
baronibus inpugnare proponit; nam comitem Warewyk
aut capite priuabit aut bonis confiscatis perpetuo
deportabit.[1]   Milites uocat ad arma, milites conducit in
castra, forestarios et sagittarios congregat, pedites in
expeditionem pugne uenire procurat.

Interim autem barones et comites ad parliamentum
suum publico citauit edicto.[2]   Ipsi uero, proprie salutis
non inmemores, ad parendum regis mandato hoc modo
se preparant.   Comes Lancastrie mille loricatos, mille et
quingentos pedites secum adduxit.   Comitiua comitis
Herfordie turba Wallensium uallata, siluestris et fera, non
erat uilis nec modica.   Comes Warewykye homines suos
de Arderne animosos ualde properanter*b* mandauit
adesse, et ceteri barones qui erant ex parte comitum,
unusquisque pro posse suo communem uallauit exer-
F.185 citum, et sic profecti sunt ad parliamentum. / Venientes
autem*c* Londonias non statim accesserunt ad regem, sed
nuntios suos prouide miserunt, qui aduentum eorum
domino regi nuntiarent et causam uocationis humiliter
inquirerent.

Cum ergo didicisset rex aduentum comitum et formam aduentus eorum, consilium suum conuocat ut
instans negotium consulte disponat; uolens etiam in-
quirere an cum comitibus expediret congredi, uincere
sperarent necne.*d*   Quidam uero, quibus de uiribus
utriusque partis iam liquide constabat, conflictum ad

a placuerit MS   *b* preparanter MS
c autem] sunt MS   *d* necne] unde c. MS
[1] *deportabit* is a legal technical term

> When flatterers tickle the attentive ear
> At once they conquer all who speak the truth.

This pest prevails today with deplorable frequency at court.

Thus our king proposes to attack certain of the barons out of revenge for Piers. Either he will have the Earl of Warwick's head, or deprive him of his goods and condemn him to perpetual exile.[1] He summons the knights to arms, garrisons his castles, collects his foresters and archers, sends for infantry arrayed for battle.

Meanwhile he calls the earls and barons to his parliament[2] by public writ. Not unmindful of their own safety they prepare to obey the king's command in this way. The Earl of Lancaster brought with him a thousand horsemen and fifteen hundred foot. The retinue of the Earl of Hereford, strengthened by a crowd of Welsh, wild men from the woodlands, was neither paltry nor mean. The Earl of Warwick summoned his stout-hearted men from Arden to come with all speed, and the other barons on the side of the earls, each according to his means, sent his quota to the common army, and thus they set out for parliament. When they reached London they did not immediately approach the king, but wisely sent messengers to announce their arrival to the lord king and humbly to enquire the cause of summons.

When the king learned of the arrival of the earls and the manner of their coming, he called together his council to despatch the immediate business by their advice; he also wished to enquire whether it was expedient for him

---

[2] Originally summoned on 23 July for Lincoln. It met from 30 September to 16 December 1312 (*Parl. Writs*, II.i.79) at Westminster. The Commons were dismissed on 16 December, and King and barons made a treaty 20 December (*Foed.* 191, 192; *Ann. Lond.* 221-9).

presens penitus dissuadebant. Nam quicquid de rege
accideret, pars regis sine dubio periret, cum regis*a* exercitum pars aduersa in duplo superaret; et hoc forsitan
ad terrorem dicebant, quia pacem bello preferre uole-
bant. Et erant eodem tempore cum rege Lodowycus
frater regis Francie et quidam cardinalis qui secum
uenerat de partibus transmarinis.[1] Hii omnem opem et
operam concordiam formandi cotidie inhibebant.*b*

Comes autem Gloucestrie mediatoris partes sustinuit,
et regem de pace et concordia erga barones suos habenda
frequenter conuenit: 'Amici tui sunt,' inquit comes,
'quos inimicos uocas. Amici tui sunt quos inprudenter
expugnas. In commodum tuum cedit quicquid faciunt.
Pro commodo tuo multa satis expendunt. Rex, si
barones tuos destruis, honorem tuum certe contempnis.
Nec tamen hoc pati tenentur, nec in aliquo delinquunt
si propria iura tuentur.' Et rex comiti sic respondit:
'Non est qui uicem meam doleat[2]; non est qui pro iure
meo aduersus istos contendat. Tu uero, nepos meus et
dux meus et notus meus, auunculum tuum deseris, et
aduersariis eius amicum te facis. Protestor amicos meos
non esse qui res meas et ius meum nituntur expungnare.
F.186 Si michi iure regio sicut aliis regibus / uti liceret, non
hominem exulatum ex quacunque causa de regia potestate ad pacem possem reuocare? Hoc iure propria sua
auctoritate me priuarunt, nam cui pacem concesseram
crudeliter necarunt. Et comes Lancastrie michi proximus agnatus, cui possent sufficere quinque comitatus
licet aliena non raperet, apud Nouum Castrum homines

---

a rege MS
b Perhaps we should write 'adhibebant'
[1] Louis of Evreux and cardinal Arnold, Cardinal of St Prisca (29
August to 13 September)
[2] 1 Sam. xxii. 8

to attack the earls, did they hope he would conquer, or not? Some, indeed, who knew clearly the strength of either side, advised strongly against fighting at present. For whatever happened to the king, his party would surely perish, since his adversaries had an army double the size of his; they said this, perhaps, to cause alarm, because they preferred peace to war. At that same time there were with the king, Louis, brother of the king of France, and a certain cardinal who had come with him from foreign parts.[1] These used their best efforts daily to bring about an agreement.

The Earl of Gloucester took the part of mediator and had frequent meetings with the king that a state of peace and harmony with the barons might be reached. 'They are your friends,' said the earl, 'whom you call enemies. Your friends are those you rashly attack. Whatever they do is for your benefit. They expend much for your advantage. King, if you destroy your barons, you indeed make light of your own honour. And they are not bound to suffer this, nor do they commit any offence if they protect their own rights.' And the king replied thus to the earl: 'There is none who is sorry for me[2]: none who fights for my right against them. But thou, my nephew, one of my generals, and my friend, desertest thy uncle, and makest friends of his adversaries. I protest that they are not my friends who strive to attack my property and my rights. If I may use my royal prerogative as other kings do, may I not recall to my peace by the royal power a man exiled for any reason whatever? Of this right they deprived me by their own authority, for the man to whom I had granted peace they cruelly put to death. And the Earl of Lancaster, my first cousin, who might have been content with five earldoms without seizing others,

meos inuasit, et quedam mei iuris secum asportauit; quod
si minor aliquis fecisset, furti posset argui, et ui bonorum
raptorum iudicio recte condempnari. Et comites ad
parliamentum uocati in dedecus regis cum magno exercitu ueniunt armati. Vnde cum mea rapuerint et
homines meos occiderint, satis est uerisimile quod michi
nolunt deferre, sed coronam rapere et alium sibi regem
preficere.' Et comes, 'Domine, si quid [in] iniuriam
tuam comites presumpserint, decet emendari; et si^a
satisfacere fuerint parati, merito debent reconciliari.
Est enim sententia uulgaris^b ut nemo in admittenda
satisfactione sit difficilis. Expedit igitur comites prius
conueniri et amicabiliter de grauaminibus per eos uobis
illatis interpellari, ut ex responsione eorum appareat an
iure uel iniuria res finem acceperit. Est enim apud
omnes consuetudo ut lenia premittantur,^{c} que si non
proficiant aspera subsequantur.'

Et annuit rex. Accessit ergo comes ille mediator ad
comites, et querelam regis ac causas iniuriarum seriatim
exposuit. Ipsi uero super hiis consulti ita responderunt:
'Nos domini regis nostri Anglie barones, et secundum
possibilitatem humane condicionis per omnia fideles, in
priuationem iuris regalis nichil presumpsimus, nichil
attemptauimus, nec in preiudicium uel incommodum
eius unquam aliquid excogitauimus. Verum est quod
F.187 proditorem quendam / exulantem, et post exilii decretum
in terra latitantem, occidi mandauimus, et hoc non in
dedecus regis nec contra pacem eius; nec propria auctoritate hoc fecimus, sed iuxta ordinationes legitimas,
assensu regis et suorum baronum editas et promulgatas,
processimus, quas nec rex sola uoluntate sua reuocare

^{a} sibi MS
^{b} uulgare MS
^{c} permittantur MS

attacked my men at Newcastle and carried off some of my property out of my jurisdiction; if any lesser man had done it, he could be found guilty of theft and rightly condemned by a verdict of robbery with violence. And the earls summoned to parliament come, to the King's shame, supported by a large army. Since they have seized my goods and killed my men, it is very likely that they do not wish to have any consideration for me, but to seize the crown and set up for themselves another king.' And the earl replied, 'Sir, if the earls have presumed to offer you wrong, it must be amended; and if they are prepared to give satisfaction, they ought justly to be reconciled. For there is a common saying that no one should make difficulties about receiving satisfaction. Therefore let the earls be met and be amicably questioned concerning the grievances advanced by them against you, so that from their answer it may be known whether the matter has been rightly or wrongly judged. For it is everywhere the usage that leniency is tried first, and if it is profitless harsh measures may follow.'

The king agreed. So the earl as mediator approached the earls, explained the king's complaint and expounded his grievances one by one. When they had taken counsel in the matter, they replied thus: 'We, as barons of our lord king of England, and faithful in all things so far as is humanly possible, have not presumed to diminish the royal prerogative in anything, nor have we attempted anything or ever continued anything to his prejudice or disadvantage. It is true that we ordered to be killed a certain exiled traitor who lurked in the land after his exile had been decreed, but this was not to the shame of the king nor against his peace; nor did we do this on our own authority, but we acted according to lawful ordinances put forth and published with the

G

potuit uel immutare. Nichil enim sine consilio et communi assensu domini regis et suorum baronum potest
statui; igitur eadem ratione nec dissolui. Nam secundum
leges ciuiles nichil tam naturale quam unumquodque
dissolui eo genere quo ligatur,[1] et alibi "omnis res per
quascunque causas nascitur per easdem dissoluitur".
Patet igitur quod pax regia ipsi proditori concessa non
ualuit, quia rex ipsam pacem contra ordinationes concessit, quas solo et proprio arbitrio tollere non potuit.'

Comes de Lancastre ad obiecta sibi per regem respondit quod in predam uel rapinam nunquam concessit[a]; homines regis non inuasit; bona regis nequaquam
asportauit, sed apud Nouum Castrum ueniens multa,
que ad regem pertinere cognouit, quasi pro derelicto
habita, et occupare uolentibus exposita, ut[b] dominum
regem conseruaret indempnem, occupauit et ad opus
regis, inuentorio de omnibus confecto, custodienda
mandauit.

Ita responderunt omnes unanimiter quod non in
contemptum regis, sed propter quosdam sibi suspectos
ad parliamentum muniti uenerunt, cum iuxta consilium
sapientis nec nudi debere[c] contendere nec inhermes nos
inimicis opponere. Ex hiis dictis satis apparere in
coronam regiam se nichil deliquisse; protestantes eis in
mentem nunquam euenisse alium regem sibi preficere
uoluisse. Et in calce sermonis hec simul adiciunt;
'Manifeste,' inquiunt, 'iam liquet quia dominus rex
F.188 occasiones querit aduersus nos. Cum / enim iam per
quinquennium et amplius, pro confirmatione regni, pro

---

[a] Perhaps for 'consensit'.
[b] ut] ad MS
[c] Hearne suggests 'debemus'.
[1] *Dig.* 50.17.35

assent of the King and his barons, which not even the king by his mere will can either revoke or change. For nothing can be enacted without the counsel and common consent of the lord King and his barons. Nor for the same reason can anything be abrogated. For according to the Civil Law nothing is so natural as that everything is loosened in the same way that it is bound,[1] and again elsewhere "every obligation is dissolved by those same causes from which it arises". It is therefore evident that the King's peace granted to that traitor was not valid, because the king granted that peace against ordinances, which by his own mere will he cannot annul.'

The Earl of Lancaster replied to the king's attack upon him, that he had never descended to plunder or booty; he had not attacked the king's men; he had never carried off the king's goods, but coming to Newcastle and finding many things, which he knew belonged to the King, lying derelict and open to all those who wished to take them, he seized them, that he might save the lord king harmless, and having made an inventory of everything, ordered them to be kept to the king's use.

The earls replied unanimously in this wise: that they had not come armed to parliament in contempt of the king, but on account of some who were suspect to them, since according to the counsel of the wise we should not engage in conflict stripped of our armour nor oppose our enemies unarmed. From these remarks they maintained it was quite clear that they had committed no crime against the Crown; protesting that it had never entered their heads to wish to set up another as king. At the end of this speech they added: 'It is abundantly clear that the lord king seeketh occasion against us. Though for five years and more we have exhausted our

augmentatione honoris regii, satis ultra uires expende-
rimus, satis tamen incassum laborauimus, quia dominus
rex omnia in dedecus eius excogitata, omnia in odium
eius adinuenta conqueritur.   Vtinam dominus noster
quod bonum est in oculis faciat; unum autem sciat,
quod cum homines eius simus, fidem ei seruabimus; sed
quamuis a nobis fidelitatem receperit et homagium,
equum et ipse nihilominus iuramentum seruare tenetur
illesum.   Et si forsan ab hoc pacto uellet recedere, nos
absque fidei lesione nequaquam teneremur acquiescere.
Roboam filius regis Salamonis, quamuis regnum iure
hereditario sibi competeret, quia tamen barones suos
iusta petentes non admisit, decima parte regni contentus,
reliquam partem penitus amisit.   Igitur si dominus rex
affectione qua decet comites et barones suos tractauerit,
si rancorem quem contra nos sine causa concepit benigne
remiserit, et proditores a curia sua dimiserit, sibi ut regi
parebimus, sibi ut domino seruiemus.'

Sub tanto rerum strepitu, dum uarii rumores hinc
inde uolarent, dum unus pacem, alter guerram predi-
caret, natus est regi filius formosus et dudum affectatus.
Impositum est autem ei nomen patris eius, nomen
Edwardus; et natus puer iste in festo Sancti Bricii,[1] quod
annuatim celebratur post festum Sancti Martini.   Hec
adoptata natiuitas tempore accepto nobis aduenit,[2] quia
duos effectus Deo disponente feliciter impleuit. Dolorem
namque regis quem ex morte Petri conceperat ualde
mitigauit, et certum heredem regno prouidit.   Nam, si
rex decessisset sine prole, pro certo mansisset corona sub
lite.   Viuat igitur iuuenis Edwardus, et, auitis patribus
assimilatus, quod singulos ditabat solus optineat.   Regis

[1] 13 November 1312
[2] 2 Cor. vi. 2

strength to strengthen the realm and to increase the
king's honour, we have laboured in vain, because the lord
king complains that everything has been designed to
put him to shame, everything fabricated out of spite.
Let our lord do what is good in his eyes. But let him
know one thing, that as we are his men, we will keep
faith with him; but although he has received homage
and fealty from us, he too is bound to keep his oath intact.
And if perchance he wishes to withdraw from this bargain,
we without breach of faith are in no way bound to agree.
Rehoboam son of king Solomon, although the realm
belonged to him by hereditary right, because he did
not admit the just claims of his barons, had to be content
with the tenth part of his kingdom, having lost the rest
utterly. Thus if the lord king treats his earls and barons
with the regard that is their due, if he freely remits the
baseless rancour that he has conceived against us and
casts out the traitors from his court, we will obey him as
king, we will serve him as lord.'

Amidst this uproar, with various rumours flying
hither and thither, while one man foretold peace, his
neighbour war, there was born to the king a handsome
and long looked-for son. He was christened Edward,
his father's name. This boy was born on St Brice's
Day,[1] which is celebrated annually after the feast of
St Martin. This long wished-for birth was timely for us,[2]
because by God's will it had two fortunate consequences.
It much lessened the grief which had afflicted the king
on Piers death, and it provided a known heir to the
throne. For if the king had died without issue, the
Crown would certainly have remained in dispute.
Long live, therefore, the young Edward, and may he
combine in his person the virtues that characterised in
turn his forbears. May he follow the industry of King

F.189 Henrici secundi sectetur / industriam, regis Ricardi notam probitatem, ad regis Henrici proueniat etatem, regis Edwardi recolat sapientiam, uiribus et specie referat cum corpore patrem.[1]

Audiens igitur rex responsiones comitum, prudentes allegationes et probabiles excusationes eorum, aduertens etiam manum ualidam ex parte baronum, et per hoc suum impediri propositum, simulatam affectionem pretendit, et uotis eorum parere promisit. Vnde ne nil uideretur egisse, mandat baronibus sub forma concordie ut petitiones eorum exponerent, et quicquid dictaret ratio indubitanter reportarent. At illi dixerunt se nichil aliud petere uelle nisi ut rex ordinationes, quarum effectus in magna sui parte iam erat suspensus, sicut ante promiserat, confirmaret, et mortem Petri proditoris suis fidelibus et legiis hominibus benigne remitteret.

Et dominus rex sic ad petita respondit: 'Excepto fiscali priuilegio ordinationes concessi, et adhuc*a* concedo; mortem Petri comitibus remitto, sed proditorem nequaquam appello.' Et comites hanc regis indulgentiam parui momenti fore dixerunt; 'nam, si rex mortem Petri remittit, suam sectam tamen non remittit, sed uxori aut filiis accusationem non tollit. At si proditoris mentionem faceret, nulli ulterius secta competeret. Et si rex comitatum Cornubie aliquo colore intendit repetere, profecto requiritur ut Petrus tanquam proditor obiisse dicatur. Nam extra hunc casum non poterit rex comitatum acquirere, nisi per Petrum uel si decessisset sine prole: sed neutra conditio potest proficere, quia Petrus moritur prole superstite. Igitur. nisi proditor Petrus habeatur,

---

a ad hoc MS
[1] An unidentified hexameter

Henry II, the well-known valour of King Richard, may he reach the age of King Henry, revive the wisdom of King Edward, and 'remind us of the physical strength and comeliness of his father'.[1]

On hearing the answers of the earls, their shrewd instances and probable excuses, and having regard to the armed strength of the barons, by which his plans might be hindered, the king showed a feigned regard for them and promised to obey their wishes. Wherefore lest he should seem to have done nothing, he commanded the barons as a basis for agreement to draw up a list of their requests, and whatever reason dictated should undoubtedly be granted. But they said that they wished to ask for nothing else than that the king should, as he had promised before, confirm the Ordinances, which were now largely in abeyance, and that he should kindly pardon his faithful and liege men for the death of Piers the traitor.

The lord king replied thus to the petitions: 'I granted the Ordinances, except the fiscal privilege, and these I still grant. I pardon the earls for the death of Piers, but I will never call him traitor.' The earls said that his royal indulgence would be of little value; 'for if the king pardons the death of Piers, yet he does not remit his suit, for he does not deprive the wife or child of their right of accusation. But if there is mention of a traitor, no further suit will lie. And if the king proposes to reacquire the earldom of Cornwall under any pretext, then it is necessary that Piers should be said to have died as a traitor. If this is not allowed, the king could not acquire the earldom, except through Piers, or if he had died without issue; but neither condition can be fulfilled because Piers died leaving issue. Therefore,

ordinationibus multum derogatur, nec comitatum Cornubie poterit rex de iure repetere.'

Sed rex baronibus ita respondit: 'Regi,' inquit,
uariare non conuenit, nec sine causa reuocare quod
prius indulgetur.[a] Omne crimen per nos fuit Petro[b] /
F.190 remissum, ergo proditorem eum reputare non possum,
quia beneficium principis decet esse mansurum. Petant
igitur barones quicquid petendum iuste putauerint;
obsequar in omnibus eorum arbitrio, sed Petro proditionem nullatenus imputabo.' Et sic hac uice sub hiis
finibus contentio recedit, sed neutra partium optata
reportauit. Reuera omne studium regis erat ut negotium
protelaret, ut sic laboribus et expensis barones afficeret.
Vnde et cito post rex a Londoniis recessit, et uersus
Wyndulsore iter arripuit ut reginam uisitaret que nuper
peperit.

Effluxerunt itaque dies anni usque ad Quadragesimam, et circa festum Annuntiationis beate Marie
sperabatur rex colloquium[1] cum baronibus Londoniis
habiturus, et habita concordia regni negotia cum comitibus dispositurus. Sed[c] rex morbo ut putabatur ficto
detentus ad diem non uenit; unde nec ipsa dissensio ad
huc finem accepit. Post Pascha misit rex Francie uiros
magnos et honoratos nuntios in Angliam, qui regem
Anglie inuitarent ad conuiuium quod parauerat filio suo
in festo Pentecostes. Voluit enim rex Francie filio suo
regi Nauarie uel cingulum militie tradere [uel] regni
diadema capiti eius imponere. Vnde rex noster statim
de suo itinere disposuit et necessaria prouideri mandauit.
Miserunt comites ad eum, consulentes ei ne regnum
suum periculo exponeret, ne ita inconsulte mare transiret, maxime cum terra ipsa esset quasi in se diuisa, et

[a] indulcitur MS   [b] Petrum MS   [c] si MS
[1] 18 March to 7 April and 6 to 9 May 1313 (*Parl. Writs*, II. i. 80, 91)

unless Piers is held to be a traitor, the Ordinances are much blemished, and the king cannot lawfully reacquire the earldom of Cornwall.'

But the King replied thus to the barons: 'It is not fitting', he said 'for the king to change or revoke without cause what he has previously granted. We pardoned Piers of every crime, therefore I cannot regard him as a traitor, because royal favours should be lasting. Therefore let the barons seek whatever they think may justly be sought; I will bow to their judgment in all things, but I will by no means charge Piers with treason.' And so on this occasion the dispute died down at this point, but neither party obtained what it had sought. Indeed the king's whole endeavour was to drag out the business, in order to wear down the barons with their labours and expenses. Shortly afterwards the king left London, and took his way to Windsor to visit the queen, who had lately given birth to a child.

So the days rolled by until Lent, and about Lady Day it was hoped that the king would hold a parliament[1] with his barons at London, and with harmony restored would dispose of the business of the realm with the earls. But the king did not come at the appointed day, detained, as was thought, by a feigned illness; whence this same quarrel still persisted. After Easter the King of France sent a distinguished embassy to England, to invite the King of England to the banquet which he had prepared for his son at Whitsuntide. For the French King wished either to knight his son, the King of Navarre, or to crown him. Whence our King at once arranged for his journey and ordered the necessary supplies to be prepared. The earls sent to him, advising him not to put his kingdom in peril by crossing the sea so unadvisedly, particularly as the land was divided against

hostis oppugnaret ciuitates et castra. Robertus enim de
Brutz Eboracum*a* iam etiam appropinquauit, et Londonias adire disposuit; nec uidetur inpossibile, ex quo
non est qui uelit resistere. Verumptamen rex a proposito
F.191 suo non recessit, sed in breui transfretare / disposuit.
Vnde nepotem suum comitem Glouernie custodem regni
constituit, et aliis comitibus sub hoc tenore rescripsit,
mandans et rogans quatinus una cum dicto comite ad
regni curam intenderent, et quicquid ius dictaret aut
ratio in reditu suo certissime reportarent.   Vnde et
festum translationis beati Thome[1] terminum prefixit in
quo Deo dante redire disposuit, et tunc presentibus eis
plenarie compleret quod promisit.

Hiis itaque peractis, rex et regina, cum ceteris electis
nauem ascendentes, tendunt in Franciam,[2] et ibidem
uenientes in maximo honore suscipiuntur per totam
patriam.   Regem nostrum et reginam saluos reducat
Deus in Angliam, illos autem destruat qui regnum per-
uertunt et regiam familiam.

Ecce nunc rex noster Edwardus sex annis complete
regnauit, nec aliquid laudabile uel dignum memoria
hucusque patrauit, nisi quod regaliter nupsit et prolem
elegantem regni heredem sibi suscitauit.   Alia fuerunt
initia regis Ricardi, qui nondum elapso triennio regni
sui probitatis sue radios longe lateque dispersit; nam
Messanas ciuitatem*b* Sicilie uno die uiriliter subiecit, et
terram Cypri in quindecim diebus potenter subiugauit.
Deinde apud Acon et in aliis partibus transmarinis [quo-
modo] se habuerit, historia Latino et Gallico sermone
digesta luculenter percurrit.   O si rex noster Edwardus
initio regni sui bene se habuisset, et consilio malorum

---

a Eboracen MS
b comitatem MS; comitatum Hearne
[1] 7 July   [2] 25-6 May 1313

itself, and an enemy might besiege his towns and castles.
For Robert Bruce was already in the neighbourhood of
York, and proposed to march on London; nor did it
seem impossible, since there was none who would resist
him. The king, however, did not change his mind,
but proposed to cross shortly. He appointed his
nephew, the Earl of Gloucester, as keeper of the realm,
and he wrote to the other earls in this sense, commission-
ing them and praying that they would, together with
the said earl, look to the interests of the kingdom, and
that whatever right or reason dictated they would report
on his return. He named the feast of the Translation
of the Blessed Thomas[1] as the day on which, God willing,
he would return, and then fulfil to those present all that
he had promised. This business concluded, the king
and queen and the others chosen to go with them took
ship and set out for France,[2] where they were received
with very great honour as they passed through the country. May God bring back our king and queen safe to
England, and destroy those who lead astray the kingdom
and the royal household.

For our King Edward has now reigned six full
years and has till now achieved nothing praiseworthy
or memorable, except that by a royal marriage
he has raised up for himself a handsome son and
heir to the throne. How differently began King
Richard's reign: before the end of the third year of his
reign he had scattered far and wide the rays of his valour.
In one day he took Messina, a city of Sicily, by force, and
subdued the land of Cyprus in a fortnight. Then, how
he bore himself at Acre and in other foreign parts
history vividly relates in the Latin and French tongues.
Oh! If our king Edward had borne himself as well at
the outset of his reign, and not accepted the counsels of

hominum non adquieuisset,*a* ex antecessoribus suis
nobilior illo nequaquam fuisset. Ditauerat enim Deus
ipsum omnium uirtutum dotibus, parem immo excellen-
tiorem fecerat aliis regibus. Nam si quis ea que regem
nostrum nobilitant*b* uellet describere, parem in terra non
F.192 poterit inuenire. Gene/rositatem eius auiti patres ostendunt, quorum successiones se iam ad decem gradus
extendunt. Diuitias habuit in principio regni sui, terram
locupletem et fauorem populi. Gener factus est regi
Francie, proximus cognatus regis Hispannie. Si ad-
hesisset baronum consilio Scotos humiliasset pro nichilo.
O si armorum usibus se exercitaret, regis Ricardi probitatem precederet. Hoc enim deposcit materia habilis,
cum statura longus sit, et fortis uiribus, formosus homo
decora facie. Sed quid moror ipsum describere? Si
tantam dedisset armis operam quantam impendidit
circa rem rusticam, multum excellens fuisset Anglia;
nomen eius sonuisset in terra. O qualis sperabatur
adhuc princeps Wallie! Tota spes euanuit dum factus
est rex Anglie. Petrus de Gauestone regem duxit in
deuium, terram turbauit, consumpsit thesaurum, tribus
uicibus exilium subiit, et postea rediens caput perdidit.
Sed adhuc remanent in regis curia de familiaribus Petri
et eius familia, qui perturbant pacem totius patrie et
regem inducunt uindictam querere. Da pacem, Domine,
diebus nostris, et rex cum baronibus fiat unanimis.

Hiis temporibus mortuus est Robertus de Wynchelse
Cantuarie antistes,[1] cuius memoria in benedictione est,
qui templum Domini in uita sua roborauit, et in diebus
suis ecclesiam protexit. De ipso enim specialiter dici
potest, 'non est inuentus similis illi qui conseruaret legem
Excelsi'.[2] Ascendit namque ex aduerso et opposuit se

---

wicked men, not one of his predecessors would have been more notable than he. For God had endowed him with every gift, and had made him equal to or indeed more excellent than other kings. If anyone cared to describe those qualities which ennoble our king, he would not find his like in the land. His ancestry, reaching back to the tenth generation, shows his nobility. At the beginning of his reign he was rich, with a populous land and the goodwill of his people. He became the son-in-law of the King of France, and first cousin of the King of Spain. If he had followed the advice of the barons he would have humiliated the Scots with ease. If he had habituated himself to the use of arms, he would have exceeded the prowess of King Richard. Physically this would have been inevitable, for he was tall and strong, a fine figure of a handsome man. But why linger over this description? If only he had given to arms the labour that he expended on rustic pursuits, he would have raised England aloft; his name would have resounded through the land. What hopes he raised as Prince of Wales! How they were dashed when he became King! Piers Gaveston led the king astray, threw the country into confusion, consumed its treasure, was exiled thrice, and then returning lost his head. But there still remain at court intimates of Piers and members of his household, who disturb the peace of the whole realm and persuade the king to seek vengeance. Give peace in our time, O Lord, and may the king be at one with his barons!

At this time died Robert Winchelsey, Archbishop of Canterbury,[1] of blessed memory, who in his lifetime strengthened the temple of the Lord, and during his pontificate protected the church. Of him especially it can be said, 'None is found like unto him to preserve the law of the Highest'.[2] For he went up into the gaps and

murum pro clero.¹ Exiit aliquando edictum ab Edwardo Cesare ut taxarentur fructus ecclesie,² et sicut talliabatur populus, ad tallagium compelleretur et clerus. Porro Robertus primas Anglie preceptum regis non est passus procedere. Dicebat enim omni iuri fore contrarium, ut*ᵃ*

F.193 in bonis clericorum haberet / rex imperium, quos etiam lex imperialis multis priuilegiis insigniuit et ab omni exactione liberos esse statuit. Hoc etiam uolunt statuta canonum; et ipsi ethnici manifestum nobis reliquerunt exemplum: quando Egiptii pre magnitudine famis seruituti regie se subiecerunt, pontifices et ceteri templorum ministri liberi remanserunt. Sed rex exasperatus, et aduersus primatem et totius Anglie clerum uehementer commotus, publica uoce promisit curialibus ut in nullo penitus deferrent clericis, sed, siue religiosis seu secularibus obuiarent, ipsos ab equis protinus deicerent et in usum proprium equos assumerent, et indistincte nullis parcerent nisi regia protectione gauderent. Verumptamen Cantuarie archiepiscopus magis cœpit esse tumidus et securus, unde in sarculum suum percussit, et in grassantes ulterius processit, et omnes regiam protectionem impetrantes excommunicauit. In tantum autem excreuit laicorum audacia ut nec ulli parcerent in archipresulis curia, quin etiam ipsum archipresulem ab equo deicerent, et omnem suppellectilem diriperent, unde archiepiscopus patienter ferens*ᵇ* iniuriam pedes coactus est ire per patriam. Denique rex ad pœnitentiam reductus, et grauiter se peccasse confessus, curialium repressit audaciam et liberam manere iussit ecclesiam. Iterum orta dissensione inter regem et archipresulem,

ᵃ ut] uel MS
ᵇ ferre MS
¹ Ezek. xiii. 5
² Luke ii. 1

stood as a wall for the clergy.[1] There went out from
Caesar Edward [I] a decree that the fruits of the church
should be taxed,[2] and as the people were tallaged, so
also were the clergy to be compelled to pay. But
Robert as primate of England did not suffer the king's
decree to take effect. He said that it would be contrary
to all law, for the king to have authority over the goods
of clerks, whom the imperial law had marked out with
many privileges, and made free from every exaction.
This too is intended by canon law; and the heathen
themselves have bequeathed us an example; when the
Egyptians for their great hunger put themselves under
the royal yoke, the priests and other servants of the
temples remained free. But the king being wrathful and
strongly roused to anger against the primate and all the
clergy, publicly announced to his officials that they
should have no consideration at all for clerks, but,
when they met regulars or secular clergy, should at once
have them off their horses and take the animals for their
own use, without discrimination, sparing none who did
not enjoy the royal protection. Nevertheless the Archbishop of Canterbury became more haughty and self-
confident, and proceeding further against the aggressors,
he struck with his hoe into his barren, weedy land and
excommunicated those who sought the royal protection.
The effrontery of the laity increased to such an extent
that they spared no one in the Archbishop's court,
even pulling the Archbishop himself off his horse, and
plundering all his goods, so that the Archbishop,
patiently bearing the wrong, was forced to go about the
countryside on foot. At length the king repented, and,
confessing that he had gravely sinned, restrained the
licence of his courtiers and gave orders for the church
to remain free. When the quarrel broke out again

procurante rege uocatus est ad curiam Romanam, et ibi
per biennium fere remansit, et fructus suos biennales
confiscatos amisit. Deinde 'mortuo rege in Angliam
rediit, et ecclesiam suam pacifice usque huc gubernauit.
Nunc autem nature debita persoluens, celestem migrauit
ad patriam, Cantuariensem ut creditur ornaturus
ecclesiam.

Anno igitur septimo regis intrante, in festo Trans-
F.194 lationis beate Thome conueniunt Londoniis[1] comites / et
barones iuxta promissum regis aduentum exspectantes,
ibidemque fere per quindenam commorantes, neque
regis copiam habuerunt, neque de regis reditu certos
nuntios acceperunt. Vnde comites, laboribus et expensis satis fatigati, sine die ad propria sunt reuersi.
Circa gulam Augusti[2] rediit dominus rex, et quasi de
recessu comitum molestus, scripsit comitibus rogans
quatinus moram suam excusatam haberent, et in festo
Sancti Mathei[3] si placeret ad parliamentum redirent, et
tunc communi consilio quicquid faciendum, quicquid
corrigendum esse prospicerent, communiter repararet.

Sed quid prosunt regi procrastinationes assidue?
Dicunt quidam, ut aduersarios suos cogat expendere, uel
mortem comitis forsan exspectat quem alias superare
non sperat. Sane peccat qui hoc audet asserere; immo
non apparet uerisimile ut rex ipse tam necessarii mortem
affectaret amici. Quis magis regi succurreret in summa
necessitate, quam cognatus eius Thomas Lancastrie?
Certe non socius eius ipse rex Francie, nec Petrus, si
uiueret, comes Cornubie. Reuera quicquid dolose actum
est in curia regis processit ex consiliariis eius, sed consilium eorum est inefficax et machinatio peritura.

---

[1] The second parliament of 1313 met on 8 July (*Parl. Writs*, II.i.94).
[2] He landed 16 July.
[3] 23 September

between the King and the Archbishop, the latter was summoned to the court of Rome at the King's instance, and there remained for almost two years, losing his revenues for two years by confiscation. On the king's death he returned to England and ruled his church in peace until the present time. But now, paying his debts to nature, he has migrated to heaven, to be an ornament, it is thought, to the church of Canterbury.

At the beginning of the seventh year of the king's reign, on the Feast of the Translation of the Blessed Thomas, the earls and barons met at London,[1] awaiting the king's promised arrival, and stayed there almost a fortnight, having no access to the king, nor any certain information of his return. So the earls, weary of the trouble and expense to which they had been put, went home *sine die*. The lord king returned about the first of August,[2] and, as if offended by the departure of the earls, wrote to them asking them to excuse his delay and please to return to parliament on the Feast of St Matthew,[3] when by common counsel he would make good with them whatever they thought should be done or corrected.

But what do these incessant delays profit the king? Some say that he could force his opponents to waste their resources, or perhaps awaits the death of an earl whom he could not hope to conquer. But he is in error who dares to assert this, for it is clearly unlikely that the king would desire the death of so necessary a friend. Who could help the king more in his dire need than his cousin Thomas of Lancaster? Certainly not his ally the King of France, nor, had he lived, Piers Earl of Cornwall. Indeed whatever wickedness was perpetrated in the king's court proceeded from his counsellors; but their advice is futile and their plots will fail. Cursed

H

Maledictus furor[a][1] eorum quia pertinax, et indignatio eorum quia diuidentur tandem a curia et dispergentur in ignominia. Iustum est enim ut suos auctores teneant peccata,[2] ne maleficia remaneant impunita.

Ad festum Sancti Mathei[3] conueniunt Londoniis comites predicti, et manserunt in eodem loco per aliquod tempus, nec regi mittentes, nec mandatum a rege recipientes. Vt autem per eos non staret quominus concordia fieret, miserunt ad dominum regem petentes quatinus sepe promissa consummaret, et baronibus suis F.195 sub fide non ficta rancorem remitteret. / Rex uero non statim annuit, sed potius ex solito negotium protelauit. Tandem quia uox publica testimonium prebuit, et rex ipse per exploratores suos manifeste cognouit, quia aut[b] petitioni comitum satisfieret, aut sibi suisque tutius esse ante tempus occurrere quam post uulneratam causam remedium querere; multa etiam instantia cardinalis et domini Lodowici precibus inductus, mandauit comitibus et baronibus quatinus, omni suspicione reiecta et securitate quam uellent petita et optenta, ad presentiam suam accederent, et beniuolentiam eius multociens requisitam pro libito reportarent.

Comites igitur in crastinum dominum regem adierunt, ipsumque flexis genibus sicut decuit salutarunt. Quos ipse benigne suscipiens protinus erexit, et singillatim singulos in osculo suscepit, ab omni delicto prius eis imposito penitus absoluit, rationabiliter petita et in posterum petenda similiter concessit, et hec omnia iureiurando et scripto, magni sigillo confirmatis,[4] roborauit. Rex etiam ad maioris foederis signum comites

---

[a] fauor MS   [b] autem MS
[1] Gen. xlix. 7   [2] Cod. 9.47.22
[3] The third parliament of 1313 met on 23 September and sat till 18 November. (Parl. Writs, II, i.102, 115)
[4] 14 October 1313. Foed. II. 230-233; Statutes of the Realm, I. 169.

be their anger[1] for it is stubborn, and their wrath, for
they shall at length be divided from the court and
scattered in disgrace. It is right that their sins should
bind those who commit them,[2] that evil-doing may
not go unpunished.

At the feast of St Matthew[3] the said earls met in
London, and there remained for some time, neither
sending to the king, nor receiving any command from
him. But that the lack of agreement might not be laid
at their door, they sent to the lord king asking him to
perform what he had so often promised, and remit his
rancour towards the barons in genuine good faith. The
king did not immediately yield, but dragged out the
business as usual. It was at length being publicly said,
as the king well knew through his spies, that he must
satisfy the earls' petition, and that it would be safer for
him and his to make answer too soon than to obtain
redress once his case had been damaged. Persuaded by
the earnestness of the cardinal [Arnold] and the prayers
of lord Louis [of Evreux], the king told the earls and
barons to lay aside all suspicion, and having asked for
and obtained the security that they wanted, to come to
his presence, and freely obtain the goodwill that they
had so often sought.

On the morrow, therefore, the earls approached the
lord king and saluted him, as was proper, on bended knee.
Receiving them graciously he at once raised them, and
kissed them one by one, wholly absolving them of
every crime of which they were accused, and granting
what they reasonably sought or should seek hereafter,
and all these things he confirmed by an oath, and granted
in writing under the great seal.[4] The better to signalise
the treaty, the king invited the earls to dinner, dining
himself next day with the Earl of Lancaster. For it

inuitauit ad prandium; ipse uero altera die in mensa comitis Lancastrie. Hic etenim mos inoleuit in Anglia ut pax confirmetur ad conuiuia.[a] Sic ergo mors Petri remittitur, et comes de Penbroke reconciliatur, et de ceteris amicis regis factum est sicut rex uoluit; sed Hugo Despenser gratiam habere non potuit. Caueat sibi de comite Lancastrie, et terram euacuet si uelit euadere. Tota terra uersa est in eius odium; pauci lugerent eius infortunium. Multis in officio suo iniuste nocuit; plures magnates et uiros diuites exheredauit, et utinam amitteret quod sic adquisiuit ut puniretur in quo deliquit. Summe Deus, auctor iustitie, falsos et perfidos a rege remoue; inter regem et barones hoc fœdus initum, Te protegente, seruetur in posterum. /

F.196   Queret forsan aliquis quid comites fecissent si regem in promissis difficilem inuenissent. Credo constanter quod regem captum sub custodia posuissent, donec eos auctores discordie penitus destruxissent. Nonne sic comes Symon de Mountefort regem Henricum tenuit et filium eius Edwardum carceri mancipauit? Sed non est tutum contra regem ceruicem erigere, quia tristes exitus frequenter solet afferre. Nam Symon ille comes Leycestrie[b] tandem apud Euesham occubuit in acie; comes de Ferrers terras perdidit; comiti Marescallie rex ipse successit; quilibet istorum regi restitit, et quilibet istorum in fine succubuit.

Sic igitur rege et baronibus suis sub forma predicta in amicitiam reuocatis, comites et ceteri magnates terre dederunt regi in subsidium guerre sue uicesimum denarium totius Anglie, cetera autem ordinanda in futurum distulerunt ad proximum parliamentum; et comes Herfordie remansit de regis familia, ceteri uero comites reuersi sunt ad propria.

[a] communia MS   [b] Lancastrie MS

has become a custom in England to clinch a peace with public banquets. In this way therefore, the death of Piers was forgiven, the Earl of Pembroke reconciled, and as for the other friends of the king matters were arranged as the king willed; but Hugh Despenser could find no favour. Let him beware of the Earl of Lancaster and leave the country if he wishes to escape. The whole land has turned to hatred of him. Few would mourn his downfall. As an unjust official he did harm to many; he disinherited many magnates and rich men. Would that he might lose what he has thus acquired, that he might be punished in his crime. All-Highest God, author of justice, remove false men and traitors from the king; may this treaty entered into by king and barons, under Thy protection, be kept hereafter.

Someone may ask what the earls would have done if they had found the king backward in making promises. I firmly believe that they would have kept the king under restraint, until they had utterly destroyed the creators of discord. Did not Earl Simon de Montfort thus bridle King Henry and consign his son Edward to prison? But it is not safe to set oneself up against the king, because often the issue is wont to be unfortunate. Even the famous Simon, Earl of Leicester, was at last laid low in battle at Evesham; the Earl Ferrers lost his estates; the king himself succeeded the Earl Marshal; each of these had resisted the king, and each of them in the end succumbed.

Thus the king and his barons being reunited in amity in this fashion, the earls and other magnates of the land gave to the king as a war-subsidy the twentieth penny of all England, but other matters to be settled they put off till the next parliament. The Earl of Hereford remained at court, but the other earls went home.

Quia prius mentionem feci de morte Cantuariensis archiepiscopi, nunc de eius successore, et quomodo successit, aduerte. Mortuo namque archipresule, prior ecclesie Christi Cantuariensis, et eiusdem loci conuentus, processerunt ad electionem, unanimi consensu elegerunt magistrum Thomam de Cobham uirum nobilem, diuini et humani iuris professorem; qui statim iter arripiens mare transiit et iuri suo prosequendo operam dedit. Due tamen cause impediebant eum. Adhuc*a* enim languente primate miserat papa bullam suam qua reseruauit sibi dispositionem archiepiscopatus et electionem futuri pontificis. Misit et rex Anglie summo pontifici, orans ut clericum suum Wygorniensem episcopum ad sedem archiepiscopalem duce[re]t promouen/dum. Hiis de causis impediebatur electus, nec eligentium sibi proficere potuit assensus, quin rege instante et multa ut creditur pecunia interueniente, dominus papa archiepiscopatum conferret, et dictum episcopum ecclesie Anglicane preficeret.

F.197

O quanta inter electum et prefectum erat differentia! Nam electus ipse flos Cantie, nobilis generis, rexerat in artibus, in decretis, et magister erat theologus, sedi Cantuariensis ecclesie satis ydoneus. Dictus uero episcopus nuper erat simplex clericus et minus competenter litteratus, sed in ludis theatralibus principatum tenuit, et per hoc regis fauorem optinuit. Vnde in familia regis assumptus post modicum tempus factus est regis thesaurarius, et de thesauraria Wygorniensis episcopus, postmodum cancellarii gessit officium et ecce, nunc promotus est in archiepiscopum. Mirantur quidam de uiri fortuna, sed ego magis miror de domino papa, cur tam excellentem personam respueret, et inydoneum scienter

a ad hoc MS

Because I made mention above of the death of the Archbishop of Canterbury, I turn now to his successor and the manner of his succession. On the death of the primate, the prior and convent of Christ Church, Canterbury, proceeded to an election, and by a unanimous vote chose Mr Thomas de Cobham, a nobleman, and a doctor of canon and civil law; who at once set out and crossed the sea to prosecute his cause. He was hindered by two circumstances. While the primate was still on his sick-bed the pope had sent his bull reserving for himself the disposition of the archbishopric and the choice of the next pontiff. Also the King of England sent to the pope, praying him that he should see fit to promote his clerk the Bishop of Worcester to the archiepiscopal see. For these reasons the archbishop-elect was frustrated, nor could the assent of the electors profit him, for at the king's instance, and, it is believed, after a large sum had passed, the lord pope granted the archbishopric and set the said bishop over the English church.

O what a difference there was between the elect and the 'preferred'! For the elect was the very flower of Kent, of noble stock; he had lectured in arts and on canon law, and was a master of theology; a man eminently fitted for the see of Canterbury. The bishop, on the other hand, had recently been a mere clerk and was scarcely literate, but he excelled in theatrical presentations, and through this obtained the king's favour. Thus he was taken into the king's household, and soon became the king's treasurer, and from the treasury became Bishop of Worcester, later Chancellor, and lo! now he is made Archbishop. Some are surprised at the man's good luck, but I rather am surprised at the lord pope, why he should reject so excellent a person, and

assumeret, cum de utriusque meritis patenter sibi constaret. Sed domina pecunia omne negotium consummat in curia. Consuetudinem et mores Romane curie, si forsan ignoras, aduerte. Amat causas, lites, iurgia, quia expediri non possunt sine pecunia; et causa que curiam semel ingreditur pene inmortalis efficitur; et hec fuit causa quare, omisso quolibet medio, licuit ad papam appellare. Quilibet etiam sola contentus esse debet ecclesia, sicut cauit capitulum *de multa*[1]; excipiuntur tamen sublimes persone, dispensationem accipiunt indistincte, sed omnes qui pecuniam dare sufficiunt. Hec miranda uanitas, hec curie detestanda cupiditas, totum orbem in sui scandalum excitauit. Multis retro temporibus exstitit inauditum, ut citramontanus eligeretur in papam; post hec nunquam eueniat ut tam uicinus F.198 homo cathedram papalem ascendat. Octo annis / et amplius papa Clemens quintus uniuersalem rexit ecclesiam, sed quicquid profuit homini euasit memoriam. Apud Vienniam consilium congregauit, et Templarios disposuit, indulgentias pro Terra Sancta concessit, infinitam pecuniam congessit, sed Terre Sancte nichil omnino profuit. Regibus concessit decimas, pauperum spoliauit ecclesias. Melius esset rectoribus papam non habere quam tot exactionibus indies subiacere. Sed an hoc possit facere non est meum discutere, quia instar sacrilegii est de potestate principis disputare.[2] Inter omnes mundi prouincias sola Anglia dominum papam*a* sentit onerosum; nam ex plenitudine potestatis multa presumit, nec princeps nec populus sibi contradicit; omnes pingues redditus sibi reseruat, atque rebellantes statim

---

a papam] ipsam MS
[1] A decree of the Fourth Lateran Council, III *Decr.* tit.v.c.28.
[2] *Cod.* 9. 29. 2

deliberately adopt an unsuitable one, when the merits
of each were clearly known to him. But My Lady
Money transacts all business in the Curia. If perchance
you are ignorant of the habit and customs of the Roman
Curia, pay heed to this. It loves causes, law suits,
quarrels, because they cannot be expedited without
money; and a case once entered upon at Rome becomes
almost immortal; and this was the cause why, all
intermediaries omitted, an appeal was allowed to the
pope. Anyone ought to be content with one church
only, as we are taught by the chapter *de multa*,[1] but
very important persons are excepted, receiving in-
discriminate dispensations, and so are all who can give
money. This astonishing vanity, this detestable greed
of the Curia, has been a scandal to the whole world.
For a long time back it has been unheard-of for a
non-Italian to be elected pope; after this may it never
happen that a man so near to us ascends the papal
throne. For eight years and more Pope Clement V
has ruled the church universal. But how it has profited
anyone escapes my memory. He brought together a
Council at Vienne, disposed of the Templars, granted
indulgences for the Holy Land, collected a vast amount
of money, but it profited the Holy Land nothing at all.
He granted tithes to kings, despoiled the churches of the
poor. It would be better for rectors not to have a pope
than to be subject to so many daily exactions. But
whether this can be done is not for me to discuss,
because it is the equivalent of sacrilege to dispute the
prince's power.[2] Amongst all the provinces of the
world England alone feels the pope a burden; for he
presumes much on his *plenitudo potestatis*; neither
prince nor people contradicts him; all fat rents he
reserves for himself, and at once excommunicates the

excommunicat; ueniunt legati et terram spoliant, ueniunt bullati et prebendas uendicant. Omnes decanatus alienigenis contulit ubi lex indigenas preferri statuit. Residentia decanorum iam nunc aboletur, et canonicorum numerus ualde desolatur. Nonne*a* sicut papa spiritualia moderatur, et sic[ut] princeps imperatorum in temporalibus dominatur? Cur igitur papa magis presumit in clericis, quam ipsa magestas et dominatio imperialis in laicis? Imperator enim sine causa a nullo quicquam exigit; dominus papa passim cum uult mutat, confert et repetit. Domine Iesu, uel papam tolle de medio, uel potestatem minue quam presumit in populo, quia priuilegium meretur amittere qui concessa sibi abutitur potestate.[1] Quid dicam de clericis qui hiis diebus accedunt ad curiam, et multa refusa pecunia tanquam in foro uenali dignitates emunt et prebendas? Si dicamus simoniam committi, ipse papa non poterit excusari, quia simonia ultro citroque est obligatoria;

F.199 sicut / enim ementem ligat sic et uendentem condempnat.[2] Sed forsan dicet papa se supra leges esse et per consequens legibus ligari non posse. Sed non debet*b* facere quod necesse habet alios prohibere, ne inde nascantur iniurie, unde iura debent procedere.[3] Ego tamen ad presens dominum papam excuso; nec ipsum excedere credamus in aliquo, quia uel honoris gratia datur, uel ad elemosinam pape redigitur quicquid ex hac causa confertur; unde liberalitas domini pape sic excitatur, sed uenditio nusquam contrahitur. Nam si quis honoris gratia in auditorio quicquam tribuit, non tamen propter hoc ipsum conducit; alioquin non ex

a nonne] nomen MS
b debere MS
[1] II *Decr.* c.xi q.3 c.63
[2] II *Decr.* c.i q.i c.6
[3] *Dig.* 8.5.15

rebellious; legates come and plunder the land, men armed with bulls come and claim prebends. He grants all deaneries to foreigners though the law has decreed that natives should be preferred. The residence of deans has already been abolished, and the ranks of the canons miserably thinned. Does he not as pope rule over spiritualities, and as prince of emperors dominate in temporalities? But why does the pope presume more upon his authority over clerks than the imperial majesty and dominion itself does over laymen? For the emperor demands nothing from anyone without cause; the lord pope, where and when he wishes, changes, bestows, and withdraws. Lord Jesus! Either take away the pope from our midst or diminish the power that he presumes to exercise over the people, for he deserves to lose his privilege who abuses the power granted to him.[1] What shall I say of the clerks who in our time beset the Curia, and with a profusion of cash buy dignities and prebends as if in a secular market? If we say that simony is committed, the pope himself cannot be excused, because simony is mutually binding; it binds the purchaser just as it condemns the seller.[2] But perhaps the pope will say that he is above the laws and consequently cannot be bound by the laws. But he ought not to do what he must needs prohibit others from doing, lest wrongs arise whence rights should have proceeded.[3] Yet at present I myself excuse the lord pope; and let us not believe that his action is in any way improper because whatever is conferred for this reason is either given as a mark of respect, or is dispensed as papal charity; so that his generosity is aroused in return, and thus a sale is nowhere contracted. For if anyone pays anything at an audience for honour's sake, he does not by this bribe

mandato sed ex conducto competeret actio. Probet autem se ipsum homo et secum diligenter deliberet, an si[bi] impetrare uel non impetrare magis expediat, quia gehenne ignis exspectat incendium, qui lesa conscientia tendit ad iudicium.

Interea Robertus de Brutz partes Northumbrorum uiolenter inuasit, uillas et burgos succendit, homines occidit, animalia eorum abegit, et multos ad tributum coegit. Nam ciues et incole, uidentes se sui regis defensione carere, et seuitiam Roberti de Brutz non posse sufferre, fecerunt pacem cum eo quam poterant, de termino in terminum soluendo certum tributum. Erat autem tributum quod modico tempore sic extorserat, quasi quadraginta milia librarum. Muros etiam uillarum et castrorum in Scotia funditus destruxit, ne superuenienti genti Anglorum munitioni forent in posterum. Cepit autem duo castra regis Anglie munitissima, Edenburghe scilicet et Rokesburghe[1]; unum per proditionem cuiusdam Vasconis qui erat cognatus Petri de Gauestone, cui rex noster custodiam castri tradiderat. Ipse periurus et proditor adhesit Roberto de Brutz et castrum prodidit.[a] Alterum castrum captum erat per industriam Jacobi Dugelas, qui erat ex / parte Scotorum. Nam ipse Iacobus quadam nocte clam ad castellum accessit, et scalas latenter allatas ad murum apposuit; et sic per eas murum ascendit, et custodibus dormientibus uel incautis socios introduxit; et quos reperiebat inuasit et castrum cepit, et eodem modo castrum de Berewyke cepisset nisi quidam canis uigiles excitasset. Deinde Robertus de Brutz ad obsidendum castrum de Stryuelyn se conuertit. Hoc quidem castrum dominus Edwardus rex Anglie senior cum toto exercitu suo per tres menses et amplius

F.200

---

[a] perdidit MS
[1] 19 February to 14 March 1314

the pope; otherwise an action would lie not *ex mandato* but *ex conducto*. But let each examine himself and diligently question himself, whether it is better to obtain or not to obtain, for he awaits the blaze of hell-fire, who proffers a blemished conscience at the judgment.

Meanwhile Robert Bruce ravaged Northumbria burning vills and towns, killing the men, driving off their cattle, and compelling many to pay tribute. For the citizens and inhabitants, seeing that their king did not defend them, and being unable to bear the savagery of Robert Bruce, made such peace with him as they could, paying a fixed tribute from term to term. The tribute which he thus extorted in a short time was of the order of 40,000 pounds. He utterly destroyed, too, the walls of the castles and towns in Scotland, lest they should later serve to protect the advancing English. He took two of the King of England's strongest fortresses, namely Edinburgh and Roxburgh[1]; one through the treachery of a certain Gascon who was Piers Gaveston's cousin, to whom our king had given the custody of the castle. This perjurer and traitor adhered to Robert Bruce and betrayed the castle. The other castle was taken through the exertions of James Douglas, who was on the side of the Scots. This James came secretly to the fort by night, brought up ladders stealthily and placed them against the wall; and by this means he climbed up the wall, and leading his companions upon the sleeping or heedless guards, attacked those he found and took the castle. He would have taken Berwick Castle in the same way had not a dog aroused the guards. Robert Bruce next addressed himself to the siege of Stirling Castle. The lord Edward the elder, King of England, laid siege to this castle with his whole army for three months and more before he could take it. When

obsedit antequam capere posset. Videns igitur custos castri obsidionem iam cœptam, uictum eorum insufficientem, Robertum et Scotos in[a] insidiis semper latentes, treugas accepit sub hoc pacto, quod aut procuraret regem Anglie ad defendendum castrum uenire, aut, si regem ad hoc inducere non posset, castrum indilate relinqueret; et hoc petitum sic initum fide media confirmatur, et dies Natiuitatis Sancti Johannis Baptiste pro termino assignatur.

Circa principium Quadragesime[1] uenerunt nuntii ad regem narrantes municipiorum Scotie destructionem, castrorum captionem et murorum in circuitu diruptionem. Venit et constabularius de Stryuelyn indicans regi quale petitum necessitate compulsus inierat; procurauit regem exercitum in Scotiam ducere, castrum suum et terram defendere.[2]

Audiens hec rex uehementer doluit, et pro castrorum captione lacrimas continere uix potuit. Mandauit igitur comitibus et baronibus quatinus in auxilium suum uenirent, et proditorem qui se regem facit expungnarent. Responderunt comites melius fore ad parliamentum omnes conuenire et ibidem unanimiter diffinire quid in hoc negotio oportet agere, quam si ita inconsulte procederent; nam et ordinationes hoc uolunt. Dixit autem F.201 rex instans negotium magna / acceleratione indigere, et ideo parliamentum exspectare non posse. Dixerunt comites ad pugnam sine parliamento uenire nolle, ne contingeret eos ordinationes offendere. Consiliarii uero et domestici regis quidam consuluerunt regi, ut debita

[a] in] et MS
[1] February 1314
[2] For the whole of this campaign see the brilliant analysis by J. E. Morris, *Bannockburn* (C.U.P. 1914). Our author ranks high among the English authorities, though rather blinded by Gloucester and (later) Hereford. Edward had already promised late in 1313 that he would go to Scotland. (*Foed.* II, 237, 238.)

the warden of the castle saw that the siege had already
begun, that their stores were insufficient, that Robert
and the Scots lay continually in ambush, he agreed to a
truce on this condition, that he would either get the
King of England to come and defend the castle, or,
if he could not persuade the king to do this, he would
give up the castle without delay. This request was
granted and the truce ratified, and the day of the
Nativity of St John the Baptist was assigned for a term.

About the beginning of Lent[1] messengers came to
the king with the news of the destruction of the Scottish
cities, the capture of the castles, and the breaching of the
surrounding walls. The constable of Stirling came, too,
and pointed out to the king how he had been compelled
by necessity to enter upon the truce. He persuaded the
king to lead an army to Scotland, to defend his castle
and the country.[2] When the king heard the news he was
very much grieved, and for the capture of his castles
could scarcely restrain his tears. He therefore summoned
the earls and barons to come to his aid and overcome
the traitor who called himself King. The earls replied
that it would be better for all to meet in parliament
and there unanimously decide what ought to be done in
this matter rather than to proceed so inadvisedly; this
moreover would be in accord with the Ordinances.
But the king said that the present business was very
urgent and he could not therefore wait for parliament.
The earls said that they would not fight without parliament, lest it should happen that they infringed the
Ordinances. Some counsellors and household officials
therefore advised the king to demand their due service
from all, and set out boldly for Scotland. It was certain
that so many would come to his aid that neither Robert
Bruce nor the Scots would resist. What of the Earl of

seruitia ab omnibus exigeret, et audacter in Scotiam tenderet. Certum esse quod tot in auxilium uenirent quibus nec Robertus Brutz nec Scoti resisterent. Quid comes Gloucestrie, quid comes de Penbroke, quid comes de Herford, Robertus de Clifford, Hugo Despenser et regis familia et ceteri barones qui sunt in Anglia? Omnes hii uenient cum suis militibus: non est magna cura de reliquis comitibus. Rex igitur debita seruitia ab omnibus exegit, et commeatui necessaria prouideri mandauit. Premisit quoque comitem de Penbrok cum manu militari, qui insidias Scotorum diligenter exploraret, et uiam regis in Scotiam prepararet.

Omnibus itaque necessariis collectis, rex et alii magnates terre cum magna multitudine curruum et quadrigarum profecti sunt in Scotiam. Cumque dominus rex ad Berewyk peruenisset, aliquantulum moram fecit ut uenturum exercitum exspectaret. Comes autem Lancastrie, comes Warennie, comes de Arundel et comes de Warewik non uenerunt, sed milites instructos qui debita seruitia pro eis impenderent ad exercitum premiserunt. Instante iam festo Sancti Johannis Baptiste, sexto uel septimo die precedente, rex noster cum uniuerso exercitu suo a Berewyk exiuit, et uersus Stryuelyn iter arripuit. Erant autem armatorum amplius quam duo milia excepta peditum turba copiosa. Fuerunt in societate illa satis sufficientes ad penetrandum totam Scotiam, et iudicio aliquorum, si tota Scotia collecta fuisset in unum, non exspectaret regis exercitum. Reuera hoc fatebatur tota comitiua, quod tempore nostro talis exercitus non ex/iuit ab Anglia. Multitudo quadrigarum, si seriatim extensa fuisset in longum, occupasset spatium uiginti leucarum.

F.202

Rex igitur, de tanta et tam clara multitudine confisus et animosus effectus, de die in diem festinanter ad locum

Gloucester, the Earl of Pembroke, the Earl of Hereford, Robert de Clifford, Hugh Despenser and the King's household and the other barons in England? All these would come with their knights: there was no need to worry about the other earls. The king therefore demanded their due service from all, and ordered the necessary stores to be provided. The Earl of Pembroke he sent ahead with a force of knights, to seek out the ambushes of the Scots, and prepare the king's route into Scotland.

When all the necessaries had been collected, the king and the other magnates of the land with a great multitude of carts and baggage-wagons set out for Scotland. When the lord king had reached Berwick, he made a short halt there to await the arrival of the army. But the Earl of Lancaster, the Earl Warenne, the Earl of Arundel, and the Earl of Warwick did not come, but sent knights equipped to do their due service for them in the army. On the sixth or seventh day before the feast of St John the Baptist, our king with all his army left Berwick and took his way towards Stirling. The cavalry numbered more than two thousand, without counting a numerous crowd of infantry. There were in that company quite sufficient to penetrate the whole of Scotland, and some thought if the whole strength of Scotland had been gathered together, they would not have stayed to face the king's army. Indeed all who were present agreed that never in our time has such an army gone forth from England. The multitude of wagons if they had been placed end to end, would have taken up a space of twenty leagues.

The king therefore took confidence and courage from so great and so distinguished a multitude and hastened day by day to the appointed place, not as if he was

I

prefixum est profectus, non tanquam exercitum ducturus
ad bellum sed magis profecturus ad Sanctum Jacobum.
Breuis erat mora capiendi sompnum, sed breuior erat
mora sumendi cibum; unde equi, equites et pedites,
labore et fame fatigati, si minus bene rem gererent non
erant culpandi.

Comes autem Gloucestrie et comes Herfordie primam
aciem regebant. Die itaque Dominica, que erat beati
Johannis uigilia, cum iam quandam siluam preteriissent
et castrum de Stryuelyn iam appropinquarent, ecce Scoti
quasi fugientes errabant sub [ne]more, quos miles quidam Henricus de Boun[1] cum Walensibus persecutus est
usque ad introitum nemoris. Gestabat enim in animo
quod, si Robertum de Brutz ibidem inueniret, uel morti
traderet uel secum captum adduceret. Cum autem eo
peruenisset, Robertus ipse a latebris silue statim exiuit;
uidensque predictus Henricus quod multitudini Scotorum resistere non posset, redire uolens ad socios equum
retorsit; sed Robertus ei restitit et securi quam manu
gerebat caput ipsius contriuit. Armiger autem eius, dum
dominum suum tueri uel uindicare conatur, a Scotis
opprimitur.

Initium malorum hoc! ipso eodem die satis acre
bellum geritur, in quo comes Gloucestrie ab equo deicitur, in quo Robertus de Clifford turpiter in fugam
conuertitur, sed et homines nostri diu Scotos persequuntur, multi ex utraque parte perimuntur. Quia uero
inclinata erat iam dies conuenit totus exercitus ad locum
F.203 ubi ipsa nocte reclinaret. Sed nulla erat / quies; totam
enim illam duxerunt insompnem. Putabant namque
Scotos potius insultum dare de nocte quam bellum ex-

---

[1] Hearne reads Doun. For a well-known Welsh family of this name see
Tout, *Edward II*, 339; but *Ann. Lond.* 231 and *Cont. Trivet.* 14 both have
Bohun or Boun.

leading an army to battle but as if he was going to St James's. Brief were the halts for sleep, briefer still for food; hence horses, horsemen and infantry were worn out with toil and hunger, and if they did not bear themselves well it was hardly their fault.

The Earl of Gloucester and the Earl of Hereford commanded the first line. On Sunday, which was the vigil of St John's day, as they passed by a certain wood and were approaching Stirling Castle, the Scots were seen straggling under the trees as if in flight, and a certain knight, Henry de Boun[1] pursued them with the Welsh to the entrance of the wood. For he had in mind that if he found Robert Bruce there he would either kill him or carry him off captive. But when he had come thither, Robert himself came suddenly out of his hiding-place in the wood, and the said Henry seeing that he could not resist the multitude of Scots, turned his horse with the intention of regaining his companions; but Robert opposed him and struck him on the head with an axe that he carried in his hand. His squire, trying to protect or rescue his lord, was overwhelmed by the Scots.

This was the beginning of their troubles! On the same day a sharp action was fought, in which the Earl of Gloucester was unhorsed, and Robert de Clifford disgracefully routed, and though our men long pursued the Scots, many were killed on either side. The day being spent, the whole army met at the place where it was to bivouac that night. But there was no rest; for they spent it sleepless, expecting the Scots rather to attack by night than to await battle by day. When day came it was abundantly clear that the Scots were prepared for the conflict with a great force of armed men. Wherefore our men, the veterans that is, and the more experienced,

pectare de die. Mane autem facto certo certius compertum est Scotos paratos ad prelium cum magna multitudine armatorum. Vnde homines nostri, milites scilicet ueterani, et hii qui magis erant experti, consilium dederunt ipso die non esse pungnaturum, sed diem crastinum magis expectandum, tum propter solempne festum tum propter laborem preteritum. Vtile quidem et honestum erat consilium apud iuuenes reprobatum, inhers et ignauum reputatum.

Comes autem Gloucestrie consuluit regi ne ipso die in bellum prodiret, sed propter festum potius uacaret, et exercitum suum ualde recrearet. Sed rex consilium comitis spreuit, et proditionem et preuaricationem sibi imponens in ipsum uehementer excanduit. 'Hodie,' inquit comes, 'erit liquidum quod nec proditor nec preuaricator sum,' et statim parauit se ad pungnandum. Interim Robertus de Brutz socios monuit et instruxit, panem et uinum prebuit, et modo quo potuit confortauit; ubi uero didicit acies Anglorum in campum deuenisse totum exercitum suum eduxit de nemore. Circiter quadraginta milia hominum secum produxit, ipsosque in tres turmas diuisit, et nullus eorum equum ascendit, sed erat unusquisque eorum leui armatura munitus, quam non faciliter penetraret gladius. Securim habebant ad latus et lanceas ferebant in manibus. Ibant etiam quasi sepes densa conserti, nec leuiter potuit talis turma penetrari. Cum autem ad hoc uentum esset ut congredi simul oporteret, Jacobus Douglas, qui prime turme Scotorum preerat, aciem comitis Gloucestrie acriter inuasit. Et comes ipsum uiriliter*a* excepit, semel et iterum cuneum penetrauit, et triumphum utique F.204 reportasset si fideles / socios habuisset. Sed ecce, subito irruentibus Scotis, equus comitis occiditur et comes in

---

a ipsum uiriliter ipsum MS

advised that we should not fight that day, but rather
await the morrow, both on account of the importance
of the feast and the toil that they had already undergone.
This practical and honourable advice was rejected by
the younger men as idle and cowardly.

The Earl of Gloucester counselled the king not to
go forth to battle that day, but to rest on account of the
feast, and let his army recuperate as much as possible.
But the king spurned the earl's advice, and, growing
very heated with him, charged him with treachery and
deceit. 'Today,' said the earl, 'it will be clear that I
am neither a traitor nor a liar,' and at once prepared
himself for battle. Meanwhile Robert Bruce marshalled
and equipped his allies, gave them bread and wine,
and cheered them as best he could; when he learned that
the English line had occupied the field he led his whole
army out from the wood. About forty thousand
men he brought with him, and split them into three
divisions; and not one of them was on horseback, but
each was furnished with light armour, not easily
penetrable by a sword. They had axes at their sides and
carried lances in their hands. They advanced like a
thick-set hedge, and such a phalanx could not easily be
broken. When the situation was such that the two sides
must meet, James Douglas, who commanded the first
phalanx of the Scots, vigorously attacked the Earl of
Gloucester's line. The earl withstood him manfully,
once and again penetrated their wedge, and would have
been victorious if he had had faithful companions. But
look! At a sudden rush of Scots, the earl's horse is
killed and the earl rolls to the ground. Lacking defenders,
and borne down by the weight of his body-armour he
could not easily arise, and of the five hundred cavalry
whom he had led to battle at his own expense, he almost

terram labitur. Ipse etiam defensore carens et mole corporis nimis oneratus faciliter exsurgere non potuit, sed inter quingentos armatorum quos suis sumptibus duxerat ad bellum, ipse fere solum occubuit. Cum enim uiderent dominum suum ab equo deiectum, stabant quasi attoniti non ferentes auxilium. Maledicta militia*ᵃ* cuius summa necessitate*ᵇ* perit audacia.

Heu! uiginti milites armati satis subuenissent comiti, sed inter quingentos fere non profuit unus. Confundat eos Dominus! Alii dixerunt comitem Gloucestrie ex incauto processu subito periisse. Certabant enim inter se ipse et comes Herfordie quis in acie alterum deberet precedere,*ᶜ* et comes Herfordie dicebat hoc sibi de iure competere eo quod constabularius sit Anglie. Alius dicebat progenitores suos semper in acie primos exstitisse, et hoc ideo ad se pertinere de consuetudine. Porro dum in hunc modum uterque certaret, et acies Scotorum acriter appropinquaret, prosiluit comes Gilbertus inordinate uolens de primo congressu triumphum reportare; sed ecce irruentibus Scotis comes excipitur et equus eius statim occiditur; quia defensore caruit ab equo deiectus, et multis uulneribus confossus, turpiter occubuit. Heu! uiginti milites armati satis subuenissent comiti, sed inter quingentos fere non profuit unus. Confundat eos Dominus!

Egidius de Argentym, miles strenuus[1] et in re militari multum expertus, dum frenum regis regeret[2] et casum comitis aspiceret, acer et anxius illuc properauit subuenire comiti, nec potuit. Fecit tamen quod potuit, et cum comite simul occubuit, honestius arbitrans cum tanto uiro succumbere quam fugiendo mortem euadere; /

ᵃ malitia MS   *ᵇ* necessarie MS   *ᶜ* procedere MS
[1] *miles strenuus* is almost a technical term in this period for a knight who had seen active service.

alone was killed. For when they saw their lord unhorsed, they stood astonished and brought him no aid. Accursed be the chivalry whose courage fails in the hour of greatest need!

Alas! Twenty armed knights could have saved the earl, but among some five hundred, there was not found one. May the Lord confound them! Some said that the Earl of Gloucester had perished suddenly by reason of his rash attack. For there was rivalry between him and the Earl of Hereford, who should take precedence in the line, and the Earl of Hereford said that this was lawfully his, because he was Constable of England. Gloucester replied that his forbears had always led the van, and therefore this pertained to him by custom. While they disputed in this fashion, and the Scottish forces were approaching rapidly, the Earl of Gloucester dashed forward in disorder, seeking the glory of the first encounter; but see! The earl is met by the on-rushing Scots and his horse immediately killed; because when thrown from his horse there was no one to defend him, he was pierced by many wounds and shamefully killed. Alas! Twenty armed knights could have saved the earl, but among some five hundred not one was found to help. May the Lord confound them.

Giles de Argentine, a fighting soldier[1] and very expert in the art of war, while in command of the king's rein,[2] watched the fate of the earl, hurried up in eager anxiety to help him, but could not. Yet he did what he could, and fell together with the earl, thinking it more honourable to perish with so great a man than to escape death by flight; for those who fall in battle for

---

[2] A member of the King's personal bodyguard; cf. *Roll of Caerlaverock* 19, for six men *De son frein guyour e guardain*, cited by H. Johnstone, *Edw. of Caernarvon* 116, which see too for the career of Giles.

F.205 nam qui in acie pro re publica perimuntur semper per gloriam uiuere intelliguntur. Eodem die Robertus de Clifford, Paganus Typetot, Willelmus Mareschal, milites preclari, potentes et strenui, a Scotis oppressi ibidem occumbunt.

Videntes hii qui cum rege nostro erant aciem comitis contritam et socios eius paratos ad fugam, dixerunt, periculosum est diutius morari sed tutius fore regem reuerti. Ad quorum dicta rex campum reliquit et uersus castrum properauit. Porro dum uexillum regis abire conspicitur, totus exercitus cito dispergitur. Ducenti milites et amplius, qui nec gladium eduxerant nec ictum quidem protulerant, in fugam conuersi sunt.

O gens inclita multis retro temporibus inuicta, cur fugis pedites que uincere solebas equites? Apud Berewyke, Dounbar et Foukyrk, triumphum reportasti, nunc Scotis peditibus terga dedisti. Sed quicquid dicant alii, non erat tecum manus Domini. Sic Benedab fortissimus rex Syrie fugatur per pedissequos principum Samarie.[1]

Dum igitur gens nostra fugeret, dum uestigia regis arriperet, ecce quedam fossa multos absorbuit, magna pars nostrorum in ipsa periit. Veniens namque rex ad castrum et credens ibidem habere refugium, tanquam hostis repellitur; pons attrahitur et porta clauditur. Vnde custos castri a plerisque proditionis expers non esse credebatur, et tamen in acie armatus quasi pro rege pungnaturus ipso die uidebatur. Verum nec custodem absoluo, nec proditionis accuso, sed consilio Dei fateor euenisse regem Anglie castrum non intrasse, quia si tunc admissus fuisset sine captione nequaquam euasisset.

[1] 1 Kings xx. 14-20

their country are known to live in everlasting glory. On the same day Robert de Clifford, Payn Tibetot, William Marshal, famous, powerful, and active knights, were overcome by the Scots and died in the field.

When those who were with our king saw that the earl's line was broken and his men ready to run, they said that it would be dangerous to tarry longer and safer for the king to retreat. At these remarks the king quitted the field, and hastened towards the castle. Moreover when the royal standard was seen to depart, the whole army quickly dispersed. Two hundred knights and more, who had neither drawn their swords nor even struck a blow, were reduced to flight.

O famous race unconquered through the ages, why do you, who used to conquer knights, flee from mere footmen? At Berwick, Dunbar, and Falkirk you carried off the victory, and now you flee from the infantry of the Scots. But whatever others may say, the hand of the Lord was not with you. Thus was Ben-hadad, a most powerful King of Syria, put to flight by the footmen of the princes of Samaria.[1]

Thus while our people fled, following in the king's footsteps, lo! a certain ditch entrapped many of them, and a great part of our army perished in it. The king coming to the castle and thinking to find refuge there, was repulsed as if he were an enemy; the drawbridge was raised and the gate closed. Wherefore the castellan was thought by many to be not innocent of treason, and yet that very day he was seen in armour arrayed for battle as if to fight for the king. I neither absolve the castellan nor accuse him of treachery, but I think it was God's doing that the King of England did not enter the castle, for if he had then been admitted he would never have escaped capture.

Cum rex sic se repulsum uidisset, nec aliud refugium
iam superesset, uersus Dounbar iter arripuit, et ibidem
ueniens nauem ascendit, ad portum de Berewyke cum
suis applicuit. Alii uero nauem non habentes per
F.206 terram ueniunt. Milites arma exuunt et / nudi fugiunt;
Scoti semper persequuntur a tergo; quinquaginta miliari-
bus durauit persecutio. Multi quidem ex nostris perimuntur, et multi similiter capiuntur. Nam incole terre,
qui prius pacem finxerant, nunc homines nostros passim
trucidabant, quare*a* proclamatum erat per dominum
Robertum de Brutz captiuos ducere et capientes lucrum
sentire. Vnde Scoti satagebant ualde magnates capere
ut multam pecuniam possent extorquere. Capti sunt
itaque comes de Herforde, Johannes Gyffard,[1] Johannes
de Wylyntone, Johannes de Segraue, Mauricius de
Bekelee, barones certe magne potentie, et multi alii quos
non oportet numerare, quorum multi de redemptione
conueniunt, et pecuniam soluentes absoluti sunt. Non
profuit ibidem cognitio, quia difficilior erat redemptio.
Quingenti et amplius putabantur mortui qui captiui
ducti sunt et postea redempti. Porro inter omnia aduersa hoc quidem exercitui nostro prospere contigit,
quod, dum gens nostra fuge presidium quereret, magna
pars Scotorum ad spolia diripienda se conuertit; quia si
omnes Scoti pariter persecutioni nostrorum intendissent,
pauci ex nostris Scotos euasissent. Vnde dum Robertus
de Brutz cum suis quadrigas nostras inuasit, plurima pars
Anglorum ad Berewyke salua peruenit. Siquidem a
seculo recordor inauditum talem exercitum coram pedi-

---

a quia MS
[1] John Giffard of Brimpsfield, later became a commander against
Llewelyn Bren. John de Wylyntone, of Wiltshire, Devon and Somerset,

When the king saw that he was thus repulsed and that no other refuge now remained to him, he turned his steps towards Dunbar, and coming there took ship. He landed with his following at the port of Berwick. Others having no ship came by land. The knights shed their armour and fled without it; the Scots continually harassed their rear; the pursuit lasted fifty miles. Many of our men perished and many, too, were taken prisoner. For the inhabitants of the countryside, who had previously feigned peace, now slaughtered our men indiscriminately, wherefore it was proclaimed by Sir Robert Bruce that they should take prisoners and hold them to ransom. So the Scots busied themselves with taking prisoner the magnates in order to extort large sums from them. There were captured the Earl of Hereford, John Giffard,[1] John de Wylyntone, John de Segrave, Maurice de Berkeley, undoubtedly barons of great power, and many others whom it is not necessary to specify, of whom many agreed for their ransoms and paying the money were set free. Cognizances were no advantage there, because ransom was then more difficult. Five hundred and more were thought to be dead who had been taken captive and were later ransomed. Indeed, amongst all their misfortunes this at least turned to the advantage of our army, that, while our people sought safety in flight, a great part of the Scottish army was occupied in plunder, because, if all the Scots alike had been attending to the pursuit of our men, few would have escaped. So while Robert Bruce with his men attacked our baggage-train, the greater part of the English came safe to Berwick. Indeed I think it is unheard-of in our time for such an army

---

whose name also occurs again at the siege of Bristol in 1316, became a contrariant. Segrave is of Segrave in Leicestershire, but moved in Marcher circles.

tibus tam subito dispersum, nisi cum flos Francie coram
Flandrensibus apud Coutray[1] cecidit, ubi nobilis ille
comes Artagensis Robertus occubuit.

O dies ultionis et infortunii, dies perditionis et op-
probrii, dies mala et execranda, nec in anni circulo
computanda; que famam Anglorum maculauit, et spoliauit Anglicos, et Scotos ditauit, in qua pretiosa supellex
nostrorum diripitur, que ducentarum millium librarum
F.207 estimatur! Tot boni proceres, iuventus / ualida, tot
equi nobiles, tot arma bellica, pretiose uestes et uasa
aurea, dies dura et breuis hora abstulit hec omnia.

Queret forsan et dicet aliquis quare percussit nos
hodie Dominus, quare subcubuimus coram Scotis, cum
uiginti annis preteritis semper uictoriam habuerimus;
reuera casus antiquorum exemplum prebent, et actus
Hebreorum manifeste respondent. Medorum rex Ser-
seles potentissimus dum Grecis bellum indiceret in classe
numerosa et multitudine contumaci, uix licuit uicto sola
cum naue reuerti.[a] Israel dum Beniamyn expungnaret
propter scelus commissum in Gabaa, de numero et for-
titudine confidens, bis in prelio ceditur, bis coram Beniamyn in fuga conuertitur.[2] Sic homines nostri, qui in
superbia et abusione uenerunt, in ignominia et con-
fusione redierunt. Certe superba nostrorum presumptio
Scotos fecit gaudere triumpho.

De superbia modernorum, et quis fructus inde proueniat, modicum si placet lector aduertat. Hodie pauper et tenuis, qui nec obolum habet in bonis, maiorem
se contempnit, et maledictum pro maledicto referre non
metuit. Sed ex rusticitate forsan hoc accidit. Veniamus
igitur ad eos qui se putant eruditos. Quis putas maiori
rixa in alium excandescit quam curialis? dum forte
rancore tumescit inferiorem non respicit, parem fastidit,

---

[a] An unidentified hexameter   [1] In 1302   [2] Judges xx. 21, 25

to be scattered so suddenly by infantry, unless when the flower of France fell before the Flemings at Courtrai,[1] where the noble Count Robert of Artois was killed.

O day of vengeance and disaster, day of utter loss and shame, evil and accursed day, not to be reckoned in our calendar; that blemished the reputation of the English, despoiled them and enriched the Scots, in which our costly belongings were ravished to the value of £200,000! So many fine noblemen and valiant youth, so many noble horses, so much military equipment, costly garments and gold plate—all lost in one unfortunate day, one fleeting hour.

Perchance some one will ask why the Lord smote us this day, why we succumbed to the Scots, when for the last twenty years we have always had the better of them; indeed antiquity offers an example, and the acts of the Hebrews clearly provide a parallel. Xerxes, most powerful king of the Medes, when he waged war upon the Greeks with a numerous fleet and stubborn army, 'was scarcely allowed in defeat to escape with a single ship'. Israel fighting Benjamin for the crime committed in Gibeah, trusting in numbers and courage, was twice defeated in battle, twice put to flight before Benjamin.[2] Thus our men, who came in pride and insolence, returned in shame and rout. Assuredly the proud arrogance of our men made the Scots rejoice in victory.

I shall turn for a moment, if it please the reader, to present-day pride and its fruits. Today the poor and needy, who has not a halfpenny to his name, despises his betters, and is not afraid to exchange a curse for a curse. This perhaps arises from rusticity. Let us come therefore to those who think themselves educated. Who do you think is inflamed with greater malice against another than the courtier? While he is greatly swollen

maiori par fieri semper intendit. Nam armiger militem, miles baronem, baro comitem, comes regem, in omni fere cultu antecedere nititur et laborat. Porro dum sumptus deficit, quia patrimonium non sufficit, ad predam se conuertunt, uicinos spoliant, subditos expilant, et in ipsos Dei ministros infamem questum exercent. Hinc est quod magnates terre uel cadunt in bello, uel moriuntur sine filio, aut sexus femineus hereditatem diuidit, et nomen patris imperpetuum euanescit. /

F.208   Post hec rex de consilio suorum relicta Berewike sub custodia tendit Eboracum, et ibidem cum comite Lancastrie et ceteris magnatibus[1] habuit consilium, et de suis infortuniis querit remedium. Dixerunt comites ordinationes obseruatas non esse, et iccirco regi deterius accidisse; tum quia rex ordinationibus stare iurauerat, tum quia archiepiscopus omnes contrauenientes excommunicauerat. Vnde nichil bene posse fieri protestantur, nisi ordinationes plenius obseruentur. Rex uero ad omnia pro communi utilitate ordinata paratum se dixit, et se ordinationes obseruare in bona fide promisit. Dixerunt comites nil uideri actum dum aliquid superesset[2] agendum, sed [si] ordinationes debeant obseruari oportet eas executioni demandari. Rex executionem concessit; nichil comitibus denegauit. Igitur cancellarius, thesaurarius, uicecomites et alii officiarii remouentur, et iuxta tenorem ordinationum noui subrogantur. Voluerunt etiam comites quod Hugo Despenser, Henricus de Beaumount[3] et quidam alii curiam regis euacuarent,

[1] 9 September 1314
[2] Lucan ii, 657
[3] Henry de Beaumont was a foreign favourite dismissed from the Council in October 1311 by the Ordainers. His sister, the lady de Vescy, was also removed from the court. He was the son of Louis de Brienne, viscount of Beaumont in Maine, grandson of John de Brienne, King of Jerusalem and Emperor of Constantinople. His brother became Bishop of Durham in 1317. (See Stubbs, *Const. Hist.* 4th ed. ii 345, 372, and N. Denholm-Young, *Collected Papers*, 165 note 3.)

with rancour he pays no heed to his inferiors, despises
his equals, is always striving to equal his betters. For in
almost every fashion the squire strains and strives to
outdo the knight, the knight the baron, the baron the
earl, the earl the king. Moreover when monies fail,
because their inheritance is insufficient, they turn to
pillage, plunder their neighbours, fleece their tenants,
and practise nefarious extortions upon the servants of
God. Hence it is that the magnates of the land either
fall in battle, or die without a son, or heiresses divide the
inheritance, and the name of their father perishes for
ever.

After this the king on the advice of his friends left
a garrison in Berwick and moved to York, and there
took counsel with the Earl of Lancaster and the other
magnates,[1] and sought a remedy for his misfortunes.
The earls said that the Ordinances had not been observed, and for that reason events had turned out
badly for the king; both because the king had sworn to
stand to the Ordinances, and because the archbishop
had excommunicated all who opposed them. Whence
they affirmed that nothing could be well done unless the
Ordinances were fully observed. The king said that he
was prepared to do everything ordained for the common
good, and promised that he would observe the Ordinances in good faith. The earls said that nothing
seemed to be done while anything remained undone[2]
but if the Ordinances ought to be observed, it was
necessary to ask for their execution. The king granted
their execution; he refused nothing to the earls. Therefore the chancellor, the treasurer, the sheriffs and other
officials were removed and fresh ones substituted
according to the tenor of the Ordinances. The earls
also wished that Hugh Despenser, Henry de Beaumont[3]

donec ad sibi obicienda responderent interrogati,*a* et
super obiectis satisfactionem prestarent conuicti; sed hoc
ad instantiam regis differtur. Hugo tamen Despenser
latitare compellitur.

De expungnatione Roberti de Brutz et recuperatione
Scotie ad proximum parliamentum distulerunt, quia
comes. Herfordie et alii barones in uinculis detenti nondum redierunt. Lugebat autem soror regis maritum
suum comitem Herfordie, et dominus rex dedit ei omnes
captiuos Scotie. Nam tempore regis Edwardi senioris
quidam capti fuerant qui usque ad presens tempus sub
carcere remanserant; inter quos erat uxor Roberti de
Brutz, episcopus de Glascou, et quidam comes iuuenis,
et alii milites Scotorum quindecim et amplius.¹ Elaboratum est interim ut comes postliminio rediret, sed [non]
F.209   promittitur, nisi multa con/ferret; et multa quidem
offeruntur, sed plura satis et que uires eius excederent
exiguntur. Tandem post uarios circuitus sic actum est,
ut Robertus de Brutz uxorem suam et ceteros captiuos
Scotorum reciperet, et comitem Herfordie sine mora
restitueret; et hac permutatione sic facta rediit comes
noster ad propria.

Post Natale Domini paucis euolutis diebus dominus
rex corpus Petri de Gauestone, sui quondam specialis
amici, ab Oxonia ad Langeleye fecit transferri. Iam
enim de capitatione ipsius biennium transiuit et amplius,
et usque nunc apud fratres Oxonie iacuit inhumatus.
Proposuerat namque rex, ut dicitur, prius mortem Petri
uindicasse, deinde corpus eius sepulture tradidisse. Sed

---

a interrogatis MS
¹ Elizabeth, Bruce's wife, Marjory his daughter, Christina Seton his
sister, Donald Earl of Mar, and Robert Wishart were all exchanged for
Hereford.

and certain others should leave the king's court, until they should answer certain objections put to them, and if convicted give satisfaction in the matters raised; but at the king's instance this was deferred. Nevertheless Hugh Despenser was compelled to go into retirement.

They postponed discussion of the struggle against Robert Bruce for the recovery of Scotland until the next parliament, because the Earl of Hereford and other barons held captive had not yet returned. But the king's sister mourned for her husband the Earl of Hereford, and the lord king gave to her all the Scottish captives. For in the time of old King Edward some had been captured who remained in prison until the present time; among them was the wife of Robert Bruce, the Bishop of Glasgow, a certain young earl, and fifteen or more other Scottish knights.[1] Meanwhile it was worked out how the earl might return from exile to his hearth, but this was only promised under many conditions; much indeed was offered, but many more demands were made upon the earl, beyond his ability to pay. At length after various goings-about, it was decided that Robert Bruce should have back his wife and the other Scottish captives, and he should restore the Earl of Hereford without delay; and when this exchange had been made our earl returned to his estates.

A few days after Christmas, the king had the body of Piers Gaveston, once his intimate friend, transferred from Oxford to Langley. For now two years and more had elapsed since he was beheaded, and till now he had lain unburied with the friars of Oxford. For the king had proposed, it is said, first to avenge Piers' death, and then consign his body to the grave. But already those

K

iam reuocati in amicitiam sunt ex quibus uidebatur rex petere uindictam. Rex apud Langeleye, ubi fratribus Predicatoribus iam pridem domum construxit, corpus sui Petri honorifice sepeliuit.

Deinde ad Purificationem beate Marie conueniunt Londiniis[1] comites et barones uniuersi, de statu regis et regni et de expungnatione Scotorum tractaturi. Et in primis eiecerunt a consilio regis Hugonem Despenser, et Walterum de Langetone episcopum Cestrie, olim thesaurarium domini regis Anglie. Postea remouerunt a curia regis familiam superfluam, regi et terre nimis onerosam, ut dicebatur. Ex illa remotione expense regis cotidiane in decem libris sunt diminute.[2] Cœpit igitur parliamentum pacifice tractari et usque ad finem Quadragesime fere protelari.

In hoc parliamento, quia negotiatores in uendendis[a] uictualibus per patriam transeuntibus modum exces-serunt, comites et barones, rei publice prospicientes, huic morbo medelam apposuerunt; unde in bobus, / porcis et ouibus, in auibus, pulcinis et columbis, et in ceteris communibus uictualibus certum pretium statuerunt. Prouisum est etiam et concessum ut Vascones uina sua ad portus Anglie transueherent, et ibidem tonellum secundum pretium in parliamento taxatum uenderent, nec Anglici ulterius tanquam forstallarii ad querenda uina transfretarent. Hec omnia per terram sic diuulgan-tur et in comitatibus [et] burgis publice proclamantur.[3]

Mauricius de Berkelee curam et custodiam uille de Berewik[4] accepit, unde ad eam tuendam sine dilatione

F.210 (left margin)

---

[a] uendidis MS

[1] 20 January to 9 March (*Parl. Writs*, II.i.137, 139, 149)

[2] cf. Tout, *Edward II*, 93 note 1

[3] *Rot. Parl.* I. 295. *Foed.* ii 263, 266

[4] 18 April 1315. The indenture for this is in Conway Davies, *Baronial Opposition to Edward II*, App. no. 46.

have been readmitted to friendship from whom the king seemed to seek vengeance. The king had Piers' body buried with honour at Langley, where he had formerly built the Dominicans a house.

Then at the Purification of the Blessed Mary the earls and all the barons met at London,[1] to treat of the state of the king and the realm, and of fighting the Scots. And first they removed Hugh Despenser from the king's council, and Walter Langton, Bishop of Chester, formerly Treasurer of the lord King of England.

Next they removed from the king's court the unnecessary members of his household, overburdensome to the king and to the land, it was said. By that displacement the daily expenses of the king's household were reduced by ten pounds.[2] Parliament therefore began to discuss matters peaceably and dragged on almost to the end of Lent.

In this parliament, because merchants going about the country selling victuals charged excessively, the earls and barons, looking to the welfare of the state, appointed a remedy for this malady; they ordained a fixed price for oxen, pigs and sheep, for fowls, chickens, and pigeons, and for other common foods. It was also provided and granted that the Gascons should carry their wines to English ports, and there sell it by the barrel according to the price assigned in parliament, and that Englishmen should not in future cross the sea as forestallers seeking wine. These matters were published throughout the land, and publicly proclaimed in shirecourts and boroughs.[3]

Maurice de Berkeley received the care and custody of the town of Berwick,[4] and he at once set out to defend it. Berwick is a strong and well-walled town situated on the coast on the borders of Scotland, very convenient for

iter arripuit. Est autem Berewyke uilla fortis et bene murata in initio Scotie super mare posita, mercatoribus in tempore pacis satis accommoda; que si proditione non fraudetur nunquam Scotie subicietur; obsidionem non formidat, dum tamen Anglia sibi succurrat. Naues enim Anglicane totam terram circueunt, et in arte nauigandi et in conflictu nauali principatum gerunt; unde, si tota Scotia Berewyk inuaderet, a parte maris timeri non oportet.

Exiit preterea a curia regis preceptum publicum, ne quis arma uel bladum uel aliquod genus uictualium ad Scotos transferret; si quis autem huius precepti transgressor inueniretur, tanquam proditor et hostis publicus puniretur. Vnde Johannes Bodetourtus[1] cum manu armata ex parte una, et alii magnates ex altera, meatus marinos obseruabant, et ne quid in subsidium hostium differretur summo opere procurabant. Itaque opere et opera eorum in breui sic actum est ut tanta esset apud Scotos bladi penuria quod pro centum solidis uenderetur quarterium frumenti in Scotia. Missi sunt etiam ad partes Northumbrorum comes de Penbrok et Bartholomeus de Bade[le]smere cum quingentis armatis ad fines illos tuendos et ad frequentes insultus Scotorum pro-

F.211 pulsandos, ut sic uirtus eorum / undique lacessita, et machinatio eorum pro parte refrenata, minus proficeret ad singula.

---

[1] John Botetourt was a King's Knight from at least 1285, promoted Banneret 23 August 1297. He was summoned to Parliament from 1-18 Ed. II, i.e. until his death in 1324. He had considerable importance as a member of the middle party. He is stated to have been an illegitimate son of Edward I (*Handbook of British Chronology*, edited for the Royal Hist. Soc. in 1939 by F. M. Powicke, 37), and from about 1286 had an active administrative career, e.g. as Constable of St Briavel's and Keeper of the forest of Dene (*C.P.R.* 4 January 1290, 412; *C.Cl.R.*, 16 April 1298, p. 156). In 1294 he was in command of the North Sea fleet (Trivet, 331-2); in 1303-4 he was Warden of the Marches of Lochmaben and Dumfries and Justiciar of Galloway (Bain, *Cal. Docs. Scotl.* 377, 446). In the last years of Edward I's reign he was much employed as a justice of *oyer et terminer* (*C.P.R.* 1302-7

merchants in time of peace, a town which will never be subject to Scotland unless we are cheated out of it by treachery. It fears no siege with England at its back. For English ships sail round the whole land, and both in the art of navigation and naval warfare they are supreme; so that if the whole of Scotland invaded Berwick, nothing would be feared from the sea.

There also issued from the king's court a public edict that no one should carry arms or corn or any kind of food to the Scots; if anyone should be found breaking this edict, he would be punished as a traitor and public enemy. So John Botetourt[1] with an armed squadron on the one side, and some other magnates on the other, kept a watch on the maritime approaches, and did their utmost to prevent anything being carried over to help the enemy. Thus by their labour and care it resulted in a short space of time that the Scots were so short of corn that a quarter of wheat was sold for a hundred shillings in Scotland. The Earl of Pembroke and Bartholomew de Badlesmere were sent to Northumbria with five hundred men-at-arms to protect the border and repel the frequent attacks of the Scots, in order that with their courage challenged on all sides, and their plots to some extent frustrated, they would profit less on each occasion.

---

passim). His commission as Admiral (the which title goes back to 1297 only) in 1315 is given in full by Clowes, *Hist. of the Royal Navy* I, 142-3. The climax of his political career (see Conway Davies, *Baronial Opposition* especially 137, 365, 390 and App. 16) was his appointment as a member of the Standing Council set up by the Parliament of York in 1318 (Tout, *Edward II*, 117). For the war in Scotland he built a good and beautiful ship of 120 oars at his own expense (C. Moor, *Knights of Edward I* (Harl. Soc. 1929) I (A-E); further, Dugdale, *Baronage*, ii.46).

It will be seen from what is said at the beginning of this note that he is unlikely to have been born later than 1264.

Dum hec aguntur in Anglia, Robertus de Brutz de aliis negotiis deliberat in Scotia. Nam exercitum copiosum adunauit, et ciuitatem de Cardoil[1] obsedit. Sane hec urbs Scotis semper erat odiosa; hec urbs Scotis semper formidanda, incursus eorum frequenter excepit et uolatus eorum multociens impediuit. Hanc igitur si capere posset, usque ad Nouum Castrum nullus sibi resisteret. Premiserat[a] quoque fratrem suum Edwardum cum electa manu militum in Hiberniam, qui gentem illam aduersus regem Anglie excitaret, et terram si posset sue dominationi subiceret. Et erat rumor quod, si ibidem ad uotum proficeret, statim ad partes Wallie se transferret, et Walenses similiter contra regem nostrum procuraret. Hec enim duo genera faciliter in rebellionem excitantur, et iugum seruitutis egre ferentes dominationem Anglorum execrantur.

Iusticiarius autem Hibernie, Edmundus Botiler nomine, audiens Scotos in terram de Huluestre appulisse, de fidelibus regis congregauit exercitum, et Scotis eorumque fautoribus fecit insultum. In primo autem congressu fugati sunt Scoti ad montana quasi greges ouium dispersi per pascua; habitant siquidem in montanis et nemoribus illius terre Hibernienses siluestres, terras non colunt, sed de animalibus et eorum lacticiniis uiuunt; et, si quandoque panibus indigeant, ad uillas Anglorum super maritima descendunt; uendunt autem animalia et comparant sibi frumenta. Hos et eorum regulos associauit sibi Edwardus contra Anglicos. Si comes de Huluestre fuerit fidelis, non est enim timendum ab eorum insidiis.

Exiuit interim falsus rumor per totam Angliam quod exercitus noster in Hibernia Scotos disperserat, quod

---

[a] promiserat MS
[1] 22 July to 1 August 1315

While this was happening in England Robert Bruce was thinking of other things in Scotland. For he had collected a large army and laid siege to the city of Carlisle.[1] This city was indeed always hateful to the Scots; it was always feared by them, for it bore the brunt of their frequent raids and was often an obstacle to their flight. If Robert Bruce could take this place there would be no resistance as far as Newcastle. He had also sent his brother Edward to Ireland with a picked force of knights, to stir up that people against the King of England, and subject the country if he could to his authority. And there was a rumour that if he achieved his wish there, he would at once cross to Wales, and raise the Welsh likewise against our king. For these two races are easily roused to rebellion; they bear hardly the yoke of slavery, and curse the lordship of the English.

The justiciar of Ireland, Edmund Butler by name, hearing that the Scots had landed in Ulster, assembled an army of loyalists, and attacked the Scots and those who abetted them. At the first clash the Scots were driven to the hills like flocks of sheep scattered over the pastures; for the Irish are woodland people and dwell in the mountains and forests of their country; they do not cultivate the land, but live on their flocks and the milk thereof; and if from time to time they need bread, they come down to the English towns on the coast, selling livestock and buying corn. With these people and their kinglets Edward allied himself against the English. If the Earl of Ulster is loyal their plots need cause no alarm.

A false report meanwhile spread throughout England that our army in Ireland had scattered the Scots, that Edward Bruce was dead, and that hardly one of the Scots remained alive. Hence Robert Bruce, both on

F.212 Edwardus de Brutz perierat, quod uix unus ex / Scotis
uiuus remanserat. Vnde Robertus de Brutz tum propter
rumores desperatos, tum quia audiuit comitem Penbrokye cum multis armatis nouiter aduenire, obsidionem
reliquit, et uersus Scotiam iter arripuit. Videntes hii
qui erant infra ciuitatem quod exercitus Scotorum
recederet,ᵃ [exierunt] post eos, diu persequentes a tergo.
Vnde in illa persecutione multi ex Scotis perierunt,
plures uero lesi, et quidam remanserunt captiui.

Mirabitur forsan aliquis in posterum quomodo gens
Scotorum audaciam resistendi concepit, et cur sic repente uirtus Anglorum defecerit. Reuera populus sine
duce facile dispergitur, et membra deficiunt cum caput
deprimitur. Olim reges Anglie, dum contra hostes
erigerent uexillum, quindecim comites et plures sequebantur ad bellum. Nunc autem quinque uel sex tantum
regi nostro ferunt auxilium. Comitatus Cornubie,
Marescallie et Cestrie in manu regis sunt hodie. Comes
Lyncolnie nuper obiit, comes Glouernie in bello cecidit,
et comes Warewykye infirmus occubuit.

De comite Gloucestrie censeo dolendum quia tam
potens et iuuenis tam premature decessit, quod heredem
de corpore suo non reliquit, et tamen uxor eius comitissa
per annum iam et amplius expectatur paritura; et licet
nunc pareret non uideo quo iure puer hereditatem
uendicaret, quia iure cauetur quod, si posthumus ultra
undecimum mensem natus fuerit, hereditatem defuncti
uendicare non poterit. Igitur si hereditas comitis ad
sorores descendat, tres partes fieri continget, et scutum
quod semper fuit integrum iam erit tripertitum. Sed
comes Warewykye si in uiuisᵇ fuisset, [fuisset] tota patria
pro eo: consilio eius [et] ingenio ordinationes prodierunt,

ᵃ resideret MS
ᵇ 'si inuiuis' Hearne; uicinius MS

account of these wild stories and because he heard that the Earl of Pembroke had recently arrived with many men-at-arms, gave up the siege and set out towards Scotland. When those who were within the city saw that the Scots were departing, they went forth after them, pursuing them for a long time. Many of the Scots perished in that pursuit, very many were wounded, and some were taken prisoner.

Someone hereafter may perhaps wonder how the Scottish race had the boldness to resist, and why the courage of the English should have so suddenly failed them. In truth, a leaderless people is easily dispersed, and the limbs fail when the head is removed. Formerly when the kings of England raised their standard against the enemy, fifteen earls and more followed them to war; but now only five or six bring aid to our king. The Earldoms of Cornwall, of the Marshal, and of Chester are today in the king's hand. The Earl of Lincoln is recently dead, the Earl of Gloucester fell in battle, and the Earl of Warwick lay ill.

We must grieve, I think, for the Earl of Gloucester, that so powerful and youthful a man should die so prematurely that he left no heir of his body, and yet the countess his wife has been expected to give birth for a year or more; and if she should now give birth, I do not see by what right the boy could claim the inheritance, because the law warns us that if a posthumous child is born after the eleventh month, it cannot claim the inheritance of the deceased. Thus, if the inheritance of the earl descends to sisters, it will fall into three parts, and the shield that was always whole will thenceforth be tripartite. But if the Earl of Warwick had been alive, the whole country would have been behind him. By his advice and skill the Ordinances were framed,

et ceteri comites eo audito multa fecerunt; in prudentia
et consilio non habuit similem. Heredem reliquit sed
F.213 ualde iuuenem. / Credo constanter quod hec uindicta
Dei, hec mutatio dextere Excelsi,[1] propter peccata et
scelera nostra duces nostros preripiat, et populus terre
indefensus intereat.

Temeritatis quidem argui possem si patriam meam,
si proprium genus, infamarem; sed, si uera loqui licet
aut conuenit, gens Anglorum pre ceteris nationibus in
tribus excedit, in superbia, in dolo et in periurio.
Modernos homines et maxime iuuenes reputo superbos
quia contumaces, et, cum superbia initium sit omnium
malorum, abierunt hodie [de] uitio in uitium, de superbia
in dolum et periurium. In omni regno circa mare
Grecum reperies multos de genere Anglorum, et uulgo
dicitur et fama nuntiat quod in hiis pre ceteris dolus
habitat. Est et species doli maxima et quidem frequens
in Anglia; de hiis loquor qui mutuum accipiunt et
statutis diebus debitum non soluunt. Iam dolo facit qui
detinet quod enim restituere oportet.[2] Omni malitie
potest obuiari, sed mali debitores non possunt castigari.
Si non mutuo, inimicus ero; si repeto, amicitias perdo.
Quid ergo melius est? Non mutuando inimicum habere,
quam*a* mutuum perdere et inimicitias nichilominus
incurrere. Merlinus de nobis*b* ait 'ue genti periure',
ostendens propter periurium aliquod excidium nobis
euenire.[3]

Omnes fere lites et placita que agitantur in regis curia
per assisas terminantur in patria. Porro cum ad assisam
uentum fuerit, qui plus dare sufficit proculdubio op-
tinebit. Heu omnis religio, omnis dignitas, et omnis

---

a quasi MS   *b* uobis MS
[1] cf. Ps. lxxvi. 11 (AV lxxvii. 10)   [2] *Dig.* 17.1.8.9
[3] 'Ve perjure genti, quia urbs inclyta propter eam ruiet' (*Geoff. Mon.*
lib.vii. c.4).

and other earls did many things only after taking his
opinion; in wisdom and council he had no peer.
He left an heir, but very young, I firmly believe
that this judgment of God, this change of the
right hand of the most High,[1] carries off our leaders
for our sins and crimes, and leaves the people of the
land defenceless.

I could indeed be accused of rashness if I defamed
my country, my own people; but, if it is permissible or
proper to speak the truth, the English race excel other
nations in three qualities, in pride, in craft, and in
perjury. Modern men, especially young ones, I regard
as proud because they are contumacious, and since
pride is the beginning of all evils, they have gone today
from vice to vice, from pride to craft and perjury. In
every kingdom bordering the Mediterranean you will
find many of the English race; it is commonly said and
rumour relates that guile pre-eminently resides in them.
There is indeed a very great kind of guile that is common
in England; I speak of those who accept a loan and fail
to pay the debt on the appointed days. For he employs
guile who witholds what he ought to restore.[2] All
malice can be withstood, but bad debtors cannot be
chastised. If I do not lend I shall be an enemy, if I
seek repayment I lose friendships. Which, therefore, is
the better? By not lending to make an enemy, or to
lose the loan and none the less incur enmity. Merlin
says of us, 'Woe to a perjured race,' showing that for
perjury no mean destruction awaits us.[3]

Almost all the lawsuits and pleas started in the
king's court are brought to an end by assizes in the
provinces. Now when it comes to an assize, he who can
give more will certainly obtain the verdict. Alas!
every religious institution, every dignity, every authority

potestas cedit pretio. Hinc quidam festiue ait,

> Manus ferens munera pium facit impium;
> Nummus iungit fœdera, dat nummus consilium.
> Nummus in prelatis est pro iure satis,
> Vos qui iudicatis nummo locum datis.

Per alia quedam signa apparet manus Dei contra /
F.214 nos extenta. Nam anno preterito tanta fuit habundantia
pluuie quod uix licuit hominibus frumenta colligere uel
horreo̓ salua recondere. Anno uero presenti deterius
euenit. Nam inundatio pluuiarum omne fere semen
consumpsit, in tantum ut*a* uaticinium Ysaye iam uideretur expletum esse; ait enim decem iugera uinearum
faciunt lagunculam unam, et triginta modii sementis
faciunt modios tres[1]: et in pluribusque locis fœnum tam
diu sub aquis latuit quod nec falcari nec colligi potuit.
Oues autem communiter perierunt et alia animalia
subita peste ceciderunt. Valde autem nobis timendum
est ne, si Dominus post hec flagella incorrigibiles nos
inueniat, homines et pecora simul disperdat; et constanter credo quod, nisi intercederet Anglicana religio,
dispersi fuissemus elapso tempore multo.

Accidit interea ut quidam miles, Adam de Banastre[2b]
nomine, de domo et familia comitis Lancastrie, perpe-
trasset homicidium, et de uenia desperans ac peccatum
suum augmentans, insurgere cœpit contra dominum
suum. Credidit enim regi placere si comitem infestaret,
qui totiens regi restiterat, qui totiens regem initum
cogerat mutare consilium. Vnde terras comitis cœpit

---

a ut] uel MS
b Danastre MS
[1] Isa. v. 10
[2] Sir Adam Banaster made a sworn confederacy with other knights
8 October 1315. He vainly attacked Liverpool on 23 October, and stole
and exhibited at Manchester the king's standard. (*V.C.H. Lancs.* ii. 198-9;
cf. *Ann. Lond.* 236-7; *Bridl.* 48.)

has its price. Hence someone says in sport:

> Some men who bring us presents, changing right from wrong;
> Money seals our treaties, money sings its song.
> Money for the prelacy surely wlll suffice.
> You who sit in judgment are paid for your advice.

By certain other portents the hand of God appears
to be raised against us. For in the past year there was
such plentiful rain that men could scarcely harvest the
corn or bring it safely to the barn. In the present year
worse has happened. For the floods of rain have
rotted almost all the seed, so that the prophecy of
Isaiah might seem now to be fulfilled; for he says that
'ten acres of vineyard shall yield one little measure
and thirty bushels of seed shall yield three bushels'[1]:
and in many places the hay lay so long under water
that it could neither be mown nor gathered. Sheep
generally died and other animals were killed by a
sudden plague. It is greatly to be feared that if the
Lord finds us incorrigible after these visitations, he
will destroy at once both men and beasts; and I firmly
believe that unless the English church had interceded
for us, we should have perished long ago.

It happened meanwhile that a certain knight,
Adam Banastre[2] by name, of the household retinue of
the Earl of Lancaster, committed homicide. Des-
pairing of pardon, he rose against his lord, thus aggravat-
ing his crime. For he believed that it would please the
king if he showed himself hostile to the earl who had so
often opposed the king and so often forced him to alter
plans already set on foot. Wherefore this knight began
to attack the earl's estates, especially the earldom of
Lancaster, and according to some accounts he raised
the royal standard, as if on the king's orders, and under
this colour he drew to himself many helpers, entered

inuadere et precipue comitatum Lancastrie, et, secundum
relatum aliquorum, quasi a rege iussus, baneriam regis
erexit, et sub hoc colore multos auxiliarios secum
assumpsit, castella comitis latenter intrauit, arma in
exercitum Scotorum preparata et multam pecuniam
simul asportauit. Erant autem quasi octingenti uiri in
auxilium eius procurati, quidam pretio conducti, quidam
mortis timore compulsi, quos uel oportuit patriam relinquere uel secum in arma concurrere. Audiens ergo
comes proditoris insaniam, et considerans rem esse periculosam, statim precepit militibus suis ut infidelem illum
F.215 prudenter inuestigarent, et inuentum / prudenter in-
uaderent. Ibant ergo armatorum quasi sexcenti in
mortem Ade de Banastre omnes accensi. Et cum
uenissent prope locum ubi congregauerat Adam exercitum suum, diuiserunt se in duas turmas ut prima
ueniens hostes inuaderet, que si non sufficeret, altera
superueniens negotium consummaret.

Hoc postquam Adam de Banastre cognouit, cum
fautoribus et complicibus suis primam turmam acriter
excepit, et ipsam sine dubio penitus dissipasset, nisi
secunda turma recenter aduenisset. Adam uero et sui
sequaces aduersarios accrescere uidentes, et multo plures
adesse putantes, iam uacillare cœperunt, et post modicum, aduersariorum impetum non ferentes, fugam
inierunt. Sed fugientes passim ceduntur a tergo. Porro
persequentium tota fuit intentio, ceterorum signiferum
Adam comprehendere, et uiuum si possent comiti pre-
sentare. Fugerat autem in quoddam horreum, et ibidem
latitabat, sed modicum; non enim diu latitare potuit qui
totam patriam uelut hostis publicus debellauit. Aduer-
sarii eius domum obsederunt et ipsum ad deditionem
sepius monuerunt; sed ipse delicti sui conscius, et quocunque se uerteret de morte securus, audaciam ex

the earl's fortresses by stealth, and carried off equipment prepared for the army of Scotland together with
a large sum of money. Some eight hundred men were
persuaded to help him, some bought by bribes, some
compelled by the fear of death, who had either to leave
the country or join him in arms. The earl, hearing
of the traitor's madness, and considering the situation
dangerous, at once ordered his knights to make careful search for this faithless man, and attack him cir-
cumspectly when they found him. So about six hundred
men-at-arms went forth thirsting for the death of
Adam Banastre. When they came near the place where
Adam had assembled his army, they split up into two
squadrons—the first to attack, and if this did not suffice,
the other coming up would finish the business.

When Adam Banastre realised this, he stood up to
the first squadron with those who aided and abetted
him, and would doubtless have utterly defeated it,
had not the second squadron rapidly appeared on the
scene. When Adam and his followers saw that their
opponents grew in numbers, and thinking that many
more were near at hand, they began to waver, and in
a little while could not withstand the attack of their
opponents, and took to flight. As they fled they were
everywhere cut down from behind. Now the whole
intention of the pursuers was to capture Adam, the
ringleader of the rest, and take him alive to the earl
if they could. Adam took refuge in a certain barn and
lay hid there but only for a while; for the man who
had brought war to the whole countryside like a
public enemy could not hide for long. His opponents
laid siege to his house and urged him more than once
to surrender; but he, conscious of his guilt, and certain
of death whichever way he turned, boldy faced his

desperatione concepit, et se aduersariis audacter opposuit, quosdam eorum occidit et plures ex eis male uulnerauit. Tandem, quia sine magno periculo uiuum capere non poterant, inpressionem in eum facientes ipsum occiderunt, et caput eius auferentes comiti detulerunt. Sic Ciba filius Botri dominum suum Dauid regem expungnauit, quem Joab princeps militie fugientem in Abbella capite priuauit.[1]

Paganus de Torboruile[2] curam terre de Glamorgan acceperat a rege, unde ministrales prius constitutos nouis subrogatis cœpit amouere; quamobrem Leulinus Bren commotus est, nec poterat Pagano quicquam loqui
F.216 pacifice. Erat autem Leulinus ille Walensis uir mag/nus et potens in partibus suis. Hic uiuente comite Gloucestrie magnum officium sub ipso gerebat, et nunc preposito Pagano potestatem sibi sublatam egre ferebat. Vnde Paganum contumeliis frequenter aggreditur, et pluribus audientibus in has minas inuehitur: 'Venient,' inquit, 'dies, et cessare faciam superbiam Pagani, reddam sibi uices quas impendit michi.' Propter quod accusatus est Leulinus apud regem quod seditiosus esset, quod occasiones rebellandi quereret, et, nisi rex diligenter precaueret, Leulinus de nouo Walenses excitaret. Audiens Leulinus conditionem suam sic apud regem deterioratam, de consilio amicorum accessit ad curiam, uolens si posset se ipsum excusare, aut saltem iniuriam suam caute palliare. Spreuit eum rex, iurans et protestans quod filius mortis esset,[3] si crimen ei obiectum manifestum

[1] 2 Sam. xx. 21

[2] 'Payn de Turbervile of Coyty, son of Richard and grandson of Gilbert, had charge of the honour of Glamorgan, the accounts for which were rendered by Gwenllian his widow, and are on the Pipe Roll 10 Ed. II 1316-17' (Clarke, *Cartae de Glamorgan*, 1034). On 10 February 1316 he was ordered to deliver Cardiff to John Giffard of Brimpsfield (*C.P.R.* 431). Humphrey

enemies with the courage of despair, killed some of them and seriously wounded many. At length, because they could not take him alive without great danger, they made a rush upon him and killed him, cut off his head and took it to the earl. So likewise did Sheba son of Bichri fight against his lord king David. Him Joab captain of the soldiery beheaded as he fled to Abel.[1]

Payn Turberville[2] had been given charge of the land of Glamorgan by the king, and began to replace the officials previously oppointed by new ones; this angered Llewelyn Bren, so that he could not speak peaceably to Payn. This Llewelyn was a Welshman, a great man and powerful in his own country. While the Earl of Gloucester was alive he had held high office under him, and now with Payn in charge he bore it hardly that his authority was taken from him. Hence he frequently attacked Payn with insults, and in the hearing of many uttered these threats against him: 'The day will come,' he said, 'when I will put an end to the insolence of Payn and give him as good as he gives me.' For this, Llewelyn was accused before the king of sedition of seeking an excuse for rebellion; and if the king had not taken great care Llewelyn would have roused the Welsh afresh. Llewelyn hearing that he was out of favour with the king, came to court on the advice of his friends, wishing if he could to excuse himself, or at least cautiously to gloss over his crime. But the king spurned him, swearing and maintaining that he should surely die[3] if the crime charged against him

---

de Bohun was appointed captain of the forces against Llewelyn Bren the next day (*ibid.* 432).
   [3] 1 Sam. xx. 31

L

foret: habuitque in mandatis ad Lyncolniam uenire, et ibidem super hiis responsum expectare.[1]

Leulinus ergo, accepto tali mandato, clam et festinanter ad partes suas rediit, et quod ante proposuerat statim patefecit. Prius quidem fecerat uerba maliuola, sed iam de uerbis peruentum est ad uerbera. Nam quadam die, dum custos de Kaerfili extra castrum curiam teneret, superuenit Leulinus cum filiis et fautoribus suis ad constabularium, captum secum abduxit, quibusdam ministris cesis et pluribus qui ad curiam illam conuenerant male uulneratis. Castrum quoque statim inuasit, sed custodibus resistentibus intrare non potuit, ulteriorem uero custodiam totam incendit. Iam palam facte sunt inimicitie; Leulinus minatur Paganum occidere. Paganus declinauit eius insidias donec accresceret uires suas.

Interim Leulinus ipse terras sub tuitione Pagani constitutas uiolenter aggreditur, cedit, incendit et depredatur. Associauerat sibi enim in auxilium quasi /
F.217 decem milia Walensium. Omnia bona sua, boues, uaccas et cetera uictualia ad montes transtulerant; nam in cauernis montium et in latebris nemorum erat eorum refugium. Hiis et aliis malis perpetratis ac domino regi notificatis, precepit rex seruis suis dicens, 'Ite uelociter, et persequimini proditorem illum, ne forte ex mora deterius eueniat, et tota Wallia contra nos insurgat.' Committiturque negotium comiti Herfordie, nam res ipsa precipue uidebatur ipsum tangere; terra enim de Breynok que ad comitem pertinet terram de Glamorgan collateralem habet, et iuxta poetam 'Tunc tua res agitur paries dum proximus ardet.'[2]

Abiit ergo comes in terram suam ut persequeretur

---

[1] *Parl. Writs*, II.ii.460
[2] Horace, *Ep.*I.18.84

was proved. He was ordered to come to Lincoln, and there await his reply on these matters.[1]

When Llewelyn received this command, he hastily and in secret returned to his own country and at once made clear what he had previously intended. He had formerly uttered malicious words, but now it had come from words to blows. For on a certain day, while the keeper of Caerphilly was outside the castle holding his court, Llewelyn with his sons and accomplices, fell upon the constable and led him away captive, Some of the servants were killed, and many who had come to the court were badly wounded. Llewelyn at once attacked the castle, too, but owing to the resistance of the guards he was unable to enter, nevertheless he burnt the whole of the outer ward. Their enmity was now quite open; Llewelyn threatens to kill Payn, but Payn avoids his snares until his forces have increased.

Meanwhile Llewelyn violently attacked the district under Payn's protection, killing, burning, and plundering. He had attracted to himself some 10,000 Welshmen, who had carried off all Payn's goods to the mountains, oxen, cows, and other victuals; for in the mountain-caves and wooded hiding-places they had their refuge. These and other wrongs were committed and reported to the king who commanded his servants saying, 'Go quickly, and pursue this traitor, lest from delay worse befall and all Wales rise against us.' He committed the business to the Earl of Hereford, as the situation seemed to affect him especially; for the land of Brecon which pertains to the earl, marches with Glamorgan, and according to the poet, 'Have a care for your eaves, if your neighbour's dwelling burns.'[2]

The earl went off to his lands to pursue Llewelyn, and both the lords Roger Mortimer helped him.

Leulinum, et uterque Rogerus de Mortimer ferebat auxilium. Willelmus de Monte Acuto[1] prefectus[a] militie regis ex parte una, Johannes Gyffard et qui cum eo erant ex altera uenerunt. Henricus de Lancastria, et alii barones et milites, terras in uicinio habentes, opem tulerunt, ut sic Walenses undique obsessi nullatenus haberent locum diffugii. Videns ergo Leulinus quod male errasset, quod ad resistendum non sufficeret,— Walenses enim bis uel ter Anglicos predantes[b] acceperant, sed semper ubique deterius reportauerant,—obtulit se comiti sub conditione; ut scilicet uitam et membra, terras et cetera bona mobilia salua liceret habere, et pro satisfactione delicti optulit magnam summam argenti; sed noluit comes eum admittere, nisi simpliciter se uellet reddere. Tandem cum exercitus noster appropinquasset et excubias Walensium iam didicisset, Leulinus suos homines sic cœpit alloqui: 'Non est,' inquit, 'tutum cum Anglis congredi; ego dedi causam negotio; ego me F.218 tradam pro toto populo: melius est enim / ut unus moriatur quam tota gens exulet uel gladio perimatur.'

Descendens[c] ergo Leulinus de montibus reddidit se comiti, subiciens se penitus regie uoluntati; misitque eum comes ad regem ut misericordiam expectaret aut legem. Hec est consuetudo Walensium ut uetus[d] insania. Si quieuerint per decennium statim respirant ad prelium, et quod multo tempore congesserint uadit in exterminium. Leulinus ap Griffyth et frater eius Dauid poterant in pace uixisse, sed rebellantes uitam per-

---

[a] profectus MS   [b] predanter MS
[c] ascendens MS   [d] Perhaps we should write 'uel potius'.

[1] Sir William Montague, of Somerset and Devon (Dugdale, *Baronage*, i, '640', '633' *recte* 644, 645) has left an account of his doings against Llewelyn Bren in the Black Mountains in Glamorgan (*Cal. Chanc. Warr.* I 437-439; March 1316). He was steward of the household in 1316-18 at 200 marks a year. His son, who held the famous tournament in Cheapside in 1331 (*Ann. Paul.* 354) was made Earl of Salisbury in 1337.

William de Montague[1] commander of the royal cavalry came from one side, and John Giffard and his company from the other.   Henry of Lancaster and the other barons and knights who had lands in the neighbourhood, brought help, so that the Welsh hemmed in on all sides had no place of refuge at all.   Llewelyn therefore, seeing that he had made a bad mistake, and that he was powerless to resist, for the Welsh had twice or thrice met the English on plundering raids but had always had the worst of the encounters, offered to submit to the earl on condition that he should have safety of life and limb, lands and moveables, and in satisfaction of his crime he offered a great sum of money, but the earl would not receive him unless he would surrender unconditionally.   At length when our army had drawn near and had already recognised the Welsh guards, Llewelyn began to address his men thus: 'It is not safe,' he said, 'to engage the English; I provoked this business; I will hand myself over for the whole people: it is better that one man should die than that the whole race should be exiled or perish by the sword.'

Coming down from the hills therefore Llewelyn gave himself up to the earl, submitting himself utterly to the king's will; and the earl sent him to the king to await his mercy or judgment.   This habit of the Welsh is an old-standing madness.   They keep quiet for ten years and are then suddenly athirst for battle, and their achievements over a long period are brought to destruction.   Llewelyn ap Gryffydd and David his brother could have lived in peace, but in rebellion they lost their lives and the principality of Wales.   And if you wish to trace the roots of this rebellious habit,

diderunt et principatum Wallie. Verum si consuete
rebellionis causam uel[is] perscrutari, hoc pro ratione
poterit assignari. Walenses, prius dicti Britones, olim[a]
quidem erant nobiles et totius Anglie regnum possi-
dentes; sed superuenientibus Saxonibus eiecti fuerunt,
et regnum [et] nomen simul amiserunt. Terra fertilis
et plana cessit Saxonibus; terra sterilis et montuosa
remansit Walensibus. Porro ex dictis Merlini prophete,
sperant adhuc Angliam recuperare. Hinc est quod
frequenter insurgunt Walenses, effectum uaticinii im-
plere uolentes; sed quia debitum tempus ignorant, sepe
decipiuntur et in uanum laborant.

Dominus rex apud Lyncolniam[1] barones conuoca-
uerat, sed propter guerram Leulini Bren, de paucis
consuluerat. Perambulatio tamen forestarum ibidem
conceditur, et comes Lancastrie principalis consiliarius
regis efficitur. Ordinationes super uictualibus prius
facte penitus dissoluuntur. Itinerantes enim per patriam
multum grauabantur. Nam ex quo processit illud
statutum, nichil uel modicum in foro reperiebatur ex-
F.219 positum, cum tamen prius habundaret forum uenali/bus,
licet cara uiderentur transeuntibus. Porro melius est
emere care quam nichil emendum ad opus inuenire.
Nam licet raritas annonam facit cariorem, habundantia
subsequens reddet meliorem.

Transeunte solempnitate Paschali cœpit caristia bladi
uehementer augeri. Non est uisa temporibus nostris in
Anglia nec audita centum [annis] retroactis tanta caristia. Nam Londoniis et locis uicinis uendebatur modius
tritici pro quadraginta denariis, et aliis partibus terre
ubi minor erat concursus hominum triginta denarii erat

[a] olim dicti MS
[1] 27 January to 20 February. *Parl. Writs*, II.i.152, 157. *Rot. Parl.*
I.351, 352.

this may be given as a reason. The Welsh, formerly
called the Britons, were once noble and owned the whole
realm of England; but they were expelled by the on-
coming Saxons and lost both name and kingdom. The
fertile plains went to the Saxons; the sterile and moun-
tainous districts remained to the Welsh. Moreover
from the sayings of the prophet Merlin they still hope
to recover England. Hence it is that the Welsh frequently rebel, hoping to give effect to the prophecy;
but because they do not know the appointed time,
they are often deceived and their labour is in vain.

The lord king had summoned the barons to Lincoln,[1]
but on account of the war of Llewelyn Bren little business
was transacted. However, the perambulation of the
forests was granted there, and the Earl of Lancaster
was made the king's chief counsellor. The regulations
formerly made about food were completely abolished.
Those who travelled about the country were indeed
suffering much hardship. For as a result of that statute
little or nothing was exposed for sale in the markets,
whereas formerly there had been an abundant market
in goods, though they seemed dear to travellers. But
it is better to buy dear than to find in case of need that
there is nothing to be had. For although scarcity of
corn raises the price, subsequent plenty will improve
the situation.

After the feast of Easter the dearth of corn was much
increased. Such a scarcity has not been seen in our
time in England, nor heard of for a hundred years.
For the measure of wheat was sold in London and the
neighbouring places for forty pence, and in other less
thickly populated parts of the country thirty pence
was a common price. Indeed during this time of
scarcity a great famine appeared, and after the famine

commune pretium. Porro durante penuria creuit et
fames ualida, et post famem dura pestilentia, ex qua
moriuntur in diuersis locis plus quam milia. A quibusdam etiam audiui relatum, quod in partibus Northumbrorum canes et equi et alia immunda sumebantur ad
esum. Hii enim propter frequentes incursus Scotorum
maiori tedio laborabant, quos maledicti Scoti suis uictualibus cotidie spoliabant. Heu terra Anglie! que olim
ex tua fertilitate aliis terris solebas subuenire, nunc
pauper et indigens cogeris mendicare. Terra fructifera
uertitur in salsuginem; aeris intemperies deuorat pin-
guedinem; seritur frumentum et procreatur lollium.
Eueniunt autem omnia a malitia habitantium in ea.[1]
Parce, Domine, parce populo tuo. Subsannant et deri-
dent nos qui sunt in circuitu nostro.[2] Dicunt tamen
sapientes astrologie has celi tempestates naturaliter
euenisse; Saturnus enim securus et frigidus asperitates
procreat inutiles seminibus; triennio iam regnans cursum
consummauit, et sibi mitis Jupiter ordine successit.
Porro Joue regnante cessabunt pluuiales unde, ualles
habundabunt frumento[a] et campi replebuntur ubertate;
etenim Dominus dabit benignitatem, et terra nostra
debit fructum suum, et cetera.[3]

Iampridem orta fuit dissensio in uilla Bristollie[4] super
consuetudinibus in portu maris et in foro, super priui-
F.220 legiis et aliis rebus, in quibus quatuordecim de / maioribus eiusdem uilleuid ebantur prerogatiuam habere.
Obstitit communitas, asserens burgenses omnes unius
conditionis esse et ob hoc in libertatibus et priuilegiis

---

[a] ferro MS
[1] Jeremiah xii. 4
[2] Ps. xliv. 14 = Vulgate Ps. xliii. 14
[3] Ps. lxxxv. 12 = Vulgate Ps. lxxxiv. 12
[4] By 10 November 1313 Bristol had been 'taken into the king's hand'
on account of the riots and siege of the castle, which had been committed to
Badlesmere (*C.P.R.* 1313-16 pp.68-9, with an account of the riots). On

came a severe pestilence, of which many thousands
died in different places. I have even heard it said by
some, that in Northumbria dogs and horses and other
unclean things were eaten. For there, on account of the
frequent raids of the Scots, work is more irksome, as
the accursed Scots despoil the people daily of their
food. Alas, poor England! You who once helped
other lands from your abundance, now poor and needy
are forced to beg. Fruitful land is turned into a salt-
marsh; the inclemency of the weather destroys the
fatness of the land; corn is sown and tares are brought
forth. All this comes from the wickedness of the inhabitants.[1] Spare, O Lord, spare thy people! For we
are a scorn and a derision to them who are round about
us.[2] Yet those who are wise in astrology say that these
storms in the heavens have happened naturally; for
Saturn, cold and heedless, brings rough weather that is
useless to the seed; in the ascendant now for three years
he has completed his course, and mild Jupiter duly
succeeds him. Under Jupiter these floods of rain will
cease, the valleys will grow rich in corn, and the fields
be filled with abundance. For the Lord shall give
that which is good and our land shall yield her increase,[3]
etc.

A long time ago discontent arose in the town of
Bristol,[4] over the customs on the harbour and the market,
over privileges and other matters in which fourteen of
the greater townsmen were understood to have a
prerogative. The 'community' opposed them, maintaining that all the burgesses were of one rank and
therefore equal in liberties and privileges. Over such

---

20 May 1315 the men of Bristol had safe-conduct to go to Warwick, where
the earl was to adjudicate (*ibid.* 289). The Earl of Pembroke and three
judges were sent to the town on 20 June 1316 and the liberties were restored
and the city pardoned in December (*ibid.* 574, 604-5).

pares existere. Super huiuscemodi rebus frequentes inter se habuerunt altercationes, donec in curia regis impetrarent iudices qui de causa cognoscerent et ipsam debite terminarent. Porro quatuordecim illi predicti procurauerant in inquisitione forenses associari. Credebantur insuper et ipsi conducti et ad partem illorum quatuordecim totaliter inclinati. Allegauit communitas libertatibus uille fore contrarium causas intrinsecas uentilari iudicio forensium; sed iustitiarii tales allegationes friuolas reputabant, unde nec libertatibus nec[a] priuilegiis eorum in hoc deferebant. Videntes ergo maiores communitatis exceptiones suas repelli, ius eorum fauore potius quam ratione confundi, conturbati nimirum exierunt ab aula ubi de consuetudine tractantur iudicia, nuntiaueruntque plebi dicentes, 'Venerunt iudices aduersariis nostris fauentes, et in preiudicium nostrum forenses admittunt, unde et iura nostra sine fine peribunt.' Ad hec uerba uulgus insipiens in seditionem uertitur, et totus populus pre tumultu timore concutitur. Redeuntes denuo cum multo comitatu uenerunt in aulam ubi ius eorum iam uertent in iniuriam. Nam pungnis et fustibus obuiam sibi turbam inuadere coeperunt, et ipsa die subito fere uiginti homines fatue peremerunt. Timor namque non uanus nobiles et ignobiles tantus inuasit ut plures per fenestras de summo solarii in plateam exilierunt, et crura uel tibias in terram decidentes enormiter leserunt. Timebant et iudices, humiliter petentes in pace recedere, quos maior uille, plebis insaniam uix tandem compescens, illesos fecit abire. /

F.221   Indictati fuerunt super hoc quasi octoginta uiri, et habita inquisitione diligenter coram iustitiariis regiis

---

[a] nec] in MS

matters they had frequent disputes among themselves, until they asked the king's court to provide judges to take cognisance of the case and duly terminate it. Now the said fourteen had so arranged matters that strangers should be on the panel, and these men were believed to have been won over and to lean wholly to the side of the said fourteen. The community alleged that it would be contrary to the liberties of the town for domestic issues to be subject to the judgment of strangers; but the justices regarded such allegations as frivolous, and would not allow them their liberties or privileges in this. The leaders of the commons seeing that their exceptions were rejected, that their rights were destroyed rather by favour than by reason, were much distressed as they left the hall where judgments are customarily given, and spoke to the people saying, 'Judges have come favourable to our opponents, and to our prejudice admit strangers, whence our rights will be lost for ever.' At these words the senseless crowd turned to rioting, and the whole populace trembled from fear of the disorder. Returning once more they entered the the hall with a large following and there turned their right to wrong. For with fists and sticks they began to attack the crowd opposed to them, and in that day nearly twenty men lost their lives for nothing. A very natural fear seized noble and commoner alike, so that many leapt out of the top-storey windows into the street, and seriously injured their legs or thighs as they fell to the ground. The judges, too, were afraid, humbly seeking to leave peacefully, but the mayor of the town, with difficulty repressing the frenzy of the populace, got them away safely.

About eighty men were indicted for this, and after a searching enquiry before the royal justices at

apud Gloucestriam condempnati, postea de comitatu
exiguntur, et non uenientes neque parentes exules fieri
precipiuntur.   Ipsi uero bene muniti continuerunt se
intra uillam suam; non parebunt regis mandato nisi per
manum ualidam.

Quatuordecim illi predicti, qui aduersabantur com-
munitati, domos et redditus relinquentes a uilla reces-
serunt; nam sub tali tempestate morari cum aduersariis
inutile censuerunt.   Per duos annos et amplius durauit
ista rebellio communitatis Bristollie, et tamen ex parte
regis pluries sunt moniti ad pacem uenire.   Maluit enim
rex pœnam grassantium si uellent mitigare, quam
plenam uindictam expetendo bonam uillam destruere.*
Perstiterunt autem ipsi semper rebelles, mandatum et
preceptum regis semper contempnentes.   Non uenerunt
uocati, non paruerunt moniti, causantes omnem processum contra eos habitum iniustum, quia priuilegiis et
libertatibus eorum omnino contrarium.

Nolens*ᵃ* ergo rex malitie eorum ulterius satisfacere,
milites et maiores de comitatu Glouernie uocantur
Londonias, quibus iniunxit in uirtute sacramenti ibidem
prestiti causam Bristollie et cuius esset iniuria patenter
edicere.   Qui omnes dixerunt communitatem Bristollie
partem sinistram fouere, et octoginta uiros auctores
iniurie.   Misit ergo Bristollie Adolmarum comitem de
Penbrok, qui uocatis maioribus communitatis dixit eis
ex parte regis: 'Dominus rex,' inquit, 'causam uestram
uentilans, uos reos inuenit, et ut iuri pareatis uos monet
et precipit.   Homicidas et reos illos tradite, et uos et

<hr>

ᵃ nolentes MS

Gloucester, were condemned, and the county ordered to produce them. As they neither came nor obeyed they were ordered to be exiled. They found good protection within the town and held out there; they will not obey the king's command unless they are forced to.

The said fourteen, who were opposing the commons, left their houses and rents and departed from the town, judging it useless to linger with their opponents during such a storm. This rebellion of the commons of Bristol lasted for two years and more, though they were many times summoned by the king to make their peace. For the king thought it better to exact a moderate penalty from the lawbreakers if they should be willing to comply, than by taking full vengeance to destroy a good town. But they persisted still in their rebellion, always disregarding the king's command and order. They did not come when they were summoned; they did not obey when bidden, pleading that the whole process against them was unjust, because it was entirely contrary to their privileges and liberties.

Unwilling any longer to put up with their wickedness the king summoned the knights and more important men of the county of Gloucester to London, and enjoined them by virtue of an oath there taken to expound openly the case of Bristol and who had suffered wrong. And they all said that the commons of Bristol had embraced the wrong cause and that the eighty men were the authors of this wrongdoing. So the king sent to Bristol Aylmer, Earl of Pembroke, who called together the leaders of the commons and spoke to them on the king's behalf: 'The lord king,' he said, 'on hearing your cause has found you guilty, and he warns and commands you to obey the law. Hand over the homicides and the guilty, and you and your town shall

uilla uestra in pace manete. Promitto quod, si sic
feceritis, dominum regem erga uos satis placabilem et
F.222 misericordem / inuenietis.' Respondit communitas:
'Nos iniurie auctores non fuimus; nos in dominum regem
nichil deliquimus. Quidam nitebantur iura nostra
tollere, et nos sicut decuit e contra defendere. Iccirco, si
dominus rex ea que nobis inponuntur remiserit, si uitam
et membra, redditus et predia nobis concesserit, sibi ut
domino parebimus, et omnia quecunque uoluerit facie-
mus; alioquin persistemus ut cœpimus, et libertates et
priuilegia nostra usque ad mortem defendemus.'

Audiens rex contumaciam eorum, et considerans rem
esse mali exempli, iussit uillam obsederi, et non recedere
donec caperentur obsessi. Et statim obsessa est uilla,
munitiones contra eam et propungnacula facta. Mauri-
cus de Berkele obseruabat uiam maris. Aderat Johannes
de Cherltone regis camerarius, Rogerus de Mortimer,
Johannes de Wylinthone, et alii barones et milites quam
plurimi, et Bartholomeus de Badesmere procurator totius
negotii. Erant etiam in castro quod est uille contiguum
uiri cum petrariis et aliis machinis facientes assultum.
Per aliquot dies obsessi nitebantur uillam defendere, quia
sperabant exteriores non longam moram facere, tum
quia comes Gloucestrie dudum prius sic uillam obses-
serat, sed infecto negotio tandem recesserat, tum quia[a]
sciebant regem in Scotiam tendere, et suorum procerum
auxilio indigere. Fefellit eos spes uacua; non recedent
nec uilla subiecta. Nam[b] petraria castri uehementius
acta conquassabat muros et edificia. Quod uidentes
oppidani turbati sunt et timore concussi, timentes totam
uillam in [destructionem ire; ita consensere in][c] dedi-

[a] quia tum MS
[b] nam] non MS
[c] This supplement is quite conjectural.

remain in peace. I promise that if you do this, the lord king will be easy with you and you will find mercy.' The commons replied: 'We were not the authors of this wrong; we have not failed the lord king in anything. Certain men strove to take away our rights, and we, as was proper, strove to defend them. Therefore if the lord king will remit his penalties, if he will grant us life and limb and rents and property, we will obey him as lord and do whatever he wishes; otherwise we shall continue as we have begun, and defend our liberties and privileges to the death.'

The king hearing of their stubbornness, and thinking that this was a bad example, ordered the town to be besieged, and not left until the besieged had been taken. Siege was laid to the town forthwith, fortifications and siegeworks made. Maurice de Berkeley guarded the approach by sea. John de Charlton, the king's chamberlain was present, Roger Mortimer, John de Wylinton, and very many other barons and knights, and Bartholomew de Baddlesmere was in charge of the whole business. There were also in the castle which lies over against the town, men assaulting it with mangonels and other engines. For some days the besieged strove to defend the town, hoping that those outside would not stay long, both because the Earl of Gloucester had long ago besieged the town, but had at length departed without taking it, and also because they knew that the king was going to Scotland, and needed the help of his magnates. This vain hope deceived them: the besiegers will not depart until the town is taken. For a mangonel of the castle, vigorously handled, beat down the walls and buildings. When the townsmen saw this they were troubled and stricken with fear, and fearing that the whole town [would be destroyed they agreed upon]

tionem et maiores capti missi sunt in carcerem. Puniri
non potuit tota multitudo, sed multis grassantibus opus
est exemplo. Iam sciunt Bristollienses se male erasse,
F.223 et rebellionem suam nichil / perfecisse. Si conditionem
pacis oblatam prius acceptassent, tota fere communitas
et bona eorum tuto remansissent, sed quia malo sunt usi
consilio relicti sunt omnes regis iudicio. Inutile quidem
fuit consilium dum utilitas priuatorum transit in commune dispendium. Sane meminisse debuerant obses-
sorum apud Bedeford finem desolatum, et eorum pariter
qui apud Kenelesworthe contra regem tenuerunt castrum[1]: illi quidem capti et omnes fere suspensi; isti uero
uel in carcerem detrusi uel in exilium deportati.

Quid est regi resistere nisi propriam uitam contemp-
nere et omnia bona pariter amittere? Nam si insulanus
contra regem insulanum rebellat, proinde ac si uinculatus
cum magistro carceris contendat. Per huiusmodi dissensiones deterioratur patria, et multipliciter leduntur
indigene; quam, si rex manum rigidam et correctricem
apponeret, sedaret facillime. Sed hodie frequenter
accidit quod, licet aliquem deliquisse constiterit, pro
muneribus iustificatur; fouetur impius, et [in] innocen-
tem culpa retorquetur. Ex hoc quippe crescit audacia
nocendi. Nam facilitas uenie incentiuum prebet delinquendi. Et si queratur cuius auctoritate fiant talia, dici
potest quod tota iniquitas originaliter exiit a curia.
Auaritia enim curialium uotis subsequitur singulorum.
Hii sunt de quibus loquitur Dauid in Psalmis 'Dextera
eorum repleta est muneribus'.[2] Iccirco nil magis utile

---

[1] Both the examples are taken from the history of Henry III: the
capture of Bedford in 1224 and that of Kenilworth in 1266.
[2] Ps. xxvi. 10. (Vulgate Ps. xxv. 10.)

surrender, and the leading captives were sent to prison.
The whole multitude could not be punished, but when
there are many lawbreakers an example is needed.
The Bristollians now know that they have made a bad
mistake, and that their rebellion has achieved nothing.
If they had formerly accepted the condition of peace
offered, almost all the commons and their goods would
have remained safe, but because they have followed
bad advice they are all at the king's mercy.
The advice indeed was useless since the advantage of
individual citizens turned to the common loss.   They
ought, indeed, to have remembered the tragic fate of
the besieged at Bedford, and of those, who held the castle
of Kenilworth against the king[1]; the former were captured and almost all hanged; the latter were cast into
prison or exiled.

What does it serve to resist the king save to throw
away one's life and lose all one's goods as well?   For
an islander to rebel against an island king is as if a
chained man were to strive with the warden of his
prison.   By quarrels of this kind the country is weakened,
and the inhabitants are injured in many ways.   If
the king applied a firm correcting hand he would very
easily subdue them.   But it often happens today that,
although someone is known to have transgressed, he
justifies himself by gifts; the wicked man is encouraged,
and guilt is fastened upon the innocent.   This increases
the presumption of the wrongdoer, for ease of pardon
is a stimulus to crime.   And if it is sought to know by
whose authority such things are done, it may be said that
the whole evil originally proceeds from the court.
The greed of courtiers pursues the offerings of in-
dividuals.   These are they of whom David speaks in
the Psalms, 'Their right hand is full of bribes.'[2]   There-

M

[et] necessarium foret in curia, quam ut rex tales collaterales haberet in camera, qui pro loco et tempore
regem excessibus suppliciter corriperent et impiorum
satellitum cum uiderint expedire facta suggerent[a];
F.224 propter quod uir / quidam religiosus et note auctoritatis
confessori domini regis misit litteras sub hiis uerbis[1]:

'Cum rex a regendo dicatur, utpote qui populum
legibus gubernare et gladio debeat ab inimicis defendere,
dum bene regit conuenienter rex appellatur; dum
populum spoliat tyrannus magis esse iudicatur. Sane
rex noster transiens per patriam bona hominum capit
et nil uel modicum aut male soluit. Sed et hii frequenter,
quibus ex tali causa aliquid debetur, ut labores euitent,
de quota remittenda faciunt pactum, ut eo citius soluatur
residuum. Olim quidem gaudebant incole regis aduen-
tantis uultum aspicere, nunc uero, quia in aduentu regis
populus leditur, recessum eius ualde prestolantur et
abeuntem[b] inprecantur ut nunquam reuertatur. Rex
etiam religiosis domibus nimis . . . .'

[*Bina folia, siue quatuor pagine, infortunio plane
dolendo interciderunt. Hearne*] . . . . ueniret.

Reuera anno preterito ordinatum erat[2] quod dominus rex sine consilio comitum et procerum nichil graue,
nichil arduum inchoaret, et comitem Lancastrie de consilio suo principaliter retineret. Sed quicquid placet
domino regi domestici comitis nituntur euertere; et
quicquid placet comiti domestici regis dicunt prodi-
torium esse; et ita ad suggestionem seminatoris zizanie
interponunt se utriusque familiares, et dominos suos, per
quos deberet terra defendi, non sinunt esse concordes.

---

[a] suggerentur MS
[b] habentem MS
[1] The language of the remonstrance closely resembles that of the
'Speculum Regis'. See the Introduction, p. xvii.
[2] 1316

fore nothing would be more useful or necessary in the
court, than that the king should have such companions
in his chamber, who, as need arose, should restrain
by their prayers the excesses of the king and point out the
doings of wicked hangers-on as should seem necessary;
wherefore a certain regular of admitted authority sent
a letter to the lord king's confessor in these words[1]:

'Since a king is so styled from the fact of ruling,
as one who should rule his people with laws, and defend
them with his sword from their enemies, he is fittingly
called king while he rules well, but when he despoils
his people he is rather adjudged a tyrant.   Indeed
our king as he passes through the country takes men's
goods and pays little or nothing or badly.   Those to
whom anything is due from such a cause, to save themselves trouble, often make an agreement to remit a
percentage, in order that the balance may be paid
quicker.   Formerly, indeed, the inhabitants used to
rejoice to see the face of the king when he came, but now,
because the king's approach injures the people, his
departure gives them much pleasure and as he goes
off they pray that he may never return.   The king
moreover too [often visits] religious houses . . . .'

[*Two leaves or four pages by a lamentable
misfortune have wholly perished.   Hearne*] . . . . come.

In fact it had been decreed the year before[2] that the
lord king should initiate nothing weighty or important
without the advice of the earls and magnates, and
should retain the Earl of Lancaster at the head of his
council.   But whatever pleases the lord king the earl's
servants try to upset; and whatever pleases the earl the
king's servants call treachery; and so at the suggestion
of the Devil the familiars of each start meddling, and
their lords, by whom the land ought to be defended,

Siquidem Robertus de Brutz iam per multos annos, cum
uastaret terras in Marchia, predia comitis semper dimisit
intacta.   Sperat enim, ut creditur, procurante comite
pœnam diu comminatam euadere, et regnum ante
uendicatum[a] sub aliquo colore pacis retinere.   Timet
forsan et comes ne rex aliquando, memor iniurie quam
F.225 exercuit comes in Petrum, / ultionem exspectet cum
uiderit oportunum.   Iccirco, ut dicitur, nititur comes
Robertum de Brutz in regno Scotie solidare, ut, si forsan
solus contra regem non possit resistere, saltem Roberti
de Brutz fretus auxilio minas regias compellat arescere;
sed in hiis an fidei transgressor, an lese magestatis reus,
comes habeatur, iudicio maiorum relinquatur: nam iure
naturali saluti proprie per fas et nefas licet consulere.
Sic Dauid fugiens a facie domini sui regis Saul sibi
prouidit, et ad regem Ghet cum suis omnibus prudenter
conuolauit.[1]

Interea mandauerat archiepiscopus Cantuariensis in
ecclesia Sancti Pauli Londoniis totius Anglie clerum
conueniri[2]; petiitque idem archiepiscopus, cum ceteris
episcopis ab aula electis, de media uel tertia parte bonorum ecclesiasticorum domino regi subueniri.   Videntes
illi pauci episcopi, qui ab ecclesia erant assumpti,
primatem suum cum maiori parte coepiscoporum in
partem domini regis inclinatum, iam in unam et eandem
sententiam conuenerunt, et petitionem archipresulis
rationabilem fieri decreuerunt; sed communitas cleri
pluribus rationibus ab huiusmodi prestatione nitebatur
absolui; tum quia[b] sine auctoritate apostolica speciali
non debet laicis de bonis ecclesiasticis aliqua portio con-

---

[a] ante uendicatum] autem uendicat MS
[b] tum quia] quia tamen MS
[1] 1 Sam. xxi. 10
[2] October 1316

are not allowed to rest in harmony. Indeed Robert
Bruce, when he devastates the district of the March,
has now for many years left the earl's estates untouched.
For he hopes, as it is believed, that with the earl's
help he will escape the long-threatened penalty, and
maintain his hold with some show of peace on the
kingdom that he claimed. The earl perhaps fears,
too, that the king, mindful of the wrong that the earl
did to Piers, is waiting for his revenge until the time is
ripe. Therefore, it said, the earl attempts to consolidate
Robert Bruce in the kingdom of Scotland, so that, if
perchance he cannot hold out alone against the king,
relying on the help of Robert Bruce he may at least
bring about a cessation of the royal threats; but whether
the earl is a breaker of faith in this or guilty of treason
may be left to the verdict of more important persons:
for by natural law it is proper to look to one's own
safety as best one may. Thus David saved himself
fleeing from the face of his lord king Saul, and with all
his men prudently took refuge with the King of Gath.[1]

Meanwhile the Archbishop of Canterbury had
ordered the clergy of all England to meet in the church
of St Paul's, London[2]; and the said Archbishop asked,
with the other bishops chosen by the court, for a half
or a third of ecclesiastical goods to be given in aid to
the king. These few bishops who had been chosen by
the church, seeing that their primate with the majority
of their fellow-bishops leaned to the king's side, now
came to one and the same conclusion, and decided that
the archbishop's reasonable request should be granted;
but the community of the clergy urged on many grounds
that they should be quit of this kind of payment;
both because without special papal authority, no portion

cedi, tum quia annona cara et annus sterilis, portioneque regis et necessariis reseruatis, non haberent rectores quid erogarent pauperibus. Responderunt prelati auctoritatem apostolicam in hoc casu non debere requiri, quia, cum rex infra regni sui terminos expungnatur, regi tanquam commune negotium gerenti communiter debet subueniri. Similiter [per] sterilitatem anni non oportet /

F.226 prestationem tam necessariam impediri, nam mediante archiepiscopo diebus oportunis fiet solutio. Tandem procuratores cleri, inportunitate petentium uicti, decimam[1] ecclesie domino regi concesserunt, et diem Purificationis proxime sequentem, et eundem anno reuoluto iterum uenientem, dies solutionis acceperunt.

Sane timendum est ne huiusmodi collecta, que grauat ecclesiam, domino regi cedat in ruinam. Nam bona ecclesie sunt bona pauperum. Nunquam pauperum, nunquam ecclesie spolia prosperum habuerunt auspicium. Certe sub Pharaone, cum ex principali decreto omnes ad solutionem quinte partis generaliter urgerentur, sacerdotes tamen fuerunt ab obseruantia et onere illius constitutionis immunes.[2] In libro etiam Numeri, ad figuram perpetue libertatis precepit Leuiticam tribum ab omni publica functione liberam esse, summi pontificis[a] duntaxat arbitrio subiacere. Quid aliud potest aut debet exigere princeps a pontificibus uel a clero, quam [ut] incessanter fiat oratio ab ecclesia ad Deum pro eo? Omnis enim pontifex ex hominibus assumptus pro hominibus constituitur in hiis que sunt ad Deum, ut offerat dona et sacrificia[3] pro rege et populo, et, si iratus

[a] summus pontifex MS
[1] The Southern Province granted a tenth on 11 October, the Northern on 23 November (Wilkins, *Conc.* ii.458).
[2] Genesis xlvii. 26
[3] Heb. v. 1

of ecclesiastical goods ought to be granted to laymen, and also because by reason of the price of grain and the failure of the harvest, when the king's portion and other necessaries had been put aside, rectors would not have the wherewithal to give to the poor. The prelates replied that in this case papal authority should not be sought; because, since the king was being attacked within the borders of his kingdom, he should be generally supported as one who was undertaking common business. Likewise so necessary a contribution ought not to be hindered by the sterility of the year, for with the mediation of the archbishop payment would be made at suitable times. At length the proctors of the clergy, overcome by the persistence of the petitioners, granted an ecclesiastical tenth[1] to the king and agreed to the feast of the Purification next following, and the same the year after, as the days for payment.

It is indeed to be feared lest this kind of contribution, which burdens the church, should bring about the lord king's ruin. For the goods of the church are the goods of the poor. Never has it augured well to despoil the poor or the church. Certainly under Pharaoh, though by the royal ordinance all in general were exhorted to pay the fifth, yet the priests were exempt from the observance of this burdensome decree.[2] Further, in the book of Numbers, as a symbol of perpetual liberty Pharoah ordered that the priestly tribe should be free from every public office, though subject to the judgement of the supreme pontiff. What else can or should the prince demand from the bishops or clergy, than that prayers should continually be offered to God by the church for him? For every high priest taken from among men is ordained for men in the things pertaining to God, that he may offer gifts and sacrifices[3]

est Dominus, sacerdos medius intercedat, et in tempore iracundie factus est reconciliatio. Iratus Dominus populum suum Israel delere decreuerat, stetitque Moises in confractione*ᵃ* in conspectu eius,[1] et motum diuine indignationis oratione placauit. Item flamma diuine animaduersionis*ᵇ* deseuiente in populo, Aaron arrepto turibulo medius inter uiuos et mortuos se flamme ob-

F.227 iecit, et cessauit / quassatio[2]; Moise orante, et manus erigente, Hebrei uicerunt; et sacerdotibus uociferantibus ad Dominum muri Jerico corruerunt. Hec est uis orationis et sacrificii; aduersus non preualebunt uectes inferi.[3] Recolat utinam dominus rex non ad oppressionem sed ad tuitionem ecclesie se potestatem gladii ab ecclesia suscepisse. Sed et locum et officium in quo posuit eum Dominus agnoscat, nec de thesauris ecclesie, que debentur pauperibus, sed de fisco vel erario*ᶜ* bellum inferat inimicis.

Instante iam uerno tempore misit rex nuntios ad curiam Romanam,[4] qui cum uenissent petierunt ex parte regis Anglie quatinus dominus papa dictum regem ab obseruatione*ᵈ* quarundam ordinationum, quibus idem rex iuramento tenebatur astrictus, dignaretur absoluere. Asserebant enim predictas ordinationes, licet de communi assensu procerum editas et confirmatas, in perniciem regni et ecclesie Anglicane periculose nimis redundare. Petierunt etiam sententiam excommunicationis in Robertum de Brutz et omnes sibi adherentes fulminari, et terram Scotorum interdicto supponi, donec idem Robertus super commissis erga regem Anglie se

---

ᵃ confirmacione MS   *ᵇ* animauersacionis MS
ᶜ fisco vel erario] fiscali erario MS   *ᵈ* ad obseruacionem MS
[1] Ps. cvi. 23. (Vulgate Ps. cv. 23.)
[2] Num. xvi. 46, 48; cf. also Ps. cvi. 30 (Vulgate Ps. cv. 33)
[3] Matt. xvi. 18
[4] The Bishops of Ely and Norwich, the Earl of Pembroke, and Bartholomew de Badlesmere were sent in 1317.

for king and people, and if God is angered, the priest may intercede as a mediator, and in time of wrath a reconciliation is made. The Lord in his wrath had decided to destroy his people Israel, and Moses stood before him in the breach,[1] and appeased by prayer the mounting anger of the Lord. Also, the fire of divine punishment going out upon the people, Aaron took up his censer and stood against the flame between the dead and the living, and the plague ceased.[2] As Moses prayed and lifted up his hands, the Hebrews conquered, and as the priests cried to the Lord the walls of Jericho fell down. This is the power of prayer and sacrifice; and the gates of hell shall not prevail against it.[3] Would that the lord king remembered that he has received the power of the sword from the church not for its oppression but to protect it. But let him acknowledge the place and office in which the Lord has placed him, and not wage war upon his enemies from the wealth of the church which belongs to the poor, but from the royal treasury.

When spring came round the king sent an embassy to the court of Rome,[4] who came and asked on the part of the King of England that the lord pope should deign to absolve the said king from the observance of certain Ordinances to which the same king was strictly bound by oath. They maintained that the said Ordinances, though published and confirmed by the common consent of the magnates, tended too dangerously to the destruction of the kingdom and the English church. They also asked for sentence of excommunication to be promulgated against Robert Bruce and all his supporters, and for the land of the Scots to be put under an interdict, until the same Robert should make good the wrongs committed by him against the King

reformaret, et regnum Scotie, quod iniuste occupare dinoscitur, penitus relinqueret. Supplicarunt insuper domino pape quatinus domino regi, qui totum thesaurum suum pro defensione regni sui et [ecclesie inpenderat], per aliquod tempus dignaretur subuenire, adicientes regem intentum, pacificato regno suo, si competeret facultas, summa deuotione contra paganos transfretare. Ad hec respondit papa regem Anglie ab obseruatione predictarum ordinationum absolui non debere, cum, sicut acceperat, fidedignorum studio fuissent confecte, F.228 quos non erat uerisimile in / preiudicium regni uel ecclesie aliquid ordinasse. Decreuit etiam dominus papa regnum Scotorum interdicto non esse supponendum donec constaret de iure partium. Denique ecclesiam uel decimas ecclesie noluit dominus papa potestati laicorum submittere, sed sue*a* tantum ordinationi reseruaret, et, si regem Anglie in subsidium Terre Sancte armari contingeret, de fructibus ecclesie, si necesse foret, sumptus habundanter ministraret. Promisit insuper dominus papa legatos in Angliam mittere,[1] qui de hiis diligenter inquirerent et auctoritate apostolica omnes controuersias fine debito terminarent.

Interim ueniente*b* tempore quo solent reges ad bella procedere, uocauit rex proceres ad parliamentum ut iuxta tenorem ordinationum, antequam procederetur ad bellum, in communi parliamento[2] deliberaretur quid esset agendum; sed die statuto adueniente non uenit comes Lancastrie. Interim sub fidelitate et homagio

---

a suae] sine MS
b inueniente MS
[1] Cardinals Gaucelin d'Euse and Luca dei Fieschi were sent. (*Foed. II* 317, 318.)
[2] A Council was held at Clarendon on 9 February, and another at London on 15 April 1317. (*Parl. Writs*, II.i.170.)

of England, and should utterly give up the kingdom of
Scotland, which he is known to have seized wrongfully.
They also besought the pope to deign to help the king
for a time, as he [had expended] all his treasure for
the defence of his realm and [of the church]; adding
that the king was determined, when he had made peace
in his realm, if opportunity offered, to cross the sea
against the pagans with the utmost devotion. To
this the pope replied that the King of England ought
not to be absolved from the observance of the said
Ordinances since they had been drawn up, as he had
been informed, by the care of trustworthy persons,
and it was not likely that they had ordained anything to the prejudice of the kingdom or the church.
The lord pope also decreed that the kingdom of Scotland was not to be put under an interdict until the
rights of the parties had been ascertained. Finally,
the lord pope refused to put the church or the tithes
of the church into the hands of laymen, but would
keep them at his own disposal, and if it happened
that the King of England took arms in aid of the Holy
Land, he should if necessary receive abundant expenses
from the fruits of the church. The lord pope also
promised to send legates to England,[1] to make diligent
enquiry about these matters, and by apostolic authority
put an end to all controversy.

Meanwhile, as the time approached at which kings
are accustomed to make war, the king summoned the
nobles to parliament in order that, according to the
tenor of the Ordinances, they should deliberate in
common parliament[2] what was to be done before
proceeding to war; but when the appointed day came
the Earl of Lancaster did not come. He was warned
in the meantime to attend parliament by reason of

monetur adesse parliamento; sed, nec sic ueniens, sub
forisfactura omnium que possidebat in Anglia, copiam
sui facere iubetur in curia. Tunc misit comes nuntios[1]
qui excusarent eum coram rege et allegarent similiter
causas absentie; qui statim iussa complentes accesserunt
ad regem dicentes: 'Domine, si placet, offendi uel mirari
non debetis, si comes Lancastrie ad parliamentum non
uenit. Timet enim quorundam insidias capitales quos
curia regia tuetur et nutrit. De inimicitiis eorum iam
constat euidenter; iam uxorem comitis in dedecus et
opprobrium eius rapuerunt, unde affectum quem erga
eum gerunt iam liquido protulerunt. Petit ergo comes
quatinus malefactores illos a familiaritate uestra uelitis
expellere, et tunc ueniet ad uos ubicunque uolueritis
F.229 assignare. Petit / etiam quod possit sine offensione
uestra de iniuria sibi illata uindictam sumere et satisfactionem qualem poterit impetrare.'

Respondit rex: 'Ego contemptum comitis uindicabo
cum potero; familiares meos expellere nolo; de raptu
uxoris sue remedium iure querat tantummodo.' Conuocatis itaque familiaribus suis et ceteris amicis, ait rex
coram omnibus: 'Ecce uidetis quomodo comes Lancastrie ad parliamentum non uenit. Videtis quomodo
mandatis nostris parere contempserit. Quid uobis
uidetur?' Dicunt quidam: 'Dignum est ut qui preceptis domini sui parere contempnit contumaciam luat,
et feodum si quod tenet, tamquam periurus consequenter
amittat. Persequatur ergo rex contemptorem suum et
comprehendat, et comprehensum sub carcere cludat uel
regno proscribat.' Alii uero dixerunt: 'Non est leue
capere comitem Lancastrie; Scoti succurrent ei et magna

---

[1] For Lancaster's behaviour see *Bridl.* 50; *Murimuth,* 271

his fealty and homage; but, as he did not so come, he was ordered on pain of forfeiting all his possessions in England, to produce his military service. At this the earl[1] sent messengers to excuse him before the king and likewise to allege the causes of his absence. They at once approached the king in fulfilment of their orders saying: 'My Lord, if it please you, you ought not to be offended or surprised at the Earl of Lancaster not coming to parliament. For he fears the deadly stratagems of certain persons who thrive under the protection of the royal court. Their enmity is already a matter of public knowledge; they have already carried off the earl's wife to his disgrace and shame, whereby they have displayed the feelings that they bear towards him. The earl therefore asks that you will expel these evildoers from your presence, and then he will come to you wherever you shall wish to appoint. He also asks that he may without offence take vengeance and such satisfaction as he can get for the wrong done to him.'

The king replied: 'I will avenge the despite done to the earl when I can; I refuse to expel my household; for the abduction of his wife let him seek a remedy in law only.' Thus having summoned his household and other friends, the king said in the presence of all: 'You see how the Earl of Lancaster has not come to parliament. You see how he scorns to obey our commands. How does it seem to you?' Some said: 'It is right that he who scorns to obey his lord's commands shall purge his contumacy, and as a perjurer lose his fief if he holds one. Let the king therefore pursue and take his despiser, and when he is taken put him in prison or exile him.' But others said: 'It is no small matter to take the Earl of Lancaster. The Scots will support

pars Wallie; sed melius est aliam uiam assumere, et prius tractare de forma concordie. Satis enim liquet ex Britonum historia quam sit plena periculis ciuilis discordia. Nam quod Julius Cesar regnum Britannie sibi subiugauit, et quod gens Saxonum fugatis Britonibus regnum occupauit, quod Normanni regimen Anglie consequenter, ex simili discordia cuncta peruenisse noscuntur.'

Interuenientibus ergo magnatibus, concessum est ut dominus rex et comes conuenirent[a] ad quendam locum sicut fieri decet ad diem amoris sine strepitu armorum. Sperabatur enim quod, si inter se rationes suas et uerba conferrent, citius efficerentur unanimes, quam per mediatores mandata partium sepe peruertentes. Sed quia secreta diuitum occultari non possunt, statim nuntiatum est comiti regem iurasse quod, si comes uix / modo[b] conuentum accederet, aut capite priuaret eum aut carceri manciparet.

F.230

Ab illa die in antea cogitauit comes regem non adire sine tutela. Congregauit sibi comes omnes sibi adherentes apud Pountefreyt castrum suum, et erat rex eo tempore apud Eboracum, ubi mandauerat exercitum suum conuenire; sed qui properabant ad regem non permittuntur cum armis transire. Obseruabat enim comes pontes, et diligenter fecit inhiberi dextrarios transduci uel arma transferri; et hoc asserebat se facere eo quod senescallus sit Anglie, cuius interest utilitatibus regni prospicere, et, si rex contra aliquem arma uellet assumere, senescallo precipue deberet innotescere. Cernens autem rex suum impediri propositum, et consilium eius pro parte denudatum, quid faceret uel quo se uer-

him and a great part of Wales; it is better to proceed
another way, and treat beforehand of a form of agreement.
For it is very clear from the history of the Britons, how
full of perils is civil discord.   For that Julius Caesar
subdued the kingdom of Britain, that the Saxon race
drove out the Britons and seized the kingdom, that the
Normans in their turn assumed the governance of
England, all these things are known to have resulted
from a like discord.'

So, at the mediation of the magnates, it was agreed
that the lord king and the earl should meet at a certain
place as is proper at a love-day without the clash of arms.
For it was hoped that if they reasoned it out between
themselves verbally, they would come to an agreement
more quickly than through mediators who often twist
the meaning of their instructions from the parties.
But because the secrets of the rich cannot be hidden,
it was immediately reported to the earl that the king
had sworn that if the earl only came to the meeting,
he would either have his head or consign him to prison.

From that day forth the earl took care not to approach the king without protection.   The earl collected
all his supporters at his castle of Pomfret, and the king
at that time was at York, where he had ordered his army
to muster; but those who were hastening to the king
were not allowed to pass by armed.   For the earl guarded
the bridges, and diligently prevented war-horses or
weapons from being taken across; and he said that he
did this because he was Steward of England, whose
business it was to look to the advantage of the kingdom,
and if the king wished to take arms against anyone
he ought first to notify the Steward.   The king seeing
that his proposal was frustrated and his plan in part
laid bare, had no idea what to do or which way to turn.

teret penitus ignorauit. Denique procurante comite de
Penbrok, interponentibus se etiam cardinalibus legatis
qui iam[a] uenerant in Angliam, sic actum est, ut in
quindena Sancti Hillarii apud Lyncolniam[1] conuenirent
uniuersi, et tunc repararentur omnia indirecta, et de
malefactoribus fieret iustitia.

Hiis itaque dispositis dominus rex cum tota comitiua
sua uersus Londonias aggreditur, et, cum uenisset prope
castrum de Pountfreit pertinens ad comitem Lancastrie,
iussit omnes suos arma resumere,[2] quia forsan timuit sibi
ubi non erat timendum, aut certe ab insipientibus processit consilium. Armati uero et per turmas distincti
processerunt quasi uillam expungnaturi; et ecce, comes
Penbrok regem alloquitur: 'Domine,' inquit comes,
'quale consilium accepisti? quid est quod ita precipi-
tanter arma sumpsisti? Aduersarius non instat, nec
F.231 aliquis nos expungnat. / Nonne omnia ad certum tempus
sunt suspensa, pacta inita, fide pariter et scriptis con-
firmata? Turpe est contra pacta uenire, credentem
fallere et fidem infringere.' Et rex ad comitem; 'Relatum est michi quod comes Lancastrie in insidiis latitat,
et nos omnes inprouisos inuadere studiose procurat.'
'Certe,' inquit comes, 'domine, non est ita. Regnum
et feodum, et uniuersa que possidet, comes ipse relinqueret priusquam huiusmodi proditionem inchoaret.'
Sic tandem ad suggestionem comitis rex ab inceptis
destitit, et uersus Londonias iter arripuit.

Rebus sic se habentibus, reuersi sunt etiam cardinales
Londonias. Processerant enim uersus Scotiam ut ibidem
legationem suum fungerentur; sed per terram Northam-

---

[a] iam qui MS
[1] This was decided on 24 September, but it was later postponed to
June, and eventually to October 1318.
[2] 1-2 October 1317

At length at the instance of the Earl of Pembroke, and by the intervention of the cardinal legates who had reached England, it was decided that they should all meet on the quinzaine of St Hilary at Lincoln,[1] and then all wrongs would be righted, and justice done upon evildoers.

When these things had been settled the lord king marched towards London with all his retinue, and when he approached the Earl of Lancaster's castle of Pomfret, he ordered all his men to take up their arms,[2] perhaps because he was afraid where there was nothing to be feared, or really because he followed unwise advice. Thus armed and divided up into squadrons they went on their way as if about to besiege the town; and lo! the Earl of Pembroke addresses the king: 'My Lord,' says the earl, 'What kind of counsel have you taken? Why have you so hastily taken up arms? No enemy presses us, no one is fighting us. Has not everything been suspended to an appointed date, agreements entered into, and faithfully set down in writing as well? It is shameful to contravene the agreement, deceive the trusting, and break faith.' The king replied to the earl: 'I have been told that the Earl of Lancaster is lying in ambush, and is diligently preparing to catch us all by surprise.' 'Indeed, my lord, it is not so,' said the earl. 'The earl would leave the kingdom, his fee, and all that he has, before he set on foot such treachery.' So at length at the earl's suggestion the king gave up his design, and made his way towards London.

This was the state of affairs when the cardinals too returned to London. They had proceeded towards Scotland to exercise their commission in that country; but as they made their way through Northumbria they were maltreated by certain robbers. For

N

himbrorum iter facientes a quibusdam predoni[bu]s male tractabantur. Nam Gilbertum quendam de Middeltone dictum cum suis complicibus obuiam habuerunt,[a] qui sarcinulas eorum scrutantes maximam summam pecunie legatis abstulerunt.[1] Suspendebant ergo legati partes legationis sue ad tempus, donec in parliamento optinerent fieri ultionem de malefactoribus illis; procedentes nichilominus spiritualiter contra dictos predones, Gilbertum de Middeltone cum suis fautoribus solempniter et publice a communione fidelium separantes. Vt expressa pœna inmanitas excessus appareat, tenorem quem ex constitutione Bonefacii viii[ui] pro parte recolui lector aduertat. Bonefacius viii[us] in titulo 'de pœnis' sic statuit[2]:—

Si quis in hoc sacrilegii genus irrepserit quod ecclesie Romane cardinalem hostiliter insecutus fuerit, percusserit aut ceperit, fieri mandauerit uel factum ratum habuerit, consilium facienti dederit uel fauorem, aut scienter receptauerit uel defensauerit eundem, tanquam reus lese magestatis per/petuo sit infamis, bannitus et intestabilis,[b] et ab omni successione repulsus; omnia edificia eius diruantur, et ut perpetuam notam infamie perpetua ruina testetur, et nullo tempore reparentur. Nullus ei debita cogatur reddere, nullus in iudicio sibi teneatur respondere, sed quicquid in bonis ipsius inuenitur, fisco uel rei publice dominio applicetur, nulla parte bonorum ad posteros eius transmissa, ut sic quodammodo cum ipso dampnentur et sua, et si quid ab ecclesia forsan optineant ipso iure beneficium perdant, de quo superior ecclesie pro sua uoluntate disponat. Insuper filii eius et nepotes per masculinam lineam descendentes, si beneficium aliquod uel etiam pontificalem dignitatem fuerint adepti, sint eis ipso iure priuati; sit talibus omnis preclusa dignitas, sit postulandi negata facultas, officium et quodlibet mi[ni]sterium publicum utrobique sic sit eis interdictum. Non credatur in iudiciis eorum assertioni; ad testimonium prorsus reddantur indigni.[c] Sit eis ad ordines ascensus inhibitus; sit ad beneficium ecclesiasticum negatus accessus; et, ut magis famosa sit eorum

F.232

<hr/>

[a] habuit MS
[b] indetestabilis MS
[c] indignum MS
[1] 1 September 1317, at Ferryhill, between Darlington and Durham
[2] cf. Sext. 5.9.5

they met a certain Gilbert called de Middeltone with his accomplices, who searched their baggage and took from them a very large sum of money.[1]   Therefore the legates postponed part of their mission for a time, until they should obtain redress in parliament for what the malefactors had done; nevertheless proceeding spiritually against the said robbers, they solemnly and in public separated Gilbert de Middeltone and his accomplices from the communion of the faithful. So that the horror of these excesses may appear from the penalty laid down, the reader may note the gist of the constitution of Boniface VIII which I have in part set forth.   Boniface VIII under the title 'Of Penalties' decreed thus[2]:—

If any one fall into this kind of sacrilege, namely that he has attacked, struck, or seized a cardinal of the Roman church, or has ordered it to be done or approved it when done, or given counsel or aid to the doer, or has knowingly received or defended him, as one guilty of treason he shall be for ever infamous, banned, and incapable of making a will, and excluded from every succession; all his buildings shall be destroyed, and that their perpetual ruin may bear witness as a perpetual mark of infamy, they shall never be repaired. No one shall be forced to pay debts to him, no-one bound to answer to him in judgment, but whatever is found of his goods shall be made over to the treasury or public funds, no part of his property shall be transmitted to his descendants, so that in a way his goods are condemned with him, and if by chance they hold anything from the church, by the same law they shall lose the benefice, which the ecclesiastical superior shall dispose of as he wills. Moreover his sons and grandsons in the male line, if they have acquired any benefice or even the episcopal dignity, are by the same law deprived of it; such persons are precluded from every dignity, denied the opportunity of postulation; office and any kind of public service is alike forbidden to them. No faith is to be placed in their statements in courts of law; they are rendered utterly unworthy of bearing witness. They may not proceed to Holy Orders; they may not receive an ecclesiastical benefice; and that their infamy may be the more notorious, for all the aforesaid all hope of dispensation is utterly taken away, and as well the persecutor

infamia, super omnibus premissis sit eis spes dispensationis penitus
adempta, et tam insecutor quam uiolente manus iniector, ipso facto
sententiam excommunicationis maioris incurrat, quam non nisi per
summum pontificem, nisi duntaxat in mortis articulo constitutus,
euadat.

Et hec quidem sententia in predictum Gilbertum et suos
fautores tam terribiliter erat promulgata.

Reuera nimis erat audax uersutia et uersuta nimis
audacia que tantis uiris non pepercit.   Cui capiti cuius-
que persone reuerentia debetur, si patribus conscriptis,
si legatis a latere pape transmissis non defertur? Ceterum
quantumcunque peccauerit*a* uir in uirum,[1] solet ecclesia
Romana humiliter petenti ueniam prestare; sed si manus
sacrilega curiam ipsam inuaserit, qua fronte, queso,
poterit ueniam postulare, cum iure caueatur quod frustra
legis auxilium inuocat qui committit in legem?[2] Denique
cuius efficacie fuerit sententia statim apparuit; nam

F.233 paucis euolutis diebus / Gilbertus capitur et coram
iustitiariis regis Londoniis condempnatur.   Deinde pro-
tractus, suspensus et exenteratus, capite truncatur.

Quia in festo Sancti Hillarii[3] dominum regem et
ceteros magnates ad parliamentum conuenire oportuit,
ex condicto conuenerunt hii qui erant de consilio domini
regis, dicentes: 'Non est bonum inire parliamentum sub
hoc modo.   Nam si dominus rex ueniat et comes Lancastrie ueniat, utique et omnes qui sunt de eorum retentione, et certe tanta et tam effrenata multitudo mali
potius quam boni foret occasio.   Iccirco melius est per
medias personas inter dominum regem et comitem Lancastrie firmam concordiam et plenam securitatem prius
reformare, ac deinde diem et locum parliamenti sicut
decet assignare.'   Et actum est.   Nam de consensu con-

---

a placuerit MS
[1] 2 Sam. ii. 25
[2] *Dig.* 4.4.37
[3] See above, p. 69.   It eventually met at York on 20 October.

as the violent layer-on of hands shall automatically incur the sentence of the greater excommunication, which he shall not escape, except at the hands of the pope alone, unless he is at the point of death.

This terrifying sentence was promulgated against the said Gilbert and his accomplices.

Indeed too rash was the cunning and too cunning the rashness that did not spare such men. To whose head, to whose person is reverence due, if it is not given to senators, to legates specially sent by the pope? However much one man sin against another,[1] the Roman church is accustomed to bestow pardon on the humble petitioner; but if the sacrilegious hand attacks the curia itself, with what assurance, I ask, can pardon be demanded, since we are warned by law that the aid of the law is sought in vain by him who breaks it?[2] At any rate the efficacy of the sentence was at once apparent; for after a few days Gilbert was taken and condemned before the king's justices at London. Then he was drawn, hanged and disembowelled and his head cut off.

Because the lord king and the other magnates were to meet in parliament on the feast of St Hilary,[3] those who were of the king's council met by agreement saying: 'It is not good to begin a parliament like this. For if the lord king comes and the Earl of Lancaster comes, and also all who are retained by them, so great and so unbridled a multitude could be an occasion of evil rather than good. Therefore it is better to restore true harmony and full confidence between the lord king and the Earl of Lancaster by intermediaries, and then appoint a day and place for parliament as is fitting.' And so it was done. The archbishops, earls and barons on the king's part and the earl's counsellors

uenerunt apud Leicestriam[1] archiepiscopi, comites et
barones ex parte domini regis, et consiliarii comitis,
tractaturi super istis negotiis. Vbi cum multa ex parte
regis peterentur quibus et comes ipse, si placeret ei,
prestaret assensum, ad nichil penitus inclinari potuit sine
plenaria obseruatione ordinationum.

Videntes igitur archiepiscopus et ceteri comites animum comitis inmobilem, concesserunt pro domino rege
et pro se ordinationes uniuersas fideliter obseruari, et
cartam testimonii sacramento singulorum et sigillorum
impressione roborari. Et comes Lancastrie e contra
domino regi et suis debitam fidelitatem et securitatem
sub fide promisit, excepta querela quam contra comitem
Warennie de raptu uxoris dudum instituit.

Hiis igitur sub tali forma concessis,[a] acceperunt diem
parliamenti apud Lyncolniam in crastino Trinitatis.[2] O
quantum nocuit ista dissensio, O quantum exsti/tit malis
occasio! Dum rex delirat cum baronibus, fiducia rebellandi datur hostibus. Sic iam amittitur tota Scotia, et
terra Northamhimbrorum iacet inculta. Vna uilla regi
remanserat in Scotia. Hec erat Berewyke fortis et ualida
et muro inexpungnabili decenter ambita. Hanc dum
rex committeret burgensium custodie, uillam tradunt
hostibus famuli perfidie.[3] Reuera nec locus tutissimus
nec uir potentissimus resistit proditoribus; sed Troia
obsessa decennio, que uinci non potuit in prelio, proditorum tandem subcubuit ingenio. Sic ille magnus
Grecorum imperator Alexander, totius orbis domitor,

F.234

---

[a] excessis MS
[1] Taken with Trokelowe, *Annales* (R.S.) 102, this passage is thought to
suggest a meeting at Leicester about 24 June 1318. See 'The Negotiations
Preceding the "Treaty" of Leake, August 1318', by B. Wilkinson, in *Studies
. . . presented to F. M. Powicke* (Oxford, 1948), 333–53, and literature there
cited. This view, however, breaks the flow of the narrative, and it may be
as well to remember that a date before 3 March is, on a strict interpretation
of the chronology of this text, just possible.

met by agreement at Leicester[1] to treat of this business. There many things were put to the earl on the king's behalf, for his assent if it seemed good to him, but he would agree to nothing at all without full observance of the Ordinances.

When the archbishop and the other earls saw that the Earl of Lancaster's mind was made up, they granted on the king's behalf and for themselves that all the Ordinances should be faithfully observed, and that the charter of witness should be confirmed by the oath of each and the imposition of their seals. And the Earl of Lancaster on his part promised on his oath due fealty and security to the lord king and his men, saving the complaint that he had long ago lodged against the Earl Warenne for the abduction of his wife.

When these things had been granted in this form, they were given a day for parliament at Lincoln on the morrow of Holy Trinity.[2] Oh! How harmful was this quarrel! How great an occasion for evil! While the king is raving against the barons, his enemies find confidence to rebel. In this way the whole of Scotland is lost and the land of Northumbria lies waste. One town alone was left to the king in Scotland. This was Berwick, sturdy and strong and well surrounded by an impregnable wall. When the king committed this town to the care of the burgesses, the treacherous slaves handed it over to the enemy.[3] Indeed there is no place safe enough nor any man powerful enough to resist traitors: Troy, besieged for a decade, though it could not be conquered in battle, at length succumbed to the wiles of traitors. So, too Alexander the Great,

---

[2] It was countermanded early in June (*Parl. Writs*, II.i.178, 181)
[3] Lost, 2-8 April 1318

cum cunctas nationes armis subicit, per familiares proditores toxicatus occubuit. Studeat amodo rex noster uel Scotiam recuperare, uel saltem terram propriam ab hostibus defendere. Nam licet Scotis fortuna semel arriserit, manum forsan retrahens ad Anglos conuolabit. Proditio, periurium et homicidium, que Roberto de Brutz regnandi dederunt initium, perducent eum tandem ad finem desolatum.

Appropinquante die parliamenti prefixo uenit rex apud Northamtoniam cum electa multitudine armatorum; ubi dum uellet omnimodo expectare magnates, apparuit quidam Oxonie qui diceret se filium regis esse et regnum Anglie iure sanguinis ad se pertinere. Dicebat enim se in cunis fuisse sublatum et regem qui nunc regnat pro ipso suppositum. Accessit autem ad aulam regiam, ubi fratres Carmeli[ta]ni cœperunt edificare, uolens ibidem seisinam capere. Peruenit itaque uerbum ad regem, et statim iussu regis capitur, et in crastino domino regi presentatur. Verumptamen coram rege constitutus priora dicta sua non negauit, sed se uerum regni heredem, regem autem iniuste regnare, constanter affirmauit. /

F.235   Huius rei celebris erat fama per totam terram, et ultra quam dici potest molestabat reginam. Cœpit igitur inter sapientes esse consultum quid in hoc casu foret agendum, ac post magnam disceptationem consideratum est inter eosdem quod qui fame principis et honori non parcit tanquam proditor capitali pœna dampnetur, sicut scriptum est, 'Qui maledixit principi morte moriatur'.[1] Itaque fatuus ille ex decreto curie

---

[1] cf. Exod. xxi. 17, xxii. 28

Emperor of the Greeks, conqueror of the whole world, though he subdued all the nations in war, was poisoned by traitors in his own household. Let our king now take thought for the recovery of Scotland, or at least for the defence of his own land against his enemies. For, though fortune has once smiled upon the Scots, perhaps she will withdraw her hand and fly over to the English. Treachery, perjury, and homicide, which brought Robert Bruce to the throne, will lead him at last to a desolate end.

As the day fixed for parliament drew near, the king came to Northampton with a chosen body of men-at-arms. While he had every intention of awaiting the magnates, there appeared at Oxford a person who said that he was the king's son and that the kingdom of England pertained to him by right of blood. He claimed that he had been taken from the cradle, and that the king who now reigned was supposititious. So he came to the royal palace, where the Carmelite friars were beginning to build, wishing to take seisin there. When word reached the king, the man was at once arrested by the king's order, and on the morrow brought before the lord king. On being brought face to face with the king he did not deny what he had said, but stated firmly that he was the true heir to the throne, and that the king had no right to reign.

The notoriety of this spread throughout the whole country, and annoyed the queen unspeakably. The wise began to take council what should be done in this case, and after much discussion it was decided amongst them that he who spares not the good fame and honour of the prince, shall suffer the extreme penalty as a traitor, as it is written: 'He who curses the ruler shall surely die.'[1] So by the verdict of the

protrahitur, ac post illam proditorum pœnam laqueo suffocatur. Reuera male uendicauit, et actionem non recte instituit, dum uitam et regnum simul amisit.

Igitur sicut predixi dominus rex apud Northamtoniam exspectabat; magnates autem erant cum eo comes de Warennia, Rogerus Dammori, Hugo Despenser pater et filius, Hugo Daudeleghe, Willelmus de Mountagu; et hii omnes cum magna sequela, ita ut reputares eos non ad parliamentum uenisse, sed potius ad bella. Quod cum audisset comes Lancastrie, licet pluries uocatus noluit accedere. Nam hos omnes prenominatos reputabat comes sibi capitales inimicos. Causas autem inimicitie breuiter, si placet, licet exponere.

Comes de Warennia comitis Lancastrie rapuit uxorem, uel saltem rapientibus prestabat assensum,[1] de quo nimirum si unus uindictam uellet expetere, et alter si posset pœnam euadere. Oderant etiam comitem reliqui omnes eo quod tueri uolebat ordinationes. Illi namque iuxta ordinationes a curia regis erant amouendi, et terras quas a domino rege acceperant similiter amissuri. Ideo insidiabantur comiti in quantum potuerunt; sed insidie eorum effectum non habuerunt; statim enim notificatur comiti quicquid contra eum machinantur inimici.

Videns igitur rex quod proficeret nichil, [nichil] ageret in omnibus que contra comitem excogitaret, F.236 pensans / etiam sibi periculosam esse huiusmodi dissensionem, eo quod Scotorum contra se firmaret rebellionem, nec posse eum contra Scotos proficere sine auxilio comitis Lancastrie; pensans etiam uillam de Berewyk turpiter amissam et uillam de Northam nouiter amittendam nisi

---

[1] 6 May 1317. See Ramsay, 86 *n.* 4

court, this fool was drawn and after that was strangled with a halter, the punishment of traitors. Indeed he had a bad claim and he did not conduct his suit aright, for he lost his life and the kingdom together.

Thus, as I have said, the lord king was waiting at Northampton: the magnates with him were the Earl Warenne, Roger D'Amory, Hugh Despenser father and son, Hugh D'Audley, William de Montague; and these were all there in great strength, so that you would have thought they had come not to parliament, but to battle. When the Earl of Lancaster heard this, though often summoned, he refused to come. For he counted all the aforenamed as his deadly enemies. The causes of this enmity may, by your leave, be briefly set forth.

The Earl Warenne abducted the Earl of Lancaster's wife, or at least gave his consent to those who did,[1] concerning which it is not to be wondered at if the one should wish to look for vengeance, and the other to escape punishment. All the others hated the earl because he wanted to uphold the Ordinances. For they, according to the Ordinances, were to be removed from the king's court and would likewise lose the lands they had received from the king. They therefore intrigued against the earl as best they could; but their plots had no effect, for the earl was at once notified of whatever his enemies contrived against him.

Thus the king seeing that he profited nothing, achieved nothing by all the plans he made against the earl, and thinking that such discord was dangerous to him, because the Scottish rebellion was taking root against him, and he could make no headway against the Scots without the aid of the Earl of Lancaster; thinking, too, that the town of Berwick had been

succurratur obsessis, qui resistere non possunt ultra
festum Sancti Michaelis; pensans et expensas inmensas
quas faciebat contra comitem, requirere quatinus, omni
rancore deposito, ad locum quem uellet accederet, ubi
cum eo super omnibus commissis pro*ᵃ* se et suis amicabiliter componeret; sed et omnes hii, contra quos diceret
se comes habere querelam, ad arbitrium comitis satisfacerent, et super hoc fideiussores, cautionem aut pig-
nora, prestarent; et ita ad instantiam domine regine,
comitis Herfordie, et aliorum nobilium quos comes
Lancastrie reputabat fideles, optentum est.

Conuenerunt igitur dominus rex et comes, et diu
familiariter alloquentes debitam amicitiam et mutuam
gratiam renouarunt, atque in signum fœderis eadem die
cibum simul acceperunt; sed et Rogerus Dammori et
ceteri, exceptis Hugone Despenser et comite de Warenna,
ad comitis presentiam humiliter accedentes, in gratiam
eius admissi sunt.[1]   Preterea quia in ordinationibus
cautum erat quod dominus rex nichil alienaret, nichil
grande uel arduum inchoaret nisi per assensum comitum
et baronum et hoc in communi parliamento solempniter
expressum, prouisum est quod eligerentur duodecim uiri
de discretioribus totius regni, quorum quatuor episcopi,
quatuor comites, et quatuor barones essent, et de hiis
tres ad minus dominum regem semper comitantes,*ᵇ* si
aliquid arduum in curia regis emergeret, auctoritas
istorum duodecim statim expediret.   Nam difficile foret,
F.237 pro singulis negotiis que solent in / curia regis accidere
omnes magnates totius regni congregare.

ᵃ per MS
ᵇ communicantes MS
[1] The terms of peace were agreed to on 9 August (*Foed.* ii.370; *Parl.
Writs*, II.i.184, 185; 123) *Rot. Parl.* I.453. Our author omits the Lancastrian banneret.

disgracefully lost and the town of Norham was on the point of being lost unless help was brought to the besieged, who could not hold out beyond Michaelmas; considering, too, the enormous expenses he incurred against the earl, asked that, all ill-feeling laid aside, the earl should go to a place of his own choosing, where a friendly agreement might be made about everything done in his name; moreover all those against whom the earl said that he had any complaint, should make satisfaction at the earl's discretion, and for this should offer sureties, caution-money, or pledges; and so at the instance of the queen, the Earl of Hereford, and other nobles whom the Earl of Lancaster accounted faithful to him, this was achieved.

So the lord king and the earl met and conversed long and intimately, with renewed friendship and mutual goodwill, and to signalise the pact they ate together on that same day. Roger D'Amory and the rest, except Hugh Despenser and the Earl Warenne, humbly presenting themselves before the earl, were received into his grace.[1] Moreover, because it had been carefully expressed in the Ordinances that the lord king should alienate nothing, and should not initiate anything important or difficult without the assent of the earls and barons and that assent solemnly expressed in common parliament, it was provided that twelve of the more discreet men of the whole realm should be elected, of whom four should be bishops, four earls, and four barons, and of these three at least should always accompany the king, in case anything difficult should arise in the king's court when the authority of these twelve would at once expedite it. For it would be difficult, in individual cases which occur from time to time in the king's court, to bring together all the magnates of the whole realm.

Nabugodonosor ille potentissimus rex Assiriorum ante annum regni sui xii^um nichil egisse legitur memorandum, quod anno uero regni sui xii° cœpit florere et gentes et regna sibi subicere. Arphaxat regem Medorum in bello deuicit, et de multis regnis unam monarchiam potenter effecit. Nec etiam rex noster Edwardus, qui xi. annis regnauit et amplius, aliquid egit quod predicari debeat in foro uel in tectis. Vtinam ad exemplum regis Nabugodonosor hostes suos nunc saltem niteretur inuadere, ut dampna et obprobria que diu sustinuit posset resarcire. Spes magna hiis diebus nobis accreuit eo quod Deus in multis prosperis regem et populum exhillarauit. In primis regi et populo Anglorum feliciter contigit quod dominus papa, cuius est dissensiones sedare, Scotis et eorum ducibus treugas biennales indixit, ut interim uiam concordie et formam pacis excogitaret. Sed Robertus de Brutz spretis^a mandatis apostolicis regem Anglie multipliciter infestauit. Visum est itaque domino pape transgressoribus pœnam infligere, et post monita censuram adicere. Igitur Robertum de Brutz et suos sequaces anathematizauit, et terram Scotorum interdicto supposuit,[1] ita ut nullus nisi ianuis clausis, interdictis et excommunicatis exclusis, diuina celebraret. Cuius efficacie fuerat interdictum dignatus est Deus ostendere ad oculum. Nam dum quadam die Robertus de Brutz peteret sibi missam celebrari, capellanus pretextu interdicti nitebatur excusari; sed iussum tiranni preualuit, et capellanus, nimio^b timore coactus, ad altare diuina

---

^a spectis MS (possibly for 'despectis')
^b nimio] non uno MS
[1] 3 September 1318 (*Foed. II*, 362, 408)

The famous Nebuchadnezzar, most powerful king of Assyria, before the twelfth year of his reign did, we are told, nothing memorable, but in that twelfth year he began to flourish and the nations and kingdoms to bow down to him. He conquered Arphaxat King of the Medes, and out of many kingdoms constructed one powerful monarchy. Neither has our King Edward who has reigned eleven years and more, done anything that ought to be preached in the market place or upon the house-tops. Would that, following the example of Nebuchadnezzar, he would now at least try to attack his enemies, so that he might repair the damage and disgrace which he has borne so long. Great hope has latterly grown up in us, because God has gladdened king and people with manifold signs of prosperity. In the first place, it turned out happily for the English people and their king that the lord pope, whose business it is to allay quarrels, imposed upon the Scots and their leaders a two-years' truce, that in the meanwhile he might devise a way of harmony and a form of peace. But Robert Bruce spurned the apostolic mandates and time and again attacked the King of England. So it seemed good to the lord pope to inflict a penalty on the transgressors, and after warnings to add censure. He therefore anathematised Robert Bruce and his followers, and placed the land of the Scots under an interdict,[1] so that no one except behind closed doors, interdicted and excommunicate persons excluded, could celebrate the holy offices. God deigned to make manifest the efficacy of this interdict. For when one day Robert Bruce asked for Mass to be celebrated for himself, the chaplain sought to be excused by reason of the interdict; but the tyrant's order prevailed, and the chaplain, overwhelmed with

celebraturus accessit. Cum autem sacerdos missam usque ad eleuationem Corporis Domini rite peregisset, sacerdos, sicut mos est, hostiam nitebatur erigere, et F.238 columba desuper ueniens manifeste cunctis / apparuit et hostiam de manu sacerdotis ereptam cunctis uidentibus asportauit. Quid aliud pretendere potest huiuscemodi uisio, nisi quod presentes ibidem indigni erant sacramento? Et hoc quidem acceptabile nobis et gratum, dum scimus hostem nostrum a Deo reprobatum, eo quod non seruauit interdictum.

Secundo dedit nobis Deus uictoriam super inimicos nostros in Hibernia. Edwardus de Brutz et sui milites, qui iam per biennium dominium ibidem usurparunt, uenientes uersus Dondalk ut uillam caperent, exercitum nostrum obuiam habuerunt; sed inito conflictu cecidit Edwardus et quingenti cum eo ualentes armati ipsa die coram nostris.[1]

[Tertio, cessauit] sterilitas illa que diu nos afflixit, et habundantia omni[um] bonorum terram Anglorum multipliciter fœcundauit. Modius tritici, qui anno preterito pro xl. denariis uendebatur, hodie pro sex denariis emptori libenter offertur. Sic olim tamdiu obsessa Samaria, ut mater filii carnibus uesceretur pro penuria uictualium, recuperauit diuina gratia. Nam caput asini, quod octoginta aureis pridie uendebatur, omnibus inmundum in crastino reputatum erat, et modius simile pro statere uno uenundatus, sicut predixerat uir Dei Heliseus.[2]

Quarto, factus est unanimis rex noster cum baronibus suis. Nam nugis postpositis[a] consilia baronum ascultat, nec est qui regem ad malum instigat amplius, quia

---

[a] prepositis MS
[1] 14 October 1318
[2] 2 Kings vi. 25; vii. 16

fear, approached the altar to celebrate Mass. But
when the priest had duly performed the office as far
as the elevation of the Body of our Lord, the priest as
usual, attempted to elevate the Host, and a dove
coming down from above clearly appeared to all,
and plucking the Host from the priest's hand carried
it off in the sight of everyone. What else can such a
vision portend, except that those present were unworthy
of the sacrament? This indeed was acceptable and
grateful to us, for we knew that our enemy had been
rebuked by God because he had not observed the
interdict.

Secondly, God gave us the victory over our enemies
in Ireland. Edward Bruce and his knights, who had
for two years usurped power there, approaching Dundalk
to take the town, came up against our army; but when
battle was joined Edward and five hundred stout
men-at-arms fell that day before us.[1]

Thirdly, the dearth that had so long plagued us
ceased, and England became fruitful with a manifold
abundance of good things. A measure of wheat,
which the year before was sold for forty pence, was
now freely offered to the buyer for sixpence. Thus it
once happened when Samaria was besieged for so
long that for lack of food a mother fed upon the flesh
of her son, that the land recovered through divine
grace. For an ass's head, which had one day sold
for eighty pieces of gold, was on the morrow held
unclean by all, and a measure of fine flour was sold
for a shekel, according to the word of the man of God
Elisha.[2]

Fourthly, the king is reconciled with his barons.
For putting aside trifles, he listens to their advice,
and now there is none to incite the king to do evil,

priuata familia que baronibus erat contraria hodie recessit ab aula.　Hiis igitur omnibus per gratiam Dei
concurrentibus, non est timendum nobis ab inimicis
nostris, sicut scriptum est ad Romanos, 'si Deus nobis-
cum, quis contra nos?'[1]

Habita concordia inter dominum regem et comitem
Lancastrie, bonum uisum est magnatibus concordiam /
F.239 et unitatem in populo facere, iniurias ulcisci et regnum
innouare.　Tunc assignati sunt et destinati ad quemlibet
comitatum uiri discreti et bone opinionis, ad audiendum
et terminandum querelas subditorum.[2]　Ministrales enim
regii auctoritate publice potestatis concutiebant simpli-
ces, spoliarunt innocentes, ut nemo negotium suum
consummaret, nisi huiusmodi officialium manum im-
pleret.　Amoti sunt omnes tales ab officio ut liberius
procederet inquisitio.[3]　Insuper ordinatum est ut conuicti[a] lesis in duplo satisfacerent, et ad officium nunquam
redirent.

Hec ordinatio terruit multos, et ad satisfaciendum induxit nondum conuictos.　Reuera de officialibus domini
regis ueraciter hoc possumus dicere, quia a minimo
usque ad maximum omnes student auaritie; a summo
iustitiario usque ad minimum pedaneum[4] iudicem,
nullus recusat accipere.　Porro, licet aliqui non exigant
uel extorqueant offerendum, nullus tamen eorum respuit
oblatum.　Verumtamen quod offertur ex gratia licenter
recipi potest, sed cum mensura; quia a nemine accipere
est ualde inhumanum, sed passim et indifferenter, tur-
pissimum.　Oporteret certe dominum regem; a maioribus
sumitur enim exemplum, et a capite diriuatur omnis

---

[a] comiti MS
[1] Rom. viii. 31　　　　[2] December 1318　　　　[3] cf. *Bridl.* 56
[4] Literally 'foot-high', so-called because they had only a low seat and
no tribunal.　They tried only trifling cases and are alluded to more than
once in the *Digest.*

because his private following which was hostile to the barons has left the court. With all these things in our favour, by the grace of God we need not fear our enemies, as it is written in the Epistle to the Romans, 'If God be for us, who can be against us?'[1]

When peace had been made between the king and the Earl of Lancaster, it seemed good to the magnates to promote peace and unity among the people, to avenge wrongs and set the kingdom on its feet. Discreet men of good reputation were assigned and appointed to each county, to hear and determine the complaints of the people.[2] For the king's servants with the authority of the state robbed the simple, and despoiled the innocent, so that no one could finish his business without greasing the official palm. All such men were removed from office that the inquest might proceed more freely.[3] Furthermore, it was decreed that those found guilty should pay the injured party double, and never be readmitted to office.

This decree terrified many and persuaded those not yet convicted to make satisfaction. Indeed, it can truly be said of the king's officials, that from the lowest to the highest they are all filled with avarice; from the Lord Chief Justice to the least petty judge[4] no one refuses a bribe. Further, though some may not demand or extort money, none of them has scorned what is offered. Yet what is freely offered may properly be received, but in due measure; for to receive from no one is scarcely human, but to do so indiscriminately is most disgraceful. Certainly [this standard] should be necessary for the king; men take example by those greater than themselves and from the head is derived all evil. Thus our famous king, Edward I, most experienced of kings, for certain crimes and

malitia. Sic ille regum prudentissimus rex noster Edwardus proximus Thomam de Weilonde capitalem
iustitiarium, propter quasdam transgressiones et oppres-
siones subditorum, omni honore, beneficio et dignitate
priuauit, et capitali pœne uel carceri perpetuo addictus
fuisset, nisi ad ordinem Minorum citius conuolasset.[a]
Sed nec corda Minorum eidem prestabat confugium,
quin idem Thomas nudatus pedes et caput subiret
exilium. Eodem tempore multi et magni uiri inter
potestates domini regis precipui, de turpibus sceleribus
F.240 conuicti, cum / magna iactura et ignominia ab officio et
dignitate repulsi sunt. Inter quos quidam clericus,[1] inter
officiales regis non minimus, de tirannide quam exercuit
ab ipsis specialibus domini regis accusatus et conuictus,
omni feodo laicali quod in regno possidebat est priuatus.
Insuper in auro et argento et uaria suppellectili ad
ualorem xxx[ta] milium marcarum perdidit, que manus
regia, utpote de bonis regis collecta, sibi confiscauit.
O quanta cura in hiis adunandis prius impendidit, et
uno die uel uno momento ualefecit! O fallax rerum copia
que, cum possessorem suum felicem facere deberet, in-
felicissimum reddit, que nec eum dormire nec saltem
unam horam in gaudio consummare permittit. Nam
sollicitudines et uigilie inimici sunt nature. Hoc est quod
Ecclesiastes deplorando conqueritur[2]; 'Vide,' inquit,
'quod est sub sole et quidem[b] frequens apud homines;
uir cui dedit [Deus] diuitias, substantiam et honorem,
et nichil deest anime eius ex omnibus que desiderat; nec
tribuit ei Deus potestatem [ut] ex eo comedat, sed homo
extraneus deuorabat illud.' Deinde addit Ecclesiastes

[a] conualescet MS
[b] quidem] qui deus MS
[1] Adam de Stratton, Deputy Chamberlain of the Exchequer, a famous
usurer for whom see N. Denholm-Young, *Seignorial Administration in England*
77-85. The sum stated is approximately correct, also the fact that lay fees
were confiscated.

oppressions done to the people deprived Thomas
de Weyland, the chief justice, of every honour, benefice
and dignity, and he would have been condemned to
death or life imprisonment, if he had not taken refuge
quickly with the Franciscans. But even the cord of
the Franciscans did not protect the same Thomas
from going into exile with bared head and feet. At
the same time many great men amongst the king's
high officials, found guilty of disgraceful crimes, were
driven from office and honour to their great loss and
disgrace. Amongst them was a certain clerk,[1] not
the least of the king's officials, who was accused and
found guilty by those same special clerks of the lord
king of tyrannous behaviour, and was deprived of all
the lay fees that he possessed in the kingdom. Moreover
he lost gold and silver and other moveables to the
value of 30,000 marks, which the crown confiscated
for itself as these had been amassed from the king's
goods. Think of the trouble he had taken to gather
all this wealth together, only to lose it all in a day,
in a moment! Oh! How deceptive is material prosperity, which ought to render its possessor happy,
yet makes him most unhappy, keeps him sleepless,
and leaves him not even one joyful hour. For anxiety
and sleeplessness are the enemies of nature. It is this
that the Preacher deplores in his lament[2]: 'See', he
says, 'what is under the sun, and indeed common
among men; a man to whom God hath given riches,
wealth, and honour, so that he wanteth nothing for
his soul of all that he desireth; yet God giveth him not
power to eat thereof, but a stranger eateth it.' Then
the Preacher adds, giving an instance, saying that

---

[2] cf. Eccles. vi. 1-4

et diffinit de talibus, dicens quod 'melior illo est abor-
tivus. Frustra enim uenit, et pergit ad tenebras, et
obliuioni dabitur nomen eius.'

Inter comitem Lancastrie et comitem de Warenna
facta est concordia per excambium quarundam terrarum,[a] quas autem comes imperpetuum possidebit hereditate. Iacturam fecit ut euitaret maius periculum, quia
de duobus malis minus malum est eligendum. Sic comes
Lancastrie aduersarios suos ad satisfactionem reduxit
caute; sed Hugonem Despenser adhuc pro libito superare
non potuit. Hugo semper et caute querit subterfugia ut
redimat tempus et euitet pericula. Nam secundum
F.241 relatum aliquorum iam adiuit / Sanctum Jacobum, quia
timuit uenire ad parliamentum.

Post Pascha conuenerunt omnes magnates terre cum
domino rege apud Eboracum,[1] et consilio facto consen-
serunt unanimiter in festo Sancte Marie Magdalene
omnes apud Nouum Castrum cum armis conuenire, et
extunc quod ad expeditionem belli pertinet, Deo dante,
feliciter inchoare. Concesserunt etiam proceres domino
regi in subsidium guerre sue xviii[um] denarium totius
Anglie.[2]

Hiis ita dispositis[b] misit dominus rex nuntios in
Scotiam qui regnum peterent, pacem offerrent, et Roberto de Brutz uitam et membra sic salua permitterent.
Sic enim decet regem facere, et pace repulsa hostes im-
petere. Sic etiam habuerunt filii Israelis in preceptis,
ut, cum ciuitatem aliquam expungnarent, pacem prius
offerrent, qua non admissa ad pungnationem citanter
rite procederent.[3] Sic Greci post raptum Helene leguntur
Troianis pacem optulisse. Sic potens ille Nabugodo-

[a] Something seems wanting here.   [b] depositis MS
[1] 6-25 May 1319 (*Parl. Writs*, II.i.197, 210)
[2] cf. *Bridl.* 56. The boroughs gave a twelfth.
[3] cf. Deut. xx. 10-12

'an untimely birth is better than he. For he cometh
in with vanity, and departeth in darkness, and his
name shall be covered with darkness.'

An agreement was made between the Earl of
Lancaster and the Earl Warenne for the exchange of
certain estates, which the Earl [Warenne] was to
possess forever hereditarily. He cut his losses to escape
a greater danger, for of two evils the lesser is to be
preferred. Thus the Earl of Lancaster shrewdly gave
satisfaction to his enemies; but as yet he could not
overcome Hugh Despenser as he wished. Always
Hugh craftily took refuge in subterfuges to gain time
and keep out of danger. Rumour affirmed that he
had already gone to St James's (Compostella), because
he was afraid to come to parliament.

After Easter all the magnates of the land met the
lord king at York,[1] and holding council they unanimously agreed that all should muster in arms at
Newcastle on St Mary Magdalen's day, and then
auspiciously proceed to initiate, God willing, the
preparations for a campaign. The nobles also granted
to the lord king as a war-subsidy the eighteenth penny
of all England.[2]

The business thus dispatched, the lord king sent
envoys to Scotland to claim the kingdom, offer peace,
and allow safety in life and limb to Robert Bruce. It
is fitting for a king to act thus, and when peace is
refused to attack his enemies. This commandment,
too, was laid upon the children of Israel, that when
they were to besiege a city, they should first offer
peace, and if this was not accepted, they should duly
make haste to the battle.[3] Thus the Greeks after the
rape of Helen are said to have offered peace to the
Trojans. Thus the mighty Nebuchadnezzar king

nosor rex Assiriorum, antequam expungnaret exteras
nationes, petiit sub pace tributum. Respondit Robertus
de Brutz se de pace regis Anglie non multum curare;
regnum Scotie suum esse et iure hereditario et iure belli
ad se pertinere. Hiis titulis dicebat se munitum esse,
protestans se nec debere nec uelle aliquem superiorem
uel dominum terrenum agnoscere.

Termino prefixo conuenerunt rex apud Nouum
Castrum,[1] comites et barones. Aderat Thomas comes
Lancastrie, comes de Penbrok, comes de Arundel et
comes de Herford, comes de Warenna et frater domini
regis comes Marescallie. Affuit etiam Hugo Despenser,
F.242 Rogerus Dammori et Hugo Daudelye, et hii tres / uice
comitis[a] Gloucestrie; hii tres enim tres sorores duxerant
que, familie[2] iudicio, comit[at]um Gloucesterie inter se
diuiserant. Aderant etiam reliqui barones Anglie, qui
domino regi certum patrocinium tenentur conferre[3]; et
multa milia peditum similiter confluxerant; et omnes
uoluntarie, eo quod dominus rex concesserat unicuique
ad summam centum librarum sine restitutione, quantum
posset in bonis hostium occupare. Item concessit dominus rex nautis omnibus, ut scilicet a parte maris hostes
uiriliter impeterent, et de spoliis hostium quantum possent suo dominio amplicarent. Hec utique concessio in
depredationem Scotorum uoluntarios multos armauit,
quia restitutio, que post concordiam frequenter fiebat,
timenda non fuit.

Profectus inde dominus rex in Scotiam apud Berewyk
cum toto exercitu primo peruenit, et hanc primam
expungnationem de consilio fore decreuit, eo quod ultro[b]

---

[a] uices comites MS
[b] ulcio MS
[1] 22 July (*Parl. Writs*, II.i.517)
[2] For this partition of 1317 see W. H. Stevenson in *E.H.R.* xii. 756
[3] cf. p. 10 *supra*

of the Assyrians, before he attacked other nations, sought peaceful tribute. Robert Bruce replied that he did not much care for the King of England's peace; the kingdom of Scotland was his and pertained to him both by hereditary right and by right of battle. He said that he was justified by these titles, and protested that he neither ought to nor would acknowledge any superior or earthly lord.

At the term arranged the king, earls, and barons assembled at Newcastle.[1] There were present Thomas Earl of Lancaster, the Earl of Pembroke, the Earl of Arundel, and the Earl of Hereford, the Earl Warenne, and the lord king's brother, the Earl Marshal. Present, too, were Hugh Despenser, Roger Damory, and Hugh D'Audley, and these three in lieu of the Earl of Gloucester. For these three had married three sisters who by a family arrangement[2] had divided the earldom of Gloucester between themselves. The other English barons were there, too, who are bound to render a fixed service[3] to the lord king; and many thousands of infantry likewise assembled; and all these came voluntarily, because the lord king had granted to each man as much of the enemies' goods as he could seize up to the value of an hundred pounds without restitution. The lord king also granted to all the sailors, so that they should eagerly attack the enemy by sea, and add to their own possessions as much of the spoils of the enemy as they could take. This right of despoiling the Scots armed many volunteers, because restitution, frequently made after a truce, was not to be feared.

The lord king set out for Scotland and first came to Berwick with his whole army, and decided on advice that this should be the first place to be besieged, because it had renounced his authority, and in order that

recesserat ab imperio suo, et ne se ipsos exponerent
periculo dum hostes inuictos dimitterent a tergo.
Diffusus est igitur exercitus uillam in circuitu a parte
terrestri, et cœperunt contra eam munitiones et propungnacula*ᵃ* properari. A parte uero maris naute qui
presunt Quinque Portubus ita obseruabant introitus et
exitus*ᵇ* ut nulli omnino pateret egressus.

Dum hec aguntur in Scotia, nec uideretur esse
timendum ab hostibus in Anglia, Iacobus Douglas cum
suis complicibus, qui semper machinationibus fuit in-
tentus, nisi Deus et Dominus omnium nobis precauisset,
magnam iacturam et dampnum inestimabile nobis in-
tulisset. Nam iuxta consilium Achitofel decem milia
uirorum sibi eligerat,[1] et reginam Anglie, que iuxta
Eboracum morabatur, rapuisse decreuerat. / Certe si
capta fuisset tunc regina, credo quod pacem emisset sibi
Scotia. Sed dissipatum est consilium proditoris Achitofel, nec passus est tantum discrimen nobis inferri Deus
Israel.[2] Nam quadam die captus est quidam explorator
apud Eboracum; et, cum uidisset se questionibus ad-
dictum, promisit, si daretur ei pœnam euadere, totam
machinationem Scotorum reuelare; et placuit pactum
maioribus ciuitatis; erant enim ibidem archiepiscopus
Eboracensis et regis cancellarius episcopus tunc Eliensis.
Explorator ille indicauit quod inimicus noster Iacobus
Douglas clam uenturus esset cum electa manu ad partes
illas, ut uidelicet reginam abduceret et quos reperiret
inprouisos simul occiderent. 'Tali,' inquit, 'die et tali
loco latitabant, et, cum tempus acceperint ydoneum,
propositum consummabunt.' Vix erat qui dictis ad-

F.243

ᵃ Hearne leaves the MS reading in doubt between ' propugnacula '
and ' expugnacula '; but cf. F.222.
ᵇ exercitus MS
[1] 2 Sam. xvii. 1
[2] cf. 2 Sam. xvii. 14

they should not expose themselves to danger by leaving an unconquered enemy in their rear. The army was therefore disposed about the town on the landward side, and they hastened to prepare fortifications and siege-works against it. By sea the sailors in charge of the Cinque Ports fleet kept so close a watch on the entrances and exits, that no one at all could come forth.

While this was happening in Scotland, and it seemed as if there was nothing to fear from enemies in England, James Douglas and his accomplices, always ready for intrigue, would have inflicted great loss and untold damage upon us, had not God, the Lord of us all, warned us in time. For according to the advice of Ahitophel he had selected ten thousand men,[1] and proposed to carry off the Queen of England, who was staying near York. Indeed if the queen had at that time been captured, I believe that Scotland would have bought peace for herself. But the counsel of the traitor Ahitophel came to nought, and the God of Israel did not suffer so great a peril to fall upon us.[2] For one day a certain spy was captured at York; and when he saw that he would be put to the question, he promised, if he should be allowed to forego the penalty, to betray the whole conspiracy of the Scots; this pact was agreeable to the citizens. The Archbishop of York and the King's Chancellor, at that time the Bishop of Ely, were there, too. The spy then explained that our enemy James Douglas was to come to those parts secretly with his chosen band, to abduct the queen and also kill all those whom he should take unawares. 'They were lying hidden' he said, 'on such a day and in such a place, and at the appropriate moment would carry out their project.' Hardly anyone believed this story, because the lord king of

hiberet credentiam, eo quod dominus rex Anglie terras
Scotorum uastare iam inciperet, et magis uidebatur
necessarium talem exercitum proprios fines defendere
quam extra propria loca per centum miliaria pungnam
appetere.   Addidit autem explorator ille quod[a] nisi
euentus rei dictis suis fidem afferret, capitalem poenam
libenter acciperet.

Tunc exierunt de ciuitate illa archiepiscopus et cancellarius, cum communi sequela sua, uicecomes et burgenses et eorum familiares, monachi et canonici et ceteri
regulares, necnon et omnes alii qui ad arma ferenda
inuenti sunt habiles, reduxerunt reginam ad ciuitatem;
deinde per aquam reducta est apud Notyngham.   Ibi
fuit tutior locus regine, nec Iacobus timendus nec eius
insidie.

Altera autem die qua iuxta uerbum exploratoris
reperiendi erant Scoti in suis latibulis, exierunt iterum
F.244 de ciuitate Eboracensi laici, clerici et religiosi.[1] / Ibant
igitur clam et sine tumultu, ut hostes inprouisos inua-
derent, ne et ipsi premuniti fugam forsan arriperent.
Verumptamen satis erant premuniti, nec tamen in fugam
conuersi.   Nam cum homines nostros inordinate uenientes aspicerent, 'Hii,' inquiunt, 'non bellatores sed uena-
tores; non multum proficient.'   Incenderunt autem Scoti
foenum multum quod erat in loco illo congestum, et
ascendit fumus late dispersus in celum.   Fumus[b] im-
pediebat uisum nostrorum, unde et quos credebant in
fugam conuersos inuenerunt paratos ad bellum.   Erant
quippe uiri ex omni Scotia electi ad preliandum apti,
ad omnem laborem apti.   Nostri uero plures in re
militari minus instructi, ad fugandum quam ad prelian-

---

[a] qui MS
[b] fumus] fug' MS
[1] The so-called Chapter of Myton, 20 September 1319

England had already begun to lay waste the lands
of the Scots, and it appeared more necessary for such
an army (as that of Douglas) to defend its own front-
iers than to seek battle a hundred miles outside its
own territory. But the spy added that if he was not
justified by events, he would willingly submit to capital
punishment.

Then the archbishop and the chancellor went forth
from the city, with their usual retinues, the sheriff
and the burgesses and their followers, the monks and
canons and other regulars, as well as anyone also who
could handle a weapon, and brought the queen back
into the city; thence she was taken by water to Notting-
ham. That was a safer place for the queen where
neither James nor his traps were to be feared.

On the second day, on which according to the
spy the Scots would be found in their lairs, the laymen,
clerks, and men of religion issued forth again from the
city of York.[1] They went stealthily and without noise,
to take the enemy by surprise, because if they were
warned they might perhaps take flight. Nevertheless
they were well enough warned, yet they did not flee. For
when they perceived our men advancing in disorder,
they said: 'These are not soldiers but huntsmen;
they will not achieve much.' So the Scots set fire to
a large amount of hay that had been gathered there,
and the rising smoke spread far and wide. The smoke
made it difficult for our men to see, so that they found
prepared for battle those whom they thought had
fled. They were indeed men picked from the whole of
Scotland for their fighting ability, fit for every task.
Many of our men on the other hand were untrained in
the art of war, and were readier to flee than to fight.
When battle was joined many of our men were killed

dum magis intenti. Inito igitur conflictu plures ex
nostris perimuntur et multi super capiuntur; sed et
Scoti in Scotiam cum suis captiuis indempnes reuertuntur, etc.

Peruenit uerbum ad regem Anglie et ad exercitum
nostrum qui morabatur in obsidione, et statim nescio
quorum consilio derelicta est penitus obsidio. Rex enim
nitebatur obuiare Scotis fugientibus per unam semitam,
et comes Lancastrie per alteram. Scoti uero felici usi*a*
duplomate per alteram uiam reuersi sunt in regionem
suam. Sed quare derelicta est obsidio tanto opere
inchoata? Dicunt quidam quod Robertus de Brutz
habuit amicos. Certe Dauid non euasisset manus Saul
regis, si non habuisset in familiaribus amicos eius.
Inputatur comiti Lancastrie quod rex recessit de obsidione; inputatur etiam eidem quod Scoti uenerunt
rapere reginam, et quod inimici regis illesi in patriam
suam sunt reuersi. Argumenta quedam proditionis
publice proclamantur, unde comes et sui sequaces
enormiter diffamantur. Vulgariter enim dicitur quod
F.245 comes ille recepit a Roberto de Brutz / xl. milia librarum,
ut sibi et suis occulte ferret auxilium; et quod in obsidione, dum omnes expungnarent murum, nullus ex
priuatis comitis fecit insultum, et uilla de Berewyk dedita
fuisset si cautela comitis nusquam repungnasset; et
Jacobus Douglas reuertens in Scotiam per exercitum
comitis transibat, comes autem inhermis per medium
Scotorum ibat.

O comes Lancastrie, cuius sunt tante diuitie, cur
pro tanta summa pecunie perdidisti famam et nomen
constantie? Vtinam non fuisset illa pecunia pro qua
fama tua periit et creuit infamia! Magna est iactura in

a usi] uisu MS

and many more taken prisoner; but the Scots returned
unharmed to Scotland with their captives, *etc.*

Word of this came to the King of England and to our
army remaining at the siege, and at once by someone's
advice the siege was completely raised. For the king
was trying to cut off the retreating Scots by one road,
and the Earl of Lancaster by the other. But the Scots
taking a fortunate short-cut returned by another road
to their territory. Why, then, was a siege given up
that had cost so much labour to begin? Some say
that Robert Bruce had friends. Certainly David would
not have escaped the hand of King Saul had he not
had friends amongst the household. It was laid at the
Earl of Lancaster's door that the king had raised the
siege; it was also said to be his fault that the Scots
had come to seize the queen, and that the king's
enemies had returned unscathed to their own country.
Some evidence of treachery was publicly spoken of,
whereby the good fame of the earl and his followers
was seriously damaged. For it was commonly said
that the earl had received forty thousand pounds from
Robert Bruce to lend secret aid to him and his men,
and that at the siege while everyone was attacking the
wall, none of the earl's retinue assaulted it, and that
the town of Berwick would have surrendered if the
earl's caution had not fought against this, and that
James Douglas on his way back to Scotland passed
through the earl's lines, and that the earl went
through the midst of the Scots.

Oh! Earl of Lancaster, whose wealth is so great, why
for such a sum of money have you lost your reputation
and a name for constancy? Would that that money
had never been, for which your reputation died and
infamy arose! There is grave damage when reputation

fame periculo, in cuius dispendio nulla est estimatio, quia cum*a* semel lesionem patitur uix uel nunquam recuperatur. Certe, si totum thesaurum tuum in munera disperges, famam tuam pristinam nunquam reuocares. O quante laudis habebas precones dum iugiter defenderes ordinationes! Fauor populi in odium conuertitur, et fama tua in infamiam commutatur. Sic licet Joab multa fortiter gessit, proditio in Abner et Amasam omnem laudem eius denigrauit.[1]

O generose comes, cur non ad mentem reuocas genus electum,[2] regalem prosapiam tuam quam infamas? Cur non aduertis, comes egregie, quantum sit crimen scelus perfidie? Nam si facta reorum*b* diuersimode puniuntur, proditores tamen iuste*c* maxima poena plectuntur. Proprium enim proditorum est pessimum finem capere, et quis unquam talem transiuit impune? Filotas quondam pungnator strenuus sub magno Alexandro, miles egregius, quia delationem proditoris triduo suppressit, ex decreto curie sententiam proditoris accepit. Eneas et ceteri Troiani, qui urbem suam inclitam prodiderunt, F.246 post mortem Priami / exules defecti Troiam*d* reliquerunt. Veniamus ad exempla domestica. Thomas Torboruile, qui regem Anglie prodidit in Francia, nouam poenam suam pertulit postmodum in Anglia.[3] Comes de Arselles, Symon Frysel, Willelmus Waleys, non quia Scoti fuerunt sed quia proditores, sententiam proditorum acceperunt.

---

a cum] tunc MS
b eorum MS
c iniuste MS
d Troiani MS
[1] 2 Sam. iii. 27; xx. 10
[2] 1 Pet. ii. 9
[3] This seems to be the meaning, though not quite accurate historically. He was a prisoner of war in France. The sentence of twenty years previ-

is in danger, whose loss none can assess, because once injured it can scarcely ever be recovered. Indeed if you scattered all your riches in gifts, you would never recover the reputation that you had of yore. Oh! What paeans of praise you had while you were manfully upholding the Ordinances! The favour of the populace has turned to hatred, your fame to infamy has changed. Thus although Joab performed many brave deeds, his treachery towards Abner and Amasab blackened all his praise.[1]

O noble earl, why do you not recall to mind the chosen generation,[2] the royal stock which you disgrace! Why do you not take thought, distinguished earl, how great a charge is the crime of broken faith! For, though the deeds of the wicked are punished in divers ways, traitors justly suffer the extreme penalty. It is proper that traitors should undergo the worst fate, and who has ever opposed this with impunity? Long ago Philotas, a valiant warrior under Alexander the Great, a distinguished soldier, because he suppressed his denunciation of a traitor for three days, by decree of the court was sentenced as a traitor. Æneas and the other Trojans, who had betrayed their famous city, on Priam's death left Troy as disheartened exiles. Let us take examples nearer home. Thomas Turberville, who betrayed the King of England in France, afterwards received a fresh sentence in England.[3] The Count of Athol, Simon Frazer, William Wallace, were sentenced as traitors, not because they were Scots, but because they were traitors. What then are

---

ously could hardly be described as 'recent'. On Turberville see the paper of Professor J. G. Edwards in *Studies . . . presented to F. M. Powicke* (1948), 296-309.

P

Quid itaque facies, comes Lancastrie? Si uiam nefariam
proponas incedere, totus mundus insurget contra te, nec
pœnam debitam poteris euadere.   Igitur uel*a* labia
dolosa de falso conuincas, uel mala opera tua in meliora
cito conuertas.

Inter cetera uitia duo sunt diuitibus ualde incon-
uenientia, cupiditas et fallacia cupiditatis socia.   Vt quid
enim cupit qui satis habundat, ut quid fallit qui alieno
non eget?   Reuera pauperes et tenues, [qui] que necessaria sunt non habent, huiusmodi uitio laborare solent.
Nam et in iudiciis testimonium eorum solet reprobari,
eo quod presumitur tales facilius posse corrumpi.   Sed
nunc cupiditas ascensiones suas ita disposuit ut pre
ceteris uitiis ueraciter dicere possit 'ego in sublimibus
habito, et tronus meus in diuitum consortio'.[1]

Sic igitur concurrunt et stant pariter simul in unum
diues et pauper, nisi quod de paupere frequenter fit
iudicium, sed contra iniuriam diuitis non est remedium.
Heu multa mala inducit cupiditas, periurium, homicidium, et machinationes innumeras.   Hec animam
hominis uenalem facit et de periculo anime nichil curat,
dum tamen id quod concupiscit adquirit.

Maledicta cupiditas, et eius commercium, per quam
caritas abiit et fides in exilium.   Ecce comites et ceteri
magnates terre, qui de patrimonio suo satis possent
decenter uiuere, iam totum tempus suum computant pro
F.247   nichilo, nisi patrimonium augeant in duplo / uel in
triplo; unde uicinos pauperes ad uenditionem pater-
narum rerum studiose sollicitant, et quos sic inducere

a uel] ut MS
[1] A parody on Ecclesiasticus xxiv. 7.   The whole of these long specula-
tions are intended to have 'rhythmical cadence and rhymed endings', i.e.
they are 'tirades'.   For this type of prose in general see K. Polheim, *Lateinische
Reimprosa* (1925).

you doing, Earl of Lancaster? If you intend to pursue a path of crime, the whole world will rise against you, nor will you be able to escape condign punishment. Therefore you must either convict of falsehood the guileful lips [of rumour], or quickly rectify your evil deeds.

Two vices amongst others are most unbecoming to the rich, avarice and the falsity that accompanies it. For what does he covet who has already overmuch, why does he resort to trickery who does not need another's goods? Indeed, the poor and needy, who have not the necessaries of life, commonly indulge in this vice. In judicial decisions their testimony is often rejected, because it is a presumption that such people are somewhat open to corruption. But now avarice has so arranged its means of ascent that beyond other vices it may truly say: 'I dwell in high places, and my throne is set in the company of the rich.'[1]

Thus rich and poor meet and stand equally side by side together, save only that judgment is frequently obtained against the poor, but there is no remedy against the evil-doing of the rich. Avarice is, alas, the source of many evils—perjury, homicide, and innumerable conspiracies. Thus does man offer up his soul for sale and for the peril of it takes no heed, so long as he obtains what he covets.

Cursed be avarice, and its dealings, through which charity has departed and faith is exiled. Observe how the earls and other magnates of the land, who could live according to their station on their inheritance, regard all their time as wasted, unless they double or treble their patrimony; wherefore they pester their poorer neighbours to sell what they have inherited, and those who will not be persuaded they plague in

non possunt multipliciter infestant, donec angustiati pro
modico forsan offerant, quod pro magno prius uendidisse
potuerant.   Et, quia res concordat materie, factum
quoddam libet*a* apponere.

Erat quidam miles uir simplex et multe innocentie
sicut ex quodam eius actu consueto potest apparere.
Nam cum seruos suos ex decreto balliui contingeret
quandoque pro transgressione facta puniri, solebat miles
ille apud balliuum pro seruis intercedere, et pœnam in-
flictam frequenter remittere.   Dicebat se ex rapinis et
spoliis nolle uiuere; magnum erat opus hoc misericordie.
Reliquit post se filios bene ualentes quorum conuersatio
placens erat apud Dominum et homines.   Venit autem
magnus quidam et potens filius diaboli, minister Sathane,
et pueros expulit a paterna hereditate.   Illi uero non
audentes querelam instituere, coacti sunt pro iure suo
modicum accipere.

Sed cum prouidentia Dei regatur mundus, ut credi-
mus, cur subcumbit innocens et floretim pius, cur non
est sumpta uindicta de nocentibus?   Sane hec uetus
querela magnos et sanctos*b* afflixit, sed et regis Dauid
animum quandoque concussit.   Cum enim rex ille propheta pressuras iustorum cerneret, et iniquos ad omnes
uite huius illecebras licentius euagari conspiceret, que-
rebat si utique esset fructus iustorum, et esset Deus
iudicans iniquos in terra.   'Mei,' inquit, 'pene moti
sunt pedes, pene effusi sunt gressus mei, quia zelaui
super iniquos, pacem peccatorum uidens.   In labore
hominum non sunt, et cum hominibus non flagellantur.

---

a quoddam libet] quod ubilibet MS
b Sanctos] Sanctos querelam MS

many ways, until they are so straitened that they perhaps offer for a song what they could earlier have sold for a good price. And since it is relevant to my theme, I am disposed to append an example.

There was a certain knight, a simple man of great innocence, as appears from a habit of his. For when it happened that by order of his bailiff his servants were punished for some misdeed, the knight used to plead with the bailiff on behalf of his servants, and often remitted the decreed penalty. He used to say that he did not wish to live on spoil and rapine. This was a great work of mercy. He left behind him flourishing sons whose way of life was pleasing to God and man. But there came a certain great and powerful son of the devil, a minister of Satan, and expelled the children from their paternal inheritance. They not daring to lodge a complaint, were forced to accept a pittance for what was theirs by law.

But since the world is ruled by the providence of God, as we believe, why is the innocent submerged and why does the wicked flourish, why is not vengeance taken of evildoers? Truly, this old complaint has troubled great men and saints, and even at times disturbed the mind of King David. For when that prophet-king perceived the oppression of the righteous, and observed the wicked turning aside unrestrainedly after all the allurements of this life, he asked if this was the reward of the just, and if God judged the wicked upon earth. 'But as for me', he said, 'my feet were almost gone, my steps had well nigh slipped. For I was envious of the foolish, when I saw the prosperity of the wicked. They are not in trouble as other men, neither are they plagued like other men. Therefore pride compasseth them about as a chain; behold these

Ideo tenuit eos superbia; ecce ipsi peccatores habun-
dantes in seculo optinuerunt diuitias.   Et dixi, ergo sine
causa iustificaui cor meum et laui inter innocentes manus
F.248 meas, et fui flagel/latus tota die.'¹   Tandem ad occulta
Dei iudicia descendens nodum questionis enucleat dicens;
'uerumptamen propter dolos posuisti eis, deiecisti eos
dum alleuarentur. Quomodo facti sunt in desolationem,
subito defecerunt, perierunt propter iniquitatem suam.'²
Manifeste igitur insinuat, qualiter diuitie fallaces et proditorie amatores suos decipiunt, et quos dolose erigunt
cum dolore prosternunt.   Beatus igitur Job in dolore et
afflictione positus eandem querelam mouet, et postea
diuine dispensationis iustitiam assignat: 'Quare impii
uiuunt, subleuati sunt et confortati diuitiis?   Semen
eorum permanet coram eis, domus eorum secure sunt et
pacate, et non est uirga Dei super eos'³; et cetera prosequitur in hunc modum.   Nunc diuine dispensationis
iudicium: 'Ducunt in bonis dies suos, et in puncto ad
inferna descendunt.'⁴   Ecce quomodo exaltati sunt sicut
cedrus Libani, et deiecit eos consilium Altissimi. Diuitie
date sunt eis in laqueum, delicie et uoluptates in cap-
turam. Super hac re similiter disputat Ieremias; 'Quare,'
inquit, 'uia impiorum prosperatur, bene est omnibus
qui male agunt et preuaricantur? Plantasti eos, radices
miserunt, proficiunt et faciunt fructum.'⁵   Et tandem
suam mittit sententiam: 'Congregabuntur,' inquit, 'in
die occisionis quasi greges ad uictimam.'⁶ Quidam etiam
poeta, dum de prosperitate impiorumᵃ conqueritur simile

ᵃ imperiorum MS
¹ cf. Ps. lxxiii (Vulgate Ps. lxxii), 2, 3, 5, 6, 12, 13
² cf. Ps. lxxiii (Vulgate Ps. lxxii), 18, 19
³ Job xxi. 7-9
⁴ Job xxi. 13
⁵ Jer. xii. 1, 2
⁶ Jer. xii. 3

are the ungodly who prosper in the world, they increase
in riches. (And I said,) Verily I have cleansed my
heart in vain, and washed my hands in innocency,
for all the day long have I been plagued.'[1]　Proceeding
at length to the secret judgments of God, he reaches
the heart of the question, saying: 'Surely thou hast
set snares for them, thou hast cast them down while
they prospered. How are they brought to desolation,
they have failed as in a moment, they have perished for
their unrighteousness.'[2]　He clearly implies how specious
and deceptive riches deceive those who pursue them,
and those whom they raise up by guile they cast down
in sorrow. The blessed Job, set in grief and affliction,
raises the same complaint, and later admits the justice
of the divine dispensation: 'Wherefore do the wicked
live, are raised up and comforted with riches? Their
seed is established before their eyes, their houses are
safe from care and peaceful; neither is the rod of God
upon them',[3] and thus he elaborates his theme. Now
this is the judgment of the divine dispensation: 'They
spend their days in wealth and in a moment go down
to the grave.'[4]　Behold how they are exalted as the
cedar of Lebanon, and the counsel of the Most High
has cast them down. Their riches are given to them for
a snare; delights and pleasures serve for their capture.
On this matter Jeremiah argues in like manner:
'Wherefore', he says, 'doth the way of the wicked
prosper, wherefore is it good for all who do evil and
utter falsehoods? Thou hast planted them, yea, they
have taken root; they grow, yea, they bring forth
fruit'.[5]　And at length he gives his opinion: 'They
shall be gathered together on the day of slaughter
like sheep for the killing.'[6]　Also a certain poet, complaining of the prosperity of the wicked, passes a

iudicium prosequitur. Ait enim, 'Tolluntur in altum, ut lapsu grauiore ruant.'[1] Ecce Dauid et Iob, Ieremias et poeta, eandem instituunt querelam, quorum similia sunt iudicia et in unum consona dicta. Certe 'quia non profertur cito contra malos sententia, absque ullo timore filii hominum perpetrant*[a]* mala'.[2] Nunc autem due semite nobis exponuntur, una uite, altera interitus, et utriusque

F.249 noti/tiam habemus. Qui ergo salutis sue tam prodigus extiterit ut relicta semita uite uiam interitus maluerit incedere, sibi imputare debet qui potuit eligere.

Audiens autem comes Lancastrie sic nomen suum diffamatum in populo, et quod publica uox et fama testimonium perhiberet de malo, accessit ad regem et dixit, 'Scitis, domine, quod fueram cum omni retentione mea uobiscum in Scotia, et quod non modicos sumptus ibidem fecerim pro uilla de Berewyk recuperanda. Sed nunc imputatur per totum regnum quod res non successit nobis ad uotum. Ego autem ora hominum obturare non possum, uerumptamen ad arbitrium boni uiri, et, si necesse fuerit, in ferro candenti*[b]* offero me purgaturum, uel, si appareat accusator et uelit se inscribere, offero me legitime innocentiam meam ostendere.' Et uidebatur oblatio comitis iusta, eo quod sola fama laborabat, nec erat transgressio manifesta. Admissa est igitur purgatio comitis cum qua[dam][3] manu parium. Sic spina in lilium, rubigo in ferrum, et scoria redit in aurum, et cetera.

Post hec exegit nouus rex Francie[4] a rege Anglie

---

a impetrant MS
b in ferro candenti] insero cadenti MS
[1] Claudian *in Ruf.* i. 22
[2] cf. Eccles. viii. 11
[3] *quadam.* 'Hearne's reading for the *qua* of his MS, possibly it is *quarta* or *quinta*,' i.e. with four or five oath-helpers.
[4] Philip V, who seized the crown on the death of his brother Louis X (5 June 1316).

similar judgment.   For he says, 'They are raised up
on high that their fall may be the greater.'¹ Behold
David and Job, Jeremiah and the poet setting up the
same plea, whose judgments are alike and whose words
are in harmony.   Indeed 'because sentence against
evil men is not executed speedily, the sons of men are
fearless to do evil'.² And now two paths are open to
us, the one of life, the other of destruction; and of each
we are informed. He therefore who remains so prodigal
of his safety that abandoning the path of life he prefers
rather to follow the way of destruction, must blame
himself, for he has had his choice.

The Earl of Lancaster hearing that his name was
thus defamed amongst the people, and that public
opinion and rumour testified against his wrongdoing,
approached the king and said, 'You know, my lord,
that I was with you in Scotland with my whole retinue,
and that I there was put to no little expense in recovering the town of Berwick. But now it is laid upon
us by the whole realm that the matter did not fall
out for us as we had wished. I cannot stop up the
mouths of men, but I offer to clear myself either by the
decision of a good man, or, if it be necessary, by the
white-hot iron, or if an accuser shall appear and wish
to put himself on record, I offer to show my innocence
by legal process.' The earl's offer seemed a fair one,
because only rumours had been brought against him;
there was no evident crime.   The earl was therefore
allowed to purge himself with the help of his peers.³
Thus the thorn turns into a lily, rust into iron, and dross
into gold, *etc.*

After this the new King of France⁴ demanded
homage from the King of England for the land of
Gascony; and because this kind of service could only

homagium pro terra Vasconie; et, quia huiusmodi seruitium non nisi personaliter prestari potuit, rex de consilio suo treugas biennales cum Scotis iniit,[1] et sic in
breui transfretare disposuit. Displicuerunt treuge quibus-
cumque proceribus eo quod status domini regis uideretur
in hoc ualde minoratus. Sane probabiliter sentirent si
onus quod regi incumbit caute declinarent. Sed nec
lex nec ratio turpiter fieri presumit quod necessitas
ineuitabilis introducit. Legitur quod in obsidionem
Troianam omnes fere mundi principes conuenerant;
F.250 isti quidem exterioribus, illi uero ad / auxilium pre-
standum obsessis. Sed nec hii nec isti erubescebant
inducias petere cum oporteret morticina comburere.
Porro non iniit rex treugas tantum quia transfretaturus
erat, sed ut eo pacto ab infestatione suorum gens Scotorum desisteret, quos tempore hiemali precipue uastare
consueuerat. Solebat enim rex annis preteritis per totam
hiemem munire Marchiam custodibus,[2] sed magis
nocebat populo oppressio custodum quam[a] persecutio
inimicorum. Scoti namque pro modico tributo Northamhimbrorum incolis ad tempus parcebant, sed hii qui ad
tutelam prepositi uidebantur cotidiane exactioni iugiter
uacabant. Preterea non potuit rex simul transfretare et
exercitum ad bellum conducere: erat enim transfretaturus post Pascha, quando solent reges preparare con-
ductum ad bella.

Vocauit igitur dominus rex barones suos apud
Eboracum[3] ut de statu regni disponerent ante recessum

---

[a] custodum quam] custodium quamque MS

[1] 21 December 1319. It is impossible to be certain if *de consilio suo*
means more than 'by advice'.

[2] Wardens of the March, now appointed as conservators of the truce
(*Foed.* 412, 416). Ramsay, 110, is in error in regarding this as their first
appearance. See R. R. Reid 'The Office of Warden of the Marches; its
Origin and Early History' in *E.H.R.* xxxii (1917) 479-96.

[3] 20 January 1320

be performed in person, king and council[1] entered
upon a two years' truce with the Scots, and so arranged
to cross the channel in the near future. The truce
annoyed certain nobles because the estate of the lord
king seemed to be much diminished by it. Their
opinion would assuredly have been right if they could
have cautiously refused the burden that lay upon the
king. But neither law nor reason assumes that to
be disgraceful which fate decrees. We read that at
the siege of Troy almost all the princes of the world
assembled; some to help the besiegers, others the
besieged. But neither the latter nor the former were
ashamed to ask for a truce when it was necessary to
burn their dead. Further, the king did not make the
truce so much because he was about to go overseas,
as because when it was made the Scots would desist
from attacking his people, whom they used to plunder
especially in winter. In past years the king had been
in the habit of strengthening the March with wardens[2]
throughout the winter, but their oppression was more
injurious to the people than the persecution of their
enemies. For the Scots used to spare the inhabitants
of Northumbria for a time in return for a moderate
tribute, but those who were supposed to be set over
them for their protection were constantly at leisure to
oppress them every day. Moreover the king could
not cross the channel and at the same time get together
an army for war: he was to go overseas after Easter
when kings are accustomed to prepare their troops
for battle.

The lord king therefore summoned his barons to
York[3] to make arrangements about the state of the
realm before his departure. The Earl of Lancaster,
as frequently happened, was summoned but did not come.

suum. Comes autem Lancastrie, sicut pluries, uocatus non uenit. Non enim decebat habere parliamentum in cameris, ut dixit. Habebat namque regem et collaterales suos sibi suspectos, et ipsos non iam clam sed manifeste protestabatur inimicos suos. Sed nonne iam dudum erat omnis controuersia et discordia sedata? Reuera sic uidebatur pluribus fuisse res gesta. Verum suspecta est pax inter magnates, ad quam non amore sed ui sublimes ueniunt potestates. Dominus rex apud Berewyke cum firmata fuisset obsidio, et uidebatur res expedienda pro nichilo, huiusmodi uerba protulisse fertur: 'Cum iniquus*a* transierit iste tumultus, ad alia negotia manus conuertemus. Nondum enim nobis excedit a memoria*b* fratri meo Petro illata quondam iniuria'; et

F.251   hoc quidem uerbum comitem non latuit: unde nimi/rum de re apud Berewyk segnius intromisit, uel, si dicere fas sit, ipsam expeditionem forsan impediuit. Sic Achilles iratus commilitonibus Grecorum fertur nocuisse, et ab armis suis diu propter uotum abstinuisse. Non uitupero comitem si sibi precaueat, nec tamen laudo si fidem infringat.

Igitur quinto sextoue die ante Natiuitatem Sancti Iohannis Baptiste transfretauit dominus rex in Franciam,[1] quem Deus pro sua pietate saluo custodiat et saluo reducat in Angliam. Precesserant autem regem frater eius Edmundus, Bartholomeus Badesmere, et quidam alii pro quibusdam negotiis domini regis ad curiam Romanam profecturi. Eo tempore uacabat in Anglia sedes episcopalis Lyncolniensis, sed canonici ante recessum regis optenta licentia unanimiter consentiebant de electione pastoris, qui quidem, magister Antonius de Bek

---

a iniqua MS   *b* ad memoriam MS

[1] The King sailed on 19 June and returned 22 July. On the discussions at Amiens see the text printed by Miss E. Pole Stuart in *E.H.R.* xli (1926) 412-415.

He stated that it was improper to hold parliament in a closet. For he regarded the king and his supporters as suspect, and without any secrecy he openly protested that they were his enemies. But had not all controversy and discord been settled a while ago? Indeed many thought that this had been done. But peace between magnates is to be regarded with suspicion when the eminent princes have arrived at it not through love but by force. When siege had been laid to Berwick and it seemed that the matter was being pursued to no purpose, the lord king is said to have uttered some such words as these: 'When this wretched business is over, we will turn our hands to other matters. For I have not yet forgotten the wrong that was done to my brother Piers'; and this remark did not escape the earl: whence he was not at all active at Berwick, indeed, if the truth be told, he perhaps hindered that expedition. Thus Achilles in wrath is said to have brought injury upon his fellow Greeks, and to have abstained long from the use of arms for a vow. I do not condemn the earl if he is consulting his own interests, nor do I praise him if he breaks faith.

On the fifth or sixth day before the Nativity of St John the Baptist the lord king crossed to France,[1] and may God in His mercy keep him in safety and bring him safely home again. His brother Edmund, Bartholomew Badlesmere, and some others who were going on the lord king's business to the court of Rome, had preceded the king. At that time the episcopal see of Lincoln was vacant in England, but before the king's departure the canons had obtained their licence and unanimously voted for the election of a pastor, named Mr Anthony Bek, a man worthy and well born and master of theology, well fitted for the church of

nominatus, fuit generosus et morigeratus, et magister
erat theologie,[a] ecclesie Lyncolniensi satis ydoneus, illius
egregii Antonii de Bek quondam Dunelmensis episcopi
et patriarche Ierosolimitani consanguineus. Habebat
dictus Bartholomeus nepotem[1] qui pro etate industris
erat. Nondum enim xxv. annos attigerat. Procurante
itaque Bartholomeo inductus est rex Anglie supplicare
domino pape pro iuuene, ut ad dictam sedem episco-
palem dignaretur eum assumere. Rogabat et rex
Francie, et Edmundus frater regis[b] Anglie, et laudabant
iuuenem omnes, personam ipsius apud dominum papam
multipliciter recommendantes. Sic igitur dominus papa,
tot et tantorum precibus sollicitatus, priorem electionem
cassauit, et iuuenem illum ecclesie Lyncolniensi prefecit.

Mirabile quidem factum, quia contra legem et ratio-
F.252 nem[c] actum: / nec uisum nec prius auditum ut tam
iuuenis preficeretur in episcopum: contra legem, cum
nemo citra xxx[ta] annos de iure cathedram pastoralem
possit ascendere, contra rationem quia nemo iuuenes
eligit duces, eo quod non constat eos esse prudentes.
Nam et Salomon incertissimum reputat inter omnia
incerta uiam adolescentis[2] in iuuentute sua. Siquidem
admiranda seculo et ridiculosa presumptio, dum iuuenis
pastorali locatur in solio. Iuuenem contingit ad regnum
sublimari, sed bene non congruit iuuenes episcopari,
quia sanguis et natura attenditur in principe, sed uirtus
et scientia requiritur in episcopo.[d] In gregibus et
armentis aper, aries et taurus, corpore et animositate
prestantior, ceterorum erit minator et ductor, sed inter

---

[a] theologus MS   [b] regis] eius MS
[c] armationem MS   [d] episcopo] princepe MS
[1] Henry Burghersh
[2] cf. Prov. xxx. 18-19. In this famous passage the Vulgate has 'et
viam viri in adolescentia' where AV reads 'and the way of a man with a
maid'.

Lincoln, who was the cousin of the famous Anthony
Bek, formerly Bishop of Durham and Patriarch of
Jerusalem. Now the said Bartholomew had a nephew[1]
who was industrious for his age: he had not yet attained
the age of twenty-five. So at the instigation of Bartholomew the King of England was persuaded to approach the lord pope on the young man's behalf, that
he might deign to promote him to the said episcopal
see. The King of France, and Edmund brother of
the King of England added their prayers, and everyone praised the youth, recommending him repeatedly
to the lord pope. So therefore the lord pope, solicited
by the prayers of so many great men, quashed the
former election and set the young man over the church
of Lincoln.

This was a remarkable act, because illegal and
unreasonable; it had never been seen nor heard of that
so young a man should be made a bishop: it was
illegal, because no one under thirty years of age can
lawfully occupy the pastoral chair, unreasonable
because no-one chooses young men as leaders, for the
reason that their prudence is an unknown quantity.
Solomon, too, held that the most uncertain of all
uncertainties was the way of a young man in his youth.[2]
Indeed it astonishes the world and is a ridiculous
presumption, for a young man to be set upon the
pastoral throne. It may happen that a young man
is raised to the kingship, but it is not at all fitting for
young men to be bishops, because breeding and natural
aptitude are looked for in a prince, but virtue and
knowledge are required of a bishop. In flocks and herds
the boar, the ram, and the bull is outstanding in
physique and courage; he will dominate and lead
the others. But amongst rational beings this rule is

rationales hic ordo non seruatur. Hodie enim quanto
quis minus sapit, tanto audacius melioribus anteuenisse[a]
presumit. Qui nichil didicit aliorum doctor efficitur, et
quasi aes sonans aut cimbalum usurpat predicationis
officium, cum sit cuneus inutilis et ydolum mutum.
Nam episcopus illiteratus preco est mutus. Apud ueteres
erat conditio sapientum inestimabiliter uenerabilis.
Hodie uero prudentia tanquam uilis et abiecta calcatur;
et quadam abhominabili mutatione stultitia in sublimi
preponitur. Hoc est quod Ecclesiastes deplorando conqueritur. 'Vidi,' inquit, 'malum quod est sub sole,
stultum in sublimi dignitate positum, et sapientes sedere
deorsum.'[1] Sacre Scripture prorsus expertes[b] onus im-
portabile dignitatis usurpant,[c] de aliena potius quam de
sua scientia presumentes. Erubescat doleatque prelatus
preesse populo nec prodesse; docentis officium assump-
F.253 sisse et in doctrina populi mutum esse. Talem / siquidem
non prefert honestas sed cupiditas, non moralitas sed
uenalitas, non scientia sed pecunia, non meritum sed
pretium, non electio sed ambitio, et, cum ad regimen
plebis et ducatum populi preficiatur, timendum est ne
relicta terra promissionis, in seruitutem incidat et in
Egiptum reuertatur. Dignitatis equidem appetitus
natione celestis est, in celo conceptus, a celo deiectus,
quando affectabat Lucifer ille a parte aquilonis cathedram erigere, collocari in excelso et fieri similis Altissimo.[2]
Timendum est itaque miseris prelatis ne, dum cathedram
erigunt ad aquilonem, id est dum indigne cathedram
ascendunt pastoralem, cum Lucifero precipitentur in
gehennam.

Qua fronte, queso, preesse presumit qui prodesse non

[a] anteuenisse] ante eum esse MS
[b] prossus ex parte MS
[c] dignitate usurpauit MS
[1] Eccles. x. 5, 6   [2] Isa. xiv. 13, 14

not kept.   For today the less a man knows, the bolder
he is to push in front of his betters.   He who has learnt
nothing is made the teacher of others, and as sounding
brass or cymbal usurps the office of preacher, though
he is a useless block and a dumb idol.   For an illiterate
bishop is a dumb herald.   With the ancients the
condition of wise men was one of untold veneration.
But today prudence is trampled underfoot as vile and
despicable; and by some detestable change foolish-
ness is exalted.   This is what the Preacher deplores,
saying: 'I have seen an evil which is under the sun.
Folly is set in great dignity, and the wise sit in low
places.[1]   Men completely ignorant of Holy Scripture
usurp a burden of dignity they cannot bear, presum-
ing on other people's knowledge rather than their
own. A prelate may well blush and grieve to find himself in command of the people without being of use, to
have taken upon himself the duty of teaching, and to
be dumb in instructing the people.   It is greed not
worth that brings such a man promotion, not morality
but venality, not knowledge but money, not merit
but bribes, not free choice but canvassing, and when
he is set up to control the multitude and lead the
people, it is to be feared that he will leave the promised
land, fall into slavery, and return to Egypt.   Indeed
the lust for dignity is of heavenly birth, conceived
in heaven, but from heaven cast down, when the
famous Lucifer attempted to raise aloft his throne
from the northern parts, to set himself on high like
to the All Highest.[2]   Thus these wretched prelates
should be alarmed when they raise their throne in
the North, lest, as they unworthily mount the pastoral throne, they be cast down with Lucifer into the pit.

 With what impudence, I ask, does he presume

Q

nouit? Nonne uideretur insanus qui omnino nauiga-
tionis ignarus in discrimine*a* tempestatis peritissimos
nautas contempneret, ipse autem in suam et aliorum
perniciem propter temeritatem magisterium nauis usur-
paret? Sed nullus hodie ab onere pontificali se excusat;
nullus inuitus trahitur aut reclamans. Vbi hodie similis
Amonio[1] reperitur, qui cum ab omni populo ad pontifi-
catus apicem peteretur, 'Oculos meos,' inquit, 'effodiam,
linguam per quam uobis placeo nisi me dimittatis
abscidam.' Certe cum ad eruditionem populi mitteret
Dominus Ieremiam, quem sanctificauerat ex utero, suam
inperfectionem propheta formidans, 'A! A! A!' inquit,
'Domine, ecce loqui nescio.'[2] Moises etiam, dum a
Domino ad liberationem*b* populi in Egiptum destinatur,
inpeditionem lingue pretendens alium mittendum humiliter inprecatur. Iccirco propter insufficientiam et
cupiditatem pontificum translata est hodie archa Dei
de Israel in Azotum, id est, a sanctitate in ignem
F.254 con/cupiscentie, et de Azoto transfertur in templum
Dagon,[3] id est, desolationis et tristitie. Nam in Matheo
scriptum est,[4] 'Cum uideritis abhominationem desolationis sedentem in templo, tunc ue pregnantibus et
nutrientibus,' ac si diceret, cum uideritis ambitiosum,
illiteratum*c* et fatuum in ecclesia Dei preminere, ue illis
qui talibus prelatis coguntur subiacere. Illi uero qui
spem salutis conceperant, exemplo*d* talium suffocantur,
qui uero uite celestis alimenta petebant nullo uerbi
Domini pabulo sustentantur. 'Paruuli,' inquit propheta,
'petierunt panem et non erat qui frangeret eis.'[5]

a discrimen MS   *b* obliberationem MS
c ambicionem illaratum MS   *d* exemplum MS
[1] See Palladius, *Historia Lausiaca* xii (*P.L.* lxxiii. 1104)
[2] Jer. i. 6
[3] cf. 1 Sam. v. 2
[4] Matt. xxiv. 15, 19
[5] Lam. iv. 4

to command, who does not know how to be of use?
Is it not altogether mad that he who is wholly ignorant
of navigation should amidst the perils of the storm
scorn the most expert sailors, while he in his rashness
seizes control of the ship to the destruction of himself
and others? But no one today excuses himself from
the burden of the pontificate; no one is dragged forth
unwillingly, or protesting. Where is one found today
like to Amonius,[1] whom all the people sought to make
their bishop? 'I will pluck out my eyes' he said,
and cut off the tongue through which I please you,
unless you suffer me to depart.' Indeed when the
Lord sent Jeremiah for the instruction of the people,
whom He had sanctified from birth, the prophet fearing his inadequacy, cried 'Ah! Lord, behold I know
not how to speak.'[2] Moses, too, when he was sent
by the Lord into Egypt for the deliverance of his people
protested his imperfection of speech, and humbly
besought Him that another might be sent. Therefore
through the insufficiency and greed of the bishops
the ark of God is today removed from Israel to Ashdod
that is from holiness to the fire of lust, and from Ashdod
to the temple of Dagon,[3] that is of desolation and grief.
For in Matthew it is written,[4] 'When you shall see
the abomination of desolation sitting in the temple,
then woe unto them that are with child, and to those
that give suck,' as if he were to say: when you shall
see the ambitious, the illiterate and the fool pre-eminent
in the church of God, woe to those who are placed
under such prelates. Indeed those who had taken
hope of safety are choked by the example of such men;
those who sought the food of celestial life are nourished
by no word of God. 'The little ones', says the prophet,
'sought bread, but there was none to break it for them.'[5]

Post reuersionem domini regis orta est magna discordia inter quosdam maiores baronum et Hugonem
Despenser filium, domini regis camerarium.   Hugo
namque, qui primogenitam heredum Gloucestrie duxerat
uxorem, et cui fere totum Glamorgan cesserat in partem,[1]
omni studio et tota mente terras uicinas dominio suo
nitebatur amplicare, et primo castrum de Neuport,
quod Hugo de Audeleghe[a] in partem accepit, fraudu-
lenter intrauit et tenuit; et castra quedam, ex regia
munificentia Rogero de Mortemer dudum collata, uehementer affectauit, et dominum regem ad repetitionem
dictorum castrorum consequenter induxit.

Preterea terram de Gower, ex quibusdam causis in
legibus Marchie preiudicium exquisitis, fisco applicari
censebat, pro eo quod Johannes Moubray in ipsam, cum
de rege teneretur in capite, sine licentia regis ingressum
fecerat; sed et dominus rex, qui uotis Hugonis pro posse
fauebat, processum quendam in predictum Johannem,
et legi Marchie preiudicialem, fieri discernebat.[b]   Ob-
F.255 stabat Johannes, obstabat et comes Herfor/die, commune
preiudicium aduertentes, domino regi ne nouam legem,
contra[c] consuetudines ab antiquo usitatas et approbatas,
induceret humiliter supplicantes.   Instabat Hugo Despenser pertinaciter dicens dominum regem tam in
Wallia quam in Anglia hac semper prerogatiua gaudere,
ut nullus sine licentia regis ingressum[d] haberet in feodum
quod de rege teneretur in capite; et, si contrarium a
quocunque foret attemptatum, feodum sic occupatum
redigeretur in fiscum.   Allegabant alii legem marchie et
consuetudines quas non licebat infringere.   Spreuit Hugo

[a] Angelegh MS
[b] decernebat Hearne
[c] contra quam MS
[d] in ingressum MS
[1] *Supra* p. xiii

After the lord king's return a great quarrel arose between some of the greater barons and Hugh Despenser the son, the lord king's chamberlain. For Hugh had married the eldest of the Gloucester heiresses, and almost all Glamorgan had fallen to his share.[1] He now put forth all his powers to extend his sway over the neighbouring lands, and began by deceitfully seizing and holding the castle of Newport, which had fallen to Hugh D'Audley's share; he also ardently coveted certain castles which Roger Mortimer had a while ago of the king's gift, and so persuaded the lord king to try to get the said castles back again.

Further, he proposed that the land of Gower, for certain reasons fabricated in order to be prejudicial to the laws of the March, should be subordinated to the royal treasury, because John Mowbray had entered it without the king's licence, although it was held from the king in chief. And the lord king, who promoted Hugh's designs as far as he could, decided that an action should lie against the said John, to the damage of the law of the March. John opposed this, as also the Earl of Hereford, pointing out the general disadvantage, humbly petitioning the lord king that he would not introduce a new law, contrary to customs used and approved from time out of mind. Hugh Despenser stubbornly insisted that the lord king had always enjoyed this prerogative in Wales as in England, that no one without the king's licence should have entry upon any fee held of the king in chief; and if on the other hand, this should be attempted by anyone, the fee so seized should be assigned to the royal treasury. Others cited the law of the March and customs which could not be infringed. Hugh took no heed of the law and customs of the March, and appeared to

et consuetudines et legem Marchie, sed et barones talia
allegantes lese maiestatis uidebatur arguere.

Tanta contumelia barones affecti indignanter reces-
serunt, et conuenientes in Wallia Hugonem Despenser
prosequendum, deponendum et penitus destruendum,
unanimiter decreuerunt. Huic autem decreto principaliter consentientes et iuramento astricti fuerunt subscripti: Johannes de Mounbray, comes de Herford, Hugo
Daudeleye, et Rogerus de Clifforde, Rogerus Dammory,
et inter alios Rogerus de Mortymer auunculus et nepos.
Isti uenerunt cum multis aliis; et manus comitis Lancastrie erat cum illis. Quilibet^a istorum Hugonem^a
diffid[er]at, quia contra singulos Hugo deliquerat:
Johannes de Moubray pro terra de Gower, quem sup-
plantare nititur Hugo Despenser; Hugo Daudeleye pro
castro detento; comes de Herford pro leso filio; Rogerus
de Clifford pro exheredatione matris, quam Hugo procurauerat in preiudicium ipsius; Rogerus Dammori,
coheres comitis Gloucestrie, inuidum suum non potest
F.256 diligere. Rogerus de Mortimer et Rogerus / de Mortimer
inimici facti sunt Hugoni Despenser quia unum spoliare
disposuit et in utrumque mortem aui sui uindicare promisit. Comes Lancastrie notam infamie, quam apud
Berewyk pertulit, imputat Hugoni, quam uult uindicari
cum tempus acceperit.

Igitur antequam rem in actum proferrent, manda-
runt domino regi quatinus Hugonem Despenser a se
dimitteret, aut electe custodie ipsum committeret, ut
certo die iudicio sisti posset, quo ad sibi obicienda
responderet; alioquin regem pro rege deinceps non
haberent, sed homagium et fidelitatem et iusiurandum
quodlibet regi prestitum penitus declinarent, et tanquam

^{a} quibus MS

accuse the barons who alleged such things of talking treason.

Deeply moved by such abuse the barons departed full of indignation, and meeting in Wales, they unanimously decided that Hugh Despenser must be pursued, laid low and utterly destroyed. The following were the leaders of these sworn confederates: John Mowbray, the Earl of Hereford, Hugh D'Audley and Roger Clifford, Roger Damory, and amongst others Roger Mortimer, the uncle and the nephew. These came with many others; and the Earl of Lancaster's hand was with them. Each of these had defied Hugh, because he had wronged each of them: John Mowbray for the land of Gower, in which Hugh Despenser had tried to supplant him; Hugh D'Audley for the castle which he had withheld; the Earl of Hereford for the wrong done to his son; Roger Clifford for the disherison of his mother, procured by Hugh to his damage; Roger Damory, co-heir of the Earl of Gloucester, could have no affection for his deadly rival. The two Mortimers were hostile because he proposed to despoil the one, and had promised to avenge the death of his grandfather upon each of them. The Earl of Lancaster blamed Hugh for the disgrace which had attached to his name at Berwick, and this he wished to avenge as occasion offered.

Thus, before they took action, they requested the lord king to dismiss Hugh Despenser, or commit him to a picked guard, in order that he could be put on trial on a certain day, when he might answer the charges against him; otherwise they would no longer have him for king, but would utterly renounce their homage and fealty and whatever oath they had sworn to him, and as men without a king, a ruler, or a judge, would

homines sine rege, sine rectore et sine iudice, pro defectu
iustitie in ultionem Hugonis propria auctoritate procederent, et uindictam qualem possent de malefactis
tantorum malefactorum expeterent.

Indignatus rex uehementer super mandato baronum,
uersus Gloucestriam[1] iter arripuit, et ultra progressus
Rogero Dammory, qui partem aduersam sustinuit, castrum de Sancto Briauello cum libertate et pertinentiis
statim abstulit,[2] et terras Hugonis Daudeleye confiscari
iussit, quia, ut rex asserit, contra iuramentum quod regi
prestiterant baronibus adhesit. Deinde cum propositum
baronum sine forma predicta suspendere non posset,
cum suo Hugone semper a latere Londonias reuertitur.

Sed propositum baronum ulterius non differtur, nam
castrum de Neuport primitus obsidentes leuiter capiunt,
et Hugonem Daudeleye, prout ius dictabat, in possessionem mittunt. Cetera castella, que Hugo Despenser
tenebat in Wallia, modico labore barones occupant, nec
custodes defendere nec Walenses, dominationem Hugonis
F.257 execrantes, tuitionem inferre procurant.[3] Erat / enim
cum baronibus fortitudo copiosa armatorum octingenti
et peditum multa milia; nec Hugo Despenser uenerat
defendere nec custodes indefensi poterant resistere.
Quicquid[a] autem pretiosum in castris reperiunt, econtra
lege iuris belli inter ipsos diuidunt. Oues, boues et
equos non dimittunt, sed quid quis tolleret sine lite
statuunt. Dignum namque iudicant ut publicentur
[bona] eius, per quem regnum et optimates regni grauiter
perturbantur.

Conuenerunt autem incole illius terre ad barones

---

[a] quicquam MS
[1] A council met at Gloucester, 5 April (*Parl. Writs*, II.i.231)
[2] *Parl. Writs*, II.ii.158 (9 April 1321)
[3] May 1321

proceed to take vengeance upon Hugh on their own
authority for default of justice, and they would take
what satisfaction they could from the perpetrators
of such enormities.

Highly incensed at the baronial decree the king
set out towards Gloucester,[1] and going beyond it at
once, took the castle of St Briavel's, with its liberty
and appurtenances, from Roger Damory who supported
the other side, and ordered Hugh D'Audley's estates
to be confiscated,[2] because, as the king asserted, he
adhered to the barons contrary to the oath which they
had sworn to the king. Then, since he could not hinder
the baronial plan without agreeing to their formula,
he returned to London with his own Hugh always
at his side.

But the baronial plan was put off no longer, for they
first besieged Newport Castle and easily took it, and
put Hugh D'Audley in possession of it, as was only
right. The barons seized without much difficulty,
the other castles which Hugh Despenser held in Wales,
for neither did the wardens defend them, nor did the
Welsh, who hated Hugh's domination, lend them any
protection.[3] Now the barons had a contingent of 800
men-at-arms and many thousand infantry. Hugh
Despenser had not come to defend the castles, nor
could the wardens alone offer resistance. Whatever
the barons found of value in the castles, contrary to
the law of war they divided between themselves. They
did not abandon the sheep, oxen, and horses, but
what each might take was agreed without dispute.
For they adjudged it right that his goods should be
confiscated, through whom the realm and its magnates
had been so grievously troubled.

However, some thirty thousand of the inhabitants

quasi xxx^a milia hominum, dicentes: 'Cesset indignatio uestra circa nos; dominationem Hugonis Despenser nunquam gratam habuimus; parati sumus unanimiter obedire mandatis uestris.' Admissi sunt sub tali pacto, ut ab homagio Hugonis Despenser penitus discederent, ut eum pro domino nunquam agnoscerent, sed domino regi per omnia fideles existerent, et uero heredi pro loco et tempore debita seruitia illesa seruarent; et hec omnia tactis sacrosanctis Euangeliis et oretenus appositis specialiter confirmarunt.

Post rem sic consummatam in Wallia, idem iudicium decreuerunt barones exercendum in Anglia. Nam omnia bona Hugonis tam patris quam filii ubicumque reperta occuparunt, disperserunt, et publicarunt. Voluntas enim comitis Lancastrie fuit ut non solum insurgerent in filium, sed ut patrem cum filio mitterent in exterminium, quia antiquum odium erga patrem conceptum tempus uindicte non uiderat acceptum. Et sic interim coniurati sunt barones marchie cum comite Lancastrie in exilium Hugonis Despenser tam patris quam filii, in persecutionem eorum, in dampnationem, in perpetuam exheredationem.[1] Igitur, sicut dixi, occupantur bona eorum, maneria spoliantur, franguntur claustra ferarum, et, forsan quia Hugo pater olim a multis pro feris regiis F.258 iniustam extorsit redemptionem, / nunc in feris propriis, quas multum dilexit, patitur ultionem. Sic Pharao submergitur quia infantes submersit[2]; sic frequenter^a iuste contingit ut quis puniatur in quo deliquit.

Cum audisset rex tantam feritatem baronum, con-

---

^a sic frequenter et sic frequenter MS

[1] Stubbs, *Introd.* lxxxviii. 'See the Indenture printed in Tyrell, III, 280.' This was made at Lancaster's famous 'Parliament' at Sherburn in Elmet.

[2] cf. Exodus i. 22; xiv. 28

of that territory came to the barons saying: 'Remit your displeasure towards us, for we have never liked the lordship of Hugh Despenser, and are all prepared to obey your orders.' They were accepted on these terms, that they would wholly renounce their homage to Hugh Despenser, that they would never acknowledge him as lord, but remain faithful to the lord king in all things, and would maintain their due services for the true heir at the proper time and place; and all these things they solemnly confirmed having touched and kissed the Holy Gospels.

When this business had been accomplished in Wales, the barons resolved that the same judgment was to be carried out in England. They seized, divided up, and confiscated all the goods of Hugh (the father as well as the son) wherever they were found. For it was the wish of the Earl of Lancaster that they should not only rise against the son, but destroy the father along with him, because he had seen no opportunity for satisfying his longstanding hatred of the father. And so for a time the barons of the March made a sworn conspiracy with the Earl of Lancaster to banish, persecute, condemn, and perpetually disinherit the Despensers, father and son.[1] Thus, as I have said, they seized their goods, plundered their manors, broke open their game-preserves, and, perhaps because the elder Hugh had once unjustly squeezed ransom from many for offences against the royal beasts of the chase, they now revenged themselves upon his own beasts, in which he had taken much pleasure. Thus Pharaoh was drowned because he had drowned the children[2]; it often happens thus that the punishment fits the crime.

When the king heard that the barons were be-

uocatis consiliariis suis [pro]posuit consilium.[1] Erant
quidam qui iustum reputabant esse iudicium inuadere et
occupare castra baronum, ut exemplum quod ipsi prestiterant retorqueretur in caput eorum. Et huic quidem
consilio dominus rex libenter acquieuisset si consentaneos
sufficientes habuisset. Alii uero sanioris consilii dissuadebant sic fieri. Dicebant enim ex huiusmodi processu nichil aliud euenire quam communem guerram
suscitare, terram destruere, et ad perditionem regni pro-
perare. Consulebant autem ut rex barones ad parliamentum[2] conuocaret, et ibidem sicut decet querelas singulorum audiret, et eas secundum leges terminaret. Vocauit
igitur barones ad parliamentum, ut interim cessaret
impetus eorum. Venerunt itaque ad parliamentum, sed
cum maxima multitudine armatorum.

Videns autem rex propositum baronum, animaduertens petitiones eorum, et quod ad hoc tendebant omnimodo, ut exterminarent priuatum suum, nitebatur
differre negotium.[a] Nolebant dilationem ferre magnates.
Noluit rex audire barones, et ita per aliquot dies suspen-
debat rex petitiones eorum, donec unanimiter omnes
unum conformauerunt decretum, mandantes domino
regi quatinus querelas eorum audiret et petitionibus
eorum secundum iustitiam satisfaceret, aut ab homagio
suo penitus discederent et alium rectorem sibi preficerent

F.259 qui iustitiam omnibus faceret et collum nocen/tium et
superborum humiliaret; et hoc quidem mandatum comes
de Penbrok et alii magnates qui uidebantur mediatores
regi deferebant,[a] qui tamen cum baronibus de[b] querelis
eorum defendendis usque ad mortem iuramentum prestiterant.[3]

[a] differrebant MS   [b] de] et MS
[1] The council was summoned to meet at Oxford on 10 May, but
afterwards called to Westminster for 17 May (*Parl. Writs*, II.ii.159).
[2] The parliament was summoned on 17 May to meet at Westminster
on 15 July, and sat until 22 August (*Parl. Writs*, II.i.234, 237)

having so savagely, he called together his advisers and
proposed a council.[1]　Some thought it would be right
to attack and seize the baronial castles, so that the
precedent which they had established should return
upon their heads.　This advice the lord king would
willingly have followed, if it had had sufficient support.
He was, however, dissuaded from doing this by others
who gave sounder advice.　They said that nothing
could emerge from such a procedure save a general
war, that it would destroy the land, and hasten the
ruin of the kingdom.　They advised the king to summon
the barons to parliament,[2] and there, as was fitting,
hear the complaints of each, and decide them according to the law.　He therefore called the barons to
parliament that their attacks might cease for a time.
So they came to parliament, but with a very great
crowd of men-at-arms.

When the king perceived the baronial design,
and heard their petitions, and that they were utterly
determined upon the expulsion of his favourite, he
strove to delay the matter.　The magnates would
not agree to this delay.　Nor would the king listen to
the barons, and so for some days the king held up their
petitions, until they unanimously agreed upon this
resolution, requesting the lord king that he should
hear their complaints and satifsy their petitions according to justice, or they would utterly renounce their
homage and set up another ruler to do justice to all and
humble the pride of the guilty and stiffnecked.　This
message the Earl of Pembroke, and other magnates
who appeared to be acting as mediators, brought
to the king, although they had taken an oath with the
barons to defend their grievances to the death.[3]

---

[3] Mid-August 1321

Tunc comes Adomarus coram rege huiusmodi uerba fertur protulisse. 'Considera,' inquit, 'domine rex, potentiam baronum; imminens aduerte periculum; nec frater nec soror te tibi debet esse carior. Noli ergo pro aliquo uiuente perdere regnum tuum. "Alpibus ille perit qui plus se diligit ullum." Nec dicat dominus rex in contumeliam suam hec a baronibus incohata; sed, quia publice utile est ut malis hominibus euacuetur patria, et ad hoc, domine rex, prestitisti iuramentum in coronatione tua; ergo si barones audieris, potenter et gloriose regnare poteris; sin autem, et a petitionibus eorum aures*a* auertis, regnum forsan et nos omnes consequenter amittes. Coniurati enim sumus, quia paribus nostris contradicere non possumus.'

Videns ergo rex quod uehementer irruerunt in eum, annuebat licet inuitus petitionibus eorum. Tunc missus est ex parte regis archiepiscopus Cantuariensis, qui barones ad Westmonasterium conuocaret, ubi coram rege conuenirent, et quod ratio dictaret sine dilatione reportarent. Nec mora, congregatis omnibus apud Westmonasterium,[1] perlecte sunt coram rege querele eorum baronum et protinus adiecte petitiones eorum, et quia nemo contradicere posset sequebatur conforme iudicium. Summam autem querele paucis uerbis libet exprimere.

Arguebatur Hugo nimium cupidus et per hoc regi minus ydoneus; arguebatur malus consiliarius; argue-/
F.260 batur conspirator et falsus; arguebatur distructor populi, exheredator corone, inimicus regis et regni. Hec omnia contra Hugonem barones allegabant, et super hiis tam patrem quam filium constanter accusabant. Non erat

---

a aures] a nostris MS
[1] Parliament sat from 15 July

At this time Earl Aylmer is said to have uttered these words in the presence of the king: 'Consider, lord king', he said, 'the power of the barons; take heed of the danger that threatens; neither brother nor sister should be dearer to thee than thyself. Do not therefore for any living soul lose thy kingdom, "He perishes on the rocks who loves another more than himself." Let not the king say, to his own injury, that this business was begun by the barons; but since it is for the common good that the country be freed from wicked men, to which end, lord king, you swore an oath at your coronation, if you will listen to the barons you shall reign in power and glory; but if, on the other hand, you close your ears to their petitions, you may perchance lose the kingdom and all of us. For we are sworn confederates, and we cannot oppose our peers.'

So the king, seeing how violently he was attacked, unwillingly granted their requests. Then the Archbishop of Canterbury was sent on behalf of the king to summon the barons to Westminster, where they should meet in the King's presence, and obtain what reason demanded without postponement. Nor was there any delay, but when all had assembled at Westminster[1] the complaints of the barons were recited before the king and their petitions added forthwith, and as no one could contradict them, appropriate judgment followed. The sum of their complaints can be expressed in a few words.

Hugh was accused of being too greedy and thus unsuitable to be with the king; he was accused of evil counsel; of conspiracy and falsehood; of being a destroyer of the people, a disinheritor of the crown, an enemy of king and kingdom. All these things the barons alleged against Hugh, and persistently accused father

qui patrem uel filium defenderet, non erat qui pro ipsis contra barones disputaret.

Tunc in conspectu domini regis, prelatorum, comitum et baronum, prolatum est iudicium in Hugonem Despenser patrem et filium.[1] Nam uterque tanquam malus et falsus domini regis consiliarius, tanquam seductor et conspirator uel exheredator corone et destructor populi, et inimicus regis et regni, condempnatur, proscribitur et exheredatur; et super hoc editum est statutum,[2] ut iudicium, tanta auctoritate firmatum, nullum reuocetur in euum.

Ecce duo uiri inter magnates terre, et ipsius regis speciales nuper precipui, natale solum et solium deseruerunt licet inuiti. Res miranda quia tam subita; subitas enim mutationes odit et miratur natura. Reuera iudicio multorum iuste accidit eis hoc infortunium. Pater namque ferus et cupidus olim multis nocuit, et excommunicationes multorum promeruit. Cum enim esset iustitiarius de foresta, multos accusauit de uenatione regia, multos nequiter exheredauit, quosdam in exilium compulit, iniquas redemptiones a pluribus extorsit, mille libratas terre per concussionem[3] adunauit, et ecce! manum Dei uel corrigentem uel prouenientem iam sensit. Communi uero iudicio iuste perdidit quod per iacturam aliorum prius congregauit. Sed nonne legitur in sacris scripturis: 'Filius non portabit iniquitatem patris'?[4]

Ad hoc uidentur respondere, uidelicet quod commoditas iniquitatis paterne ad filium debuit deuenire;

---

[1] 19 August 1321
[2] *Statutes of the Realm.* i. 181; *Rot. Parl.* iii. 363
[3] *concussionem* legal technical term used several times in *Dig.* 47. 13
[4] Ezek. xviii. 20

and son alike of these enormities. There was no-one
to defend either father or son, no-one to speak for them
against the barons.

Then in the presence of the lord king, the prelates,
earls, and barons, judgment was given against the
Despensers[1] father and son. Each was found guilty,
proscribed, and disinherited, as an evil and false
counsellor of the lord king, as a seducer and conspirator
or disinheritor of the crown and a destroyer of the
people, and an enemy of the king and kingdom. And
concerning this a statute was published,[2] that the
judgment, confirmed by such weight of authority,
should never be reversed.

Observe now how two men, counted amongst the
magnates of the land, and until recently the particular
intimates of the king himself, reluctantly left their
native soil and splendour. An astonishing business
because so sudden: for nature abhors and marvels at
sudden changes. But in the opinion of many this
misfortune fell upon them justly. For the brutal and
greedy father had in the past wronged many, and
promoted the excommunication of many. As a justice
of the forest he had accused many of breaches of the
royal rights of hunting, many he had vilely disinherited,
some he forced into exile, extorted unjust ransoms
from many, collected a thousand librates of land by
means of threats,[3] and behold now he feels the hand of
God arising to correct him. By a general judgment
he justly lost what he had gathered together from the
losses of others. But is it not written in the Holy
Scriptures: 'The son shall not bear the iniquity of
the father'?[4]

By way of reply it may be said that as the benefit of
the father's wickedness must devolve upon the son, it was

R

iustum fuit ut paternum uitium communiter redundaret
F.261 in filium. Sed et secundum quosdam malitia / filii
preponderabat paterne seueritati. Nam de regio fauore
confisus omnia pro imperio agebat, omnia captabat,
nulli nec alicui quantumcunque auctoritatis deferebat,
coheredibus suis moliebatur insidias; sic, si fieri posset,
per occasiones fictas uterque partem suam amitteret, et
ipse solus solidum comitatum optineret. Ipsi uero,
auxilio freti baronum, malitie eius occurrerunt. Nam
et patrem et filium simul in exilium agitarunt. Verumptamen iudicio fidedignorum barones in persecutione sua
excesserunt modum. Nam, si causas exilii iustas inuenerunt, bona tamen eorum non iuste occuparunt.
Quare maneria eorum destruxerunt, quamobrem a
familiaribus redemptiones extorserunt? Si iustam causam prius habuerunt, ius et iniuriam modo conver-
terunt. Sic Saul rex dum percussit Amalec Deo placuit,[1]
sed, postquam ad predam uersus armentis pepercit et
gregibus, Deo displicuit, quia quod non debuit perpe-
trauit. Cartas autem remissionis quas a rege barones
impetrarunt*a* non sicut decuit exegerunt, et iccirco
commodo earum postmodum caruerunt. Sic Babilonii
induxerunt regem inuitum, ut Danielem mitteret in
lacum leonum,[2] et, quia hoc iniuste fecerunt, pœnam
condignam postmodum pertulerunt.

Hiis itaque gestis Hugo pater transmarinas partes se
transtulit; Hugo uero filius in mari remansit, quem
dominus rex tutele nautarum de Portubus obnixe com-
mendarat. Et factus est Hugo belua marina insidians
mercatoribus qui transibant. Maria occupauit, merces

---

a impetrauit MS
[1] I Sam. xv. 9, 15
[2] Dan. vi. 16

right that the son should share in the paternal guilt. According to some the malice of the son outweighed the father's harshness. For confident of the royal favour he did everything at his own discretion, snatched at everything, did not bow to the authority of anyone whomsoever, set traps for his co-heirs; thus, if he could manage it, each would lose his share through false accusations and he alone would obtain the whole earldom. But they, relying on the help of the barons, were a match for his wickedness. For they drove both father and son into exile at the same time. Yet in the judgment of some worthy persons the barons went too far in their persecution. For even if they found just reasons for banishment, they did not justly seize their goods. Why did they destroy their manors, for what reason did they extort ransoms from their retinues? Though formerly their cause had been just, they now turned right into wrong. Thus King Saul pleased God when he smote Amalek,[1] but afterwards, when he spared their herds and flocks for plunder, he angered God, because he had done what he ought not to have done. The charters of pardon which the barons sought from the king, were not demanded in due form, and so they later had no profit from them. Thus the Babylonians persuaded the unwilling king to cast Daniel into the lions' den,[2] and because they did this unjustly they afterwards suffered the punishment they deserved.

When this affair was settled the elder Hugh betook himself to foreign lands; but Hugh the son remained at sea, as the lord king had urgently commended him to the protection of the sailors of the Cinque Ports. And he became a sea-monster, lying-in-wait for merchants as they crossed his path. He was master of the seas,

eorum et cetera bona, et nulla nauis transibat intacta,
sed in grandem nauem Ianuensem quam uulgo appellant
dromonem inuasit, et nautis peremptis infinita bona que
naui inerant*a* ad suos usus sequestrauit.[1] /

F.262   Interim dominus rex magnates illos, qui Hugonem
in exilium compulerant, expungnare decreuit, pro eo
quod castella exulantium occupauerant, et maneria
exulantium tam patris quam filii turpiter destruxerant;
et quia bona exulum, que fisco magis applicari debuerant, in suos usus sumpserant et consumpserant; et licet
dominus rex huiusmodi transgressiones diceretur re-
misisse, et unicuique cartam concessisse, dicebat tamen
et protestabatur se inuitum hoc fecisse et uoluntatem
coactam nullam esse.

Igitur dominus rex Bartholomeum de Badelesmere
primitus expungnauit, et castrum ipsius apud Ledes[2]
personaliter obsedit. Tunc congregati sunt maiores de
Marchia [ut] succursum obsessis prestarent, sed prohi-
bitio comitis Lancastrie fecit quominus auxilium promissum inferrent. Comes enim dictum Bartholomeum
odio habuit, et plures transgressiones sibi imposuit, ob
quas uel carcere perpetuo uel saltem exilio dignum fore
decreuit; et sic obsessi in castro succursu caruerunt,
unde et non*b* ualentes resistere castrum reddiderunt.[3]
Reperit autem rex infra castrum predones, homicidas et
proditores; et hos quidem protrahi iussit, illos suspendit
et reliquos carceri mancipauit. Voluit enim rex exemplum aliis prebere, ut nullus de cetero audeat contra
eum munitiones tenere. Sicut enim nullus potest in
terra castra sine regis licentia construere, ita nec fas est
contra regem in regno castra defendere.

a inierant MS   *b* nunc MS
[1] Edward III later paid 8,000 marks compensation. (*Foed.* II. 941)
[2] October 1321. This is Leeds in Kent.
[3] Late October

their merchandise and chattels, and no ship got through unharmed. He attacked a great Genoese ship, commonly called a dromond, killed the crew, and appropriated to himself the vast wealth that he found in it.[1]

Meanwhile the lord king determined to attack those magnates who had forced Hugh into exile, because they had seized the fortresses of the banished men, and had disgracefully destroyed the manors of both father and son; and further because they had taken for their own use and wasted the goods of the exiles, which ought rather to have gone to the treasury; and although the lord king might be said to have pardoned these trespasses, and to have granted a charter to each man, he nevertheless protested that he had done this unwillingly and that a grant under coercion was void.

So to begin with the lord king attacked Bartholomew de Badlesmere, and personally besieged his castle at Leeds.[2] The greater Marchers assembled to bring help to the besieged, but the Earl of Lancaster's prohibition made it impossible to send the promised aid. For the Earl hated this Bartholomew, and laid many trespasses at his door, for which he adjudged him worthy of perpetual imprisonment or at least exile; and so those besieged in the castle lacked help, and not being strong enough to resist they surrendered the castle.[3] Within it the king found robbers, homicides, and traitors; some he ordered to be drawn, others to be hanged, and the rest imprisoned. For the king wished to make an example of them, so that no one in future would dare to hold fortresses against him. For just as no one can build castles in the land without the king's licence, so it is wrong to defend castles in the kingdom against the king.

Deinde misit[1] rex manus et occupauit cetera castra Bartholomei, et comitis Herfordie, Rogeri Dammory et Hugonis de Audeleye; nec inuenti sunt aliqui resistentes, quia ultio sumpta de hiis apud Ledes uehementer terruit omnes. Extendit etiam rex manus ad maneria baronum qui Hugonis procurauerant exilium, et bona eorum occupauit; sed et omnes adherentes eis et eorum fautores uniuersos depredauit. /

F.263 Cum igitur occupasset rex munitiones baronum a parte orientali, idem disposuit faciendum in parte occidentali.[2] Tunc congregauit exercitum copiosum iturus in Marchiam, ut magnates expungnaret qui occupabant partem illam. Ibi enim fuit tutissimum refugium baronum, et regi sine manu ualida difficile penetrandum.

Conuenerunt autem in auxilium domini regis duo fratres sui, uidelicet Thomas comes Marescallus et Edmundus comes Cantie, pro etate strenui.[3] Sed et comes de Penbrok diuertebat se ad partem regis eo quod comes Lancastrie imposuerat se proditionis. Expertus erat comes Lancastrie, ut dixit, hominem illum infidum et uarium, et baronibus indixerat auxilium eius repudiandum. Eratque cum rege comes de Arundel propter affinitatem Hugonis Despenser; comes de Warenna et comes de Rychmund adheserunt domino regi, et alii barones potentes et multi. Isti promiserunt domino regi auxilium prestare et iniuriam sibi illatam pro posse uindicare. Robertus le Ewer,[4] qui alio modo dicitur Aquarius, erat

---

[1] November   [2] December

[3] Thomas of Brotherton was born 1 June 1300; Edmund Earl of Kent *b.* on 5 August 1301.

[4] The *Aquarius* who led the infantry. His duties at court were to dry the king's clothes and prepare his bath. Robert was dismissed by the Ordainers (*Chron. Ed. I & II.* i. 199). The functions sound like those of a Chamberlain's deputy; the younger Despenser was Chamberlain at this time. Robert le Ewer, a King's yeoman in 1318 (*C.P.R.* 136) was a violent and ungrateful person. He was tenant for life by the King's gift, of the manor of Warblington, Hants (*Misc. Inq.* ii. 148, 277, 309) and Constable

Then the king sent a force[1] to seize the other castles of Bartholomew, and of the Earl of Hereford, of Roger Damory, and of Hugh D'Audley; nor were any found to resist, because the vengeance exacted from those at Leeds had terrified them exceedingly. The king also laid his hands on the manors of the barons who had brought about Hugh's exile, and seized their goods; he also plundered all their adherents and all their supporters.

When therefore the king had seized the baronial strongholds in the East, he made ready to do the same in the West.[2] He got together a numerous army to go to the March and attack the magnates who had seized those parts. For it was there that the barons had their safest refuge, and it was difficult for the king to penetrate it without a strong force.

His two brothers came to the lord king's help, namely Thomas, Earl Marshal, and Edmund Earl of Kent, active soldiers considering their age.[3] The Earl of Pembroke went over to the king's side because the Earl of Lancaster had accused him of treachery. The Earl of Lancaster knew, as he said, that this man was faithless and fickle and had pointed out to the barons that his help should be rejected. There was also with the king the Earl of Arundel on account of his kinship with Hugh Despenser; Earl Warenne and the Earl of Richmond adhered to the lord king and many other powerful barons. These promised to lend aid to the lord king and to avenge the wrong done to him in so far as in them lay. Robert le Ewer,[4] otherwise

---

of Odiham in 1320; but on 18 August of that year he was ordered to be imprisoned, as he had threatened to slay persons sent to arrest him (*C.Cl.R.* 179, 260, 236). On 9 June 1321 he was pardoned, being granted Odiham Castle again (*C.P.R.* 505, 586, 595). In 1322 he defaulted again, and was dead by 8 January 1323 (*C.P.R.* 199, 206, 232).

dux peditum, et Fulco filius Warini militie conduxit
exercitum.

Robertus le Ewer nomen sumpsit a re, quia in aula
regis aquam solebat ministrare. Fulco filius Warini,
qui nunc militat, nomen et cognomen antecessorum
suorum portat. Nam Fulco filius Warini[1] primus in
diebus regis Iohannis miles fuit famosus, cui successit
Fulco secundus, homo remissus et tepidus. Successit isti
Fulco tertius, miles fortis et strenuus et in Hispannia
contra paganos pluries expertus. Sic frequenter euenit
quod post probum improbus et e contra succedit; et talis
genologia ratione forte non caret. Nam probitas uiri
per comparationem lucidius apparet. Sic figulus iuxta
F.264 artem suam quedam uasa ad hono/rem, quedam com-
ponit ad contumeliam,[2] ut hec que facit ad honorem
comparatione deteriorum maiorem habeant decorem.

Igitur dominus rex cum exercitu suo uersus Cyren-
cestriam iter arripuit, et ibidem propter Natale Domini
per aliquot dies perhendinauit. Barones autem pre-
occupauerant Gloucestriam; quamobrem rex diuertebat
Wygorniam,[3] nec ibidem transiuit Sabrinam, quia barones ex parte aduersa custodiebant ripam. Premisit
quoque rex apud Bruggenorthe uiros armatos et pedites
qui preparent transitum suum. Restiterunt domini de
Mortimer necnon et grauem ei[a] fecerunt insultum. Nam
magnam partem uille incenderunt, et de seruis regis
plurimos occiderunt. Reliquit autem rex uillam ad
sinistram, et sic adiuit ad Salopiam,[4] ut ibidem transiret

---

[a] eius MS
[1] Fulk Fitz-Warin II, lord of Whittington Castle near Oswestry, Salop,
and Wantage, Berks, is famous as the hero of the Romance of Fulk Fitz-
Warin (Rolls Series) for which see J. Vising, *Anglo-Norman Language and
Literature* (Oxford, 1923), p. 6of.
[2] Rom. ix. 21
[3] 2 January 1322; 9 January at Droitwich; 13 January at Newport
[4] 15-24 January

called the waterbearer, was in command of the infantry, and Fulk FitzWarin led the cavalry.

Robert le Ewer derived his name from the fact that he was wont to serve the water in the king's hall. Fulk FitzWarin, now on active service, bore the name and Christian name of his ancestors. For the first Fulk FitzWarin was a famous knight in the days of King John,[1] who was succeeded by Fulk the Second, a remiss and lukewarm man. To him succeeded Fulk the Third, a brave and active knight who often proved his worth against the pagans in Spain. So it frequently happens that a valiant man is succeeded by one less worthy and *vice versa*; and such a pedigree is not perhaps without design. For a man's worth appears more clearly by comparison. Thus the potter of his art makes some vessels unto honour, and some to dishonour,[2] so that those which he makes unto honour have the greater glory by comparison with those of less worth.

So the lord king and his army set out towards Cirencester, and stayed there for some days to keep Christmas. The barons had already occupied Gloucester, so the king turned aside to Worcester,[3] but did not cross the Severn there because the barons held the opposite bank. The king also sent ahead a force of cavalry and infantry to prepare his crossing at Bridgnorth. The lords Mortimer likewise offered resistance and made a serious attack upon the King. They burned a great part of the town and killed very many of the king's servants. Leaving the town on the left, the king reached Shrewsbury,[4] in order to cross thence into the March. The barons there could have hindered the king's march if they had wished, but the lords Mortimer would not agree to this, because the Earl

in Marchiam. Poterant ad hec barones si uoluissent cursum regis impedisse; sed domini de Mortymer noluerunt ulterius consentire, eo quod iuxta placitos dies non uenit comes Lancastrie: timebant enim aliquid magnum aggredi sine comite. Iccirco sine comite noluerunt domino regi amplius resistere. Vnde uidentes quod comes non succurreret in articulo necessitatis, relictis sociis, reddiderunt se uoluntati domini regis.[1] Reliqui uero comites uehementer attoniti comitem Lancastrie adierunt, et ea que sic gesta erant in lacrimis narrauerunt. Comes autem in protectionem suam omnes recepit, et pro communi querela defendenda sub iureiurando auxilium promisit.

Rex igitur, relicta Salopia,[2] in Marchiam transiuit, et quia nemo restitit omnia castella faciliter occupauit. Veniensque rex apud Herfordiam[3] episcopum loci[4] acriter increpauit, eo quod contra naturalem dominum / suum barones sustinuit, unde et plurima bona ipsius in ultionem confiscauit.

Deinde rediit rex apud Gloucestriam,[5] et Mauricium de Berkelee recepit in gratiam suam. Iussit eum nichilominus in custodiam mitti et castrum de Berkelee cum omnibus bonis suis pariter confiscari. Exinde misit rex illos de Mortymer ad Turrim Londoniarum ut ibidem remanerent, ne forte prioris facti pœnitentes ad socios suos barones resilirent.

Dum autem rex moram faceret in uilla Gloucestrie, oblatus est quidam miles[6] de partibus Herfordie, et

F.265

---

[1] They had safe-conduct 17 January and submitted 22 January (*Foed. II* 471, 472; *Parl. Writs*, ii.175, 176).

[2] 25 January

[3] 29 January to 4 February

[4] Adam de Orleton, 1317-27

[5] 6 February

[6] This was Roger de Elmerugge, late sheriff of Herefordshire (*Cal. Fine Rolls*, 5 January 1322; the identification is given by Baker's *Chroniculum*, p. 171 in Maunde Thompson's edition). He was a Worcestershire man,

of Lancaster had not come at the appointed days;
for they were afraid to attempt any large-scale operation
without the Earl.   They therefore did not wish to
resist the lord king further without the Earl.   Then,
seeing that the Earl would not help them in their time
of need, they deserted their allies, and threw themselves on the king's mercy.[1]   The other earls were
very much astonished and approached the Earl of
Lancaster, and in tears told him what had happened.
The Earl received them all into his protection, and for
the prosecution of their common grievance he promised
aid under oath.

The king, therefore, leaving Shrewsbury,[2] crossed
to the March and as no one opposed him he easily
took all the castles.   Coming to Hereford,[3] he upbraided
the bishop of the place[4] for supporting the barons
against their natural lord, and he confiscated many
of his goods by way of revenge.

The king then returned to Gloucester[5] and received
Maurice de Berkeley into his grace.   Nevertheless
he ordered him to be arrested, and confiscated
Berkeley Castle with all his goods as well.   The lords
of Mortimer the king sent to the Tower of London,
where they were to remain, lest repenting of what
they had done they should return to their baronial
allies.

While the king was staying in the town of Gloucester
a certain Herefordshire knight[6] was brought before
him, and the king was informed that this knight had

---

but had lands in Herefordshire, which the escheator, John Walwayn, was
told to release to his widow in July 1322 (*Cal. Close Rolls*, p. 582).   For his
baronial companions, Roger Mortimer of Chirk and others, see *Cal. Pat.
Rolls*, p. 101, 15 February 1322.

notificatum est regi quod miles ille officium uicecomitis gesserat, et nichilominus cum baronibus equitauerat, et quod, in illa secta quam barones dabant militibus pro notitia, in contumelia regis placita comitatus tenuerat. Vnde decretum est militem illum tanquam proditorem fore puniendum; sed rex ex gratia pœnam proditorum remisit, sed suspendendum fore decreuit, et suspensus est miles ille in secta predicta, ut sicut patebat pœna pateret et causa.

Eodem tempore uenit Andreas de Herkelee[1] miles de partibus borialibus ad regem dicens; 'Ecce, domine, treuge Scotorum iam finite, Robertus de Brutz fines Anglorum inuasu incendit, depredatur et cedit. Non est qui populum defendit, non est qui pro populo se murum opponit.[2] Iccirco, domine mi rex, bonum esset, aliis negotiis postpositis,[a] populo oppresso primitus succurrere, qui sine auxilio regis sui seuitie Scotorum non possunt resistere.' Respondit rex: 'Scias,' inquit, 'Andrea, pro certo, quod si michi Robertus de Brutz immineret a tergo, et homines meos, qui tot et tanta enormia michi intulerunt, a fronte conspicerem, proditores illos inuaderem, et Robertum de Brutz inpersecutum dimitterem. Nimi/rum si Scoti, qui nullo uinculo michi tenentur obnoxii, regnum meum inuadunt, cum hii, qui fidelitate et homagio michi tenentur astricti, contra me insurgunt, homines meos spoliant et uillas incendunt; si dominum expungnant serui, quanto magis extraneus?' Sic ait Dauid rex cum persequeretur eum Absolon et male-

F.266

[a] prepositis MS
[1] Sir Andrew Harclay was sheriff of Cumberland from 1311. As 'the victor of Boroughbridge' he was created Earl of Carlisle, 25 March 1322, and Warden of the Scottish marches. For his intrigues with the Scots, against the king's specific orders (*C.P.R.* 1318-22, p. 692) he was arrested, and after trial by a special commision he was executed, 3 March 1323.

exercised the office of sheriff, and nevertheless had ridden with the barons, and that, wearing the livery that the barons gave to their knights as a distinguishing mark, he had held the pleas of the county to the King's damage. So it was decreed that this knight should be punished as a traitor, but the king graciously remitted the penalty of treason, and decided that he should be hanged, and hanged he was in the said livery; that as the penalty was manifest so too should be the cause.

At the same time Andrew Harclay,[1] a northern-country knight, came to the king saying: 'Behold, lord, the Scottish truce is at an end; Robert Bruce attacking the English frontier, burns, plunders and kills. There is none to defend the people, none to stand as a wall in front of the people.[2] Therefore, my lord king, it would be good if, putting aside other business, you came at once to the aid of your hard-pressed people, who without their king's aid cannot resist the savagery of the Scots.' The king replied: 'You may know for certain, Andrew, that if Robert Bruce threatens me from behind, and my own men, who have committed such enormities against me, should appear in front, I would attack the traitors and leave Robert Bruce alone. Small wonder if the Scots, who are in no way bound to me, invade my kingdom, while those who are bound to me by fealty and homage rise against me, plunder my men and set fire to my towns; if the servants attack their lord, how much more will a foreigner?' Thus said king David when

---

(See J. E. Morris in *Trans. Cumb. and Westm. Arch. Soc.*, new ser., iii. 307; Tout, *Place of Edward II*, 205 and documents cited in Conway-Davies, *Baronial Opposition*, 137, 265.)

    [2] Ezek. xiii. 5

diceret ei Semei: 'Ecce,' inquit, 'filius meus querit
animam meam; quanto magis hic filius Jemini*ᵃ* maledicit
michi?'¹ et non permisit aliquem nocere ei.

Dixit autem rex ad militem: 'Reuertere ad partes
tuas et serua munitiones tibi commissas; ego uero per-
sequar proditores meos ubicunque se conuertant, et non
reuertar donec deficiant.' Iussit itaque dominus rex
uiros fortes et armatos et pedites ex singulis comitatibus
congregari, et copiosum exercitum ad inimicos debellan-
dum festinanter adunari. Inimicos suos omnes appellat
quos pars baronum secum sustentat, sicut scriptum est
'Qui non est mecum contra me est.'² Iccirco bis uel
ter proclamari fecit solempniter quod omnes hii qui ad
partem baronum diuert[er]ant infra certum diem ad
pacem regis redirent; alioquin uelut hostes publici regi
puniendi sine spe redeundi extunc remanerent.

Circa idem tempus³ Hugo Despenser pater et filius
reuersi sunt ab exilio, eo quod reconciliatio eorum et
pax nutu regio proclamata foret in regno.⁴ Redierunt,
inquam, in Angliam quia rex nouit eos exulasse per
inuidiam. Poterant adhuc barones ad pacem uenisse,
ueniam et misericordiam regis forsan impetrasse, sed
modo quicquid agunt aut machinantur in confusionem
et dampnationem totaliter operantur. Nam, de protectione comitis Lancastrie nimis elati, resistentes cedunt,
patientes spoliant, nec parcunt alicui, et ad maiorem /
F.267 dampnationem suam castrum ipsius regis apud Tykhulle
inuadunt, et ad captionem castri toto nisu licet incassum
laborant.

Dominus rex nimirum super hiis uehementer com-

ᵃ Genui MS
¹ 2 Sam. xvi. 11   ² cf. Luke ix. 50   ³ January 1322
⁴ The Archbishop had declared their sentences illegal, 1 January
1322. Edward received the younger Despenser into his peace a week later.
(*Ann. Paul.* 301)

Absalom pursued him and Shimei cursed him: 'Behold', he said, 'my son seeketh my life; how much more may this Benjamite curse me',[1] and he did not permit anyone to harm him.

So the king said to the knight: 'Return to your own country and keep the strongholds committed to you; I shall pursue my traitors whithersoever they betake themselves, and I shall not turn back until they are brought to nought.' So the lord king ordered a force of cavalry and infantry to be assembled from each county, and hastily collected a numerous army to subdue his enemies. For so he styled all those who supported the baronial party, as it is written: 'He who is not for me is against me.'[2] Therefore twice or thrice he had it solemnly proclaimed that all those who had gone over to the baronial party should return to the king's peace by a certain day; otherwise from henceforth they were to remain as public enemies of the king to be punished without hope of restoration.

About the same time[3] the Despensers, father and son, returned from exile, because their reconciliation and reception into the King's peace at his mere will was to be published in England.[4] They returned to England, I say, because the king knew that they had been banished out of malice. The barons could still have come to peace, seeking the king's pardon and mercy, but now whatever they do or contrive works to their confusion and total loss. For, puffed-up by the Earl of Lancaster's protection, they killed those who opposed them, plundered those who offered no resistance, sparing no one, and to their greater guilt attacked the king's own castle at Tickhill, and to take it put forth their best efforts, though in vain.

The lord king was certainly very much enraged at

motus apud Couentriam¹ iter arripuit, et ibidem exercitum uenturum per aliquot dies exspectauit. Exinde conduxit exercitum usque ad magnum fluuium qui dicitur Trente. Est autem ibidem pons magnus qui uiam prebet transeuntibus. Premisit quoque rex ad pontem cuneum fortem armatorum et peditum, scire uolens anᵃ aliquis impediret transitum suum. Venerat autem comes Lancastrie cum omni sequela sua in uillam de Burghtone ex parte alia.

Cumque iam fuisset compertum quod rex disposuit transire fluuium, misit comes uiros fortes armatos et pedites qui pontem defenderent. Verum cum per tres pluresue dies inter se partes dimicassent,² ac ad eundem conflictum in crastinum rediissent, reperit rex uadum superius, ubi transiit ipse et reliqua pars exercitus. Audientes itaque barones et iam uidentes quod rex flumen transisset, pontem reliquerunt, equos ascenderunt et fugam inierunt. Sed quare fugit comes Lancastrie qui totiens solebat regi resistere, precipue cum haberet secum comitem Herfordie et clariorem militiam totius Anglie? Reuera magna erat nunc manus regis et ualida. Habebat enim circiter omnibus numeratis trecenta milia numero.³

Mandauerat comes Roberto de Hoylond,⁴ quem preposueratᵇ gazis suis, quatinus exercitum conduceret de uiris fortissimis, et certum diem ueniendi statuit; sed prefixo die Robertus non uenit, immo preuaricator in causa domini sui reddidit se domino regi; unde comitis

---

ᵃ aut MS; utrum Hearne
ᵇ proposuerat MS

¹ A general summons for 28 February at Coventry had been ordered on 13 February (*Parl. Writs*, II.ii.547, 548).
² 8-10 March
³ Possibly a scribal error for 30,000, since our author is careful with figures, but he has already assessed the baronial army at 30,000.

this and set out for Coventry,[1] where he awaited the arrival of his army for some days. Thence he led his army to the great river called Trent. There is there a great bridge which offers a passage to those who wish to cross. The king sent forward to the bridge a strong phalanx of cavalry and infantry, wishing to know if there would be any opposition to his crossing. But the Earl of Lancaster had arrived with all his retinue at the town of Burton on the other side.

When it was known that the king proposed to cross the river, the Earl sent horse and foot to defend the bridge. But when the two sides had fought together for three or more days,[2] and returned to the same battle on the morrow, the king found a ford higher up, where he himself crossed with the remainder of his army. When the barons heard, and now saw for themselves that the king had crossed the river, they left the bridge, took horse, and fled. But why does the Earl of Lancaster, so often accustomed to resist the king, now take to flight, particularly as he had with him the Earl of Hereford and the flower of English chivalry? The king's forces were indeed now great and powerful. For he had about 300,000 men all told.[3]

The Earl had ordered Robert Holland,[4] whom he had put in charge of his treasure, to bring an army of his best men, and had arranged a day for his coming; but on the appointed day Robert did not come, but as an apostate in his lord's cause deserted to the lord

---

[4] Robert Holland of Holland in Lancashire, was sometime Justice of Chester. His treachery to the earl in 1322 was perhaps decisive in destroying the baronial cause before Boroughbridge. He was beheaded at Harrow in 1328 (*Ann. Paul.* 342). See also Tout, *Chapters*, ii. 185-7; Conway Davies, *Baronial Opposition*, 503-4; Dugdale, *Baronage* ii. 73.

S

sequaces auxilium parum adesse*ᵃ* uidentes pontem reliquerunt, equos ascenderunt, [et fu]ge[runt]. /

F.268   Persequebatur rex fugientes usque ad castrum de
Totbury,¹ quod erat comitis Lancastrie, inuenitque rex
ianuas apertas, eo quod post fugam comitis nullus aude-
bat resistere. Sed et custos castri de Keneleworthe,
audita fuga comitis, reddidit statim castrum in manus
uicecomitis. Repperit autem rex apud Tottebury
Rogerum Dammori in extremis laborantem; erat enim
infirmitas ad mortem, quia non uixit ultra tertium diem;
et bene quidem et honeste sibi contigit quod ad finem
desolatum cum sociis non durauit. Iste Rogerus olim
pauper miles et tenuis ob industriam et probitatem suam
factus est regis specialis, quamobrem dedit ei rex neptem
suam in uxorem, et de comitatu Gloucestrie que contingebat eam*ᵇ* tertiam partem; sed quia cum baronibus
contra regem tenuit, notam ingratitudinis a multis
reportauit.

Comes igitur Lancastrie et comes Herfordie, cum
omnibus sibi adherentibus, in fugam conuersi, ad Pountfreit peruenerunt. Ibidem aliquantam moram facientes,
tandem diffinito consilio uersus Scotiam iter arripuerunt.
In Scotiam sperabant habere confugium, quia Robertus
de Brutz, ut dictum erat, contra regem promiserat
auxilium.

Cumque apud Borbrigge² uenissent ut ibidem saltem
una nocte requiescerent, ecce Andreas de Herkelee miles
strenuus, cui iam de fuga comitis innotuerat, qui etiam
progressum eius et propositum plenius explorauerat,
quasi cum quatuor milibus uirorum uenerat quos ad
locum illum repente conduxerat. Audientes autem
comites, qui erant infra uillam quasi iam hospitati, quod

ᵃ abesse MS   *ᵇ* Hearne suggests 'ei'
¹ 11-13 March   ² 16 March

king; hence the Earl's followers seeing that not enough help was present left the bridge, took horse, and fled.

The king pursued the fugitives to Tutbury Castle,[1] which belonged to the Earl of Lancaster, and he found the gates open, because after the Earl's flight no one dared to offer resistance. The warden of Kenilworth Castle, too, on hearing of the Earl's flight, at once surrendered the castle to the sheriff. At Tutbury the king found Roger Damory at the point of death; he was indeed at his last gasp for he did not live beyond the third day. And indeed it turned out well and honourably for him that he did not endure with his comrades to the bitter end: This Roger was once a poor and needy knight who by his industry and valour had received the king's special favour, wherefore the king gave him his niece in marriage, and her third share of the earldom of Gloucester; but because he sided with the barons against the king, many marked him down as ungrateful.

Thus the Earl of Lancaster and the Earl of Hereford, with all their adherents, were put to flight and came to Pomfret. After a short delay there it was decided to press on towards Scotland. They hoped to find a refuge in Scotland, because Robert Bruce, as was said, had promised help against the king.

When they reached Boroughbridge,[2] that there at any rate they might rest for a night, who should be there but Andrew Harclay, that active soldier, already aware of the Earl's flight. He had fully informed himself of the Earl's order of march and his plans, and had arrived with some four thousand men, whom he had led with all speed to that place. The earls were settling into their lodgings in the town, when they heard that Andrew and his followers had

uenerat Andreas et sui sequaces ad expungnandum
eos totaliter, exierunt uillam bipertito*a* cum aduersariis
congressuri.   Comes Herfordie cum suis armatis per
F.269 pontem transiuit, sed nullus / eorum equum ascendit.
Erat enim pons strictus, nec uiam equitibus ad bellum
procedentibus prebere potuit.   Comes Lancastrie cum
suis militibus ad uadum fluminis uiam arripuit.   Sed
Andreas de Herkeleye, tanquam miles prouidus, ad
utrumque exitum cuneum armatorum sapienter statuit.
Comes Herfordie partem aduersam primitus aggreditur;
decertando male uulneratus tandem occiditur.   Tres uel
quatuor milites in ipso certamine cum comite perierunt.
Rogerus de Clifford et alii quamplurimi male uulnerati
ad uillam redierunt.   Alii uero, dum uadum transire
nituntur, ab ymbre sagittarum misere*b* atteruntur; sed
post mortem comitis Herfordie sua uirtus tepuit militie,
et statim reuertuntur.   Pepigit autem comes Lancastrie
cum Andrea de Herkelee de treuga et pace seruanda
usque in crastinum; et hoc facto rediit unusquisque ad
hospitium suum.[1]   Ipsa uero nocte uicecomes Eboraci
cum magna cohorte uenerat inimicos regis inuadere;
cuius auxilio fretus Andreas de Herkelee uillam intrauit
summo mane, et cepit comitem Lancastrie et omnes
pene reliquos milites et scutarios sine uulnere, et per-
ducens Eboracum reclusit in carcerem.   Quidam*c* equos
reliquerunt, et exuentes*d* arma sua ueteres attritas uestes
quesierunt sibi, et more mendicantium uiam incesserunt.
Sed cautela non profuit, nam nec unus quidem famosus
ex omnibus euasit.

O monstrum! uidere uiros purpura et bisso nuper

a bipertitam MS
b So Stubbs; usum MS. Hearne suggests ' usque ' or ' usquequaque.'
c euitare MS
d exeuntes MS

come to destroy them utterly, so they left the town to meet their opponents in two columns. The Earl of Hereford crossed by the bridge with his men-at-arms, but none of them was mounted. For the bridge was narrow, and offered no path for horsemen in battle array. The Earl of Lancaster with his knights made their way to the ford of the river. But Andrew Harclay, like a prudent knight, had shrewdly stationed a force of men-at-arms opposite each crossing. The Earl of Hereford forthwith attacked the enemy, but at length fell badly wounded in the fighting and died. Three or four knights were killed with the earl in that conflict. Roger de Clifford and very many others returned to the town badly wounded. Others, trying to cross the ford, were lamentably cut up by a shower of arrows; but after the death of the Earl of Hereford their zeal for battle cooled off, and they at once retreated. But the Earl of Lancaster made a truce with Andrew Harclay to keep the peace until the morrow; and when this was done each returned to his lodging.[1] On that same night the sheriff of York came with a large force to attack the king's enemies; relying on his help Andrew Harclay entered the town very early, and taking the Earl of Lancaster and almost all the other knights and esquires scatheless, led them off to York and imprisoned them. Some left their horses and putting off their armour looked round for ancient worn-out garments, and took to the road as beggars. But their caution was of no avail, for not a single well-known man among them all escaped.

O calamity! To see men lately dressed in purple

---

[1] As Ramsay, 126, remarks if he 'was not absolutely besotted in his self-importance', he might have been expected to take instant flight.

indutos nunc attritis uestibus incedere, et uinctos in
compedibus recludi sub carcere! Res miranda et certe
nutu Dei et auxilio promota, quod tam rara manu
subito superatur tanta militia. Pars*a* enim comitis
numero armatorum partem persequentium excessit in
F.270 septuplum. Capti sunt enim cum comite Lancastrie / et
ceteris baronibus milites ualentes centum et amplius. Sed
et scutariorum non minus*b* ualentium multo maiorem
credo fuisse numerum. Quare igitur non restitissent et
pro salute sua uiriliter dimicassent? Reuera cor delin-
quentium semper est pauidum et ideo minus ualens ad
negotium. Videbant totam patriam a fronte excitatam,
et per hoc uiam eorum impeditam. Sciebant a tergo
imminere regis exercitum, et propter hoc cursum retro-
gradum non esse securum. Vnde quasi homines non
habentes consilium nec etiam tempus ad deliberandum,
inciderunt in manus inimicorum, etc.

Quarto quintoue die post captionem comitis Lancastrie ueniens rex apud Pontfreit[1] iussit adduci comitem
sine dilatione, et statim iussu regis adducitur, et in
quadam noua turri per noctem illam recluditur. Fertur
comes turrim illam nouiter construxisse, et regem captum
in ipsa recludendum perpetuum decreuisse, sed et leonem
more Lumbardorum principem constituisse. Hec erat
fama uulgaris, sed non audiui testem ueritatis.

In crastinum producitur comes in aulam coram iustitiariis assignatis, et singillatim species transgressionis, ac
pro quolibet articulo adicitur pœna specialis, uidelicet,
ut primo protraheretur, deinde suspenderetur, ac pos-

---

a per MS
b unus MS
[1] Edward II was at Pontefract 22-30 March (Stubbs); Ramsay, 127,
says 19 March, citing *Foed.* II. 478.

and fine linen now attired in rags, bound and imprisoned in chains! A marvellous thing and one indeed brought about by God's will and aid, that so scanty a company should in a moment overcome so many knights. For the Earl's side were more than seven times as numerous as their adversaries. There were captured with the Earl of Lancaster and the other barons more than a hundred valiant knights. The number of esquires no less valiant was, I believe, much greater. Why therefore should they not have stood and fought manfully for their safety? Indeed the criminal is always fearful and so less effective in action. They saw that the whole countryside was up-in-arms in front of them, and thus their advance was blocked. They knew that the king's army threatened them from the rear, and therefore their retreat was not secure. Thus as men having no plan nor even time to deliberate, they fell into the hands of their enemies, *etc.*

On the fourth or fifth day after the capture of the Earl of Lancaster, the king coming to Pomfret[1] ordered him to be brought up without delay. He was at once brought up by the king's command, and for that night he was shut up in a certain new tower. It is said that the Earl had recently built that tower, and determined that when the king was captured he should be imprisoned in it for life, and so to have made the prince a lion after the manner of the Lombards. This was the common story, but I have not heard evidence of its truth.

On the morrow the Earl was led into the hall before the justices assigned for the purpose, and charged one by one with his crimes, and to each charge a special penalty was attached, namely, that first he should be drawn, then hanged, and finally decapitated.

tremo capite truncaretur. Sed ob reuerentiam regii
sanguinis pœna protractionis est remissa, suspensio
suspensa, sed pœna pro omnibus decreta. At comes,
uolens se in aliquibus excusare, nitebatur quedam statim
allegare; sed iustitiarii noluerunt ipsum audire quia
uerba dampnatorum sicut nec nocent nec possent proficere. Tunc ait comes: 'Fortis est hec curia, et maior
imperio, ubi non auditur responsio nec aliqua admittitur
excusatio.' /

F.271   O spectaculum! uidere comitem Lanacstrie, qui nuper
erat terror totius patrie, in castro proprio et domo
iudicium recipere. Deinde educitur comes extra castrum, et ascendens quoddam uile iumentum conductus
est ad capitolium. Tunc comes quasi orando caput
extendit, et spiculator bis uel ter percutiens caput amputauit. Et hec acta sunt mense Martii anno regni
quintodecimo.

O comes Lancastrie! ubi est dominatio tua, ubi sunt
diuitie tue, quibus sperabas omnes subicere et nullum
contra te posse resistere? Si in primeua fide perdurasses,
ad desolatum nequaquam peruenisses. Si Sampson in
cautela et Salomon in deuotione perstitissent, nec hic
uiribus nec ille sapientia priuatus fuisset. Forte latens
causa, non presens sed preterita, comitem puniuit.
Comes Lancastrie caput Petri de Gauestone olim abstulit, et nunc iussu regis comes Lancastrie caput perdidit.
Sic uicem pro uice, forsan non iniuste, comes reportauit,
sicut scriptum est in sacris litteris: 'Eadem mensura qua
mensi fueritis remetietur uobis.'[1] Sic Abner occidit
Asael percutiens in inguine,[a] sed Abner non euasit; nam

----

[a] igne MS
[1] Luke vi. 38

But out of reverence for his royal blood the penalty
of drawing was remitted, as also that of hanging, and
one punishment was decreed for all three. The Earl,
however, wishing to speak in mitigation of his crimes,
immediately tried to make some points; but the judges
refused to hear him, because the words of the condemned
can neither harm nor be of any profit. Then the Earl
said: 'This is a powerful court, and great in authority,
where no answer is heard nor any excuse admitted.'
Here was a sight indeed! To see the Earl of Lancaster,
lately the terror of the whole country, receiving judgment in his own castle and home. Then the Earl was
led forth from the castle, and mounted on some worthless
mule was led to the place of execution. Then the
Earl stretched forth his head as if in prayer, and the
executioner cut off his head with two or three strokes.
And this happened in March in the fifteenth year of
the reign.

O Earl of Lancaster! Where is thy might, where
are thy riches, with which thou hadst hoped to subdue
all, with none to resist thee? If thou hadst been stead-
fast in faith, thou wouldst never have been brought to
nought. If Samson had remained cautious and Solomon
devout, the one would not have been deprived of his
strength nor the other of his wisdom. Perhaps a
hidden cause, not immediate but remote, brought
punishment upon the Earl. The Earl of Lancaster
once cut off Piers Gaveston's head, and now by the
king's command the Earl himself has lost his head.
Thus, perhaps not unjustly, the Earl received measure
for measure, as it is written in Holy Scripture: 'For
with the same measure that ye mete withal it shall be
measured to you again.'[1] Thus Abner killed Asahel,
striking him under the fifth rib, but Abner did not

postea interiit consimili uulnere.[1] Sic in principio
Judicum[2] cepit Judas regem Bezel et uinxit captiuum,
ac summitates manuum eius prescidit et pedum. Tunc
ait rex ille captus, 'Merito fecit hoc michi Dominus,
ego enim lxx. reges in bello ceperam et omnes hac

[*Desunt sex folia*]

tempore comes Wyntoniensis,[3] licentiatus a rege ad
partes australes se transtulit ut maneria sua uisitaret,
quia post destructionem iam dudum non uidit. Cum
audis loqui de comite Wyntoniensi, intellige de Hugone
Despenser seniore. /

F.272   Accessit itaque Robertus Lewer ad maneria comitis
Wyntoniensis, et cepit ibidem uictualia et alia necessaria
pro sua uoluntate. Visitauit etiam maneria Henrici
Thyeys[4] et Warinii de Insula, comiti Wyntoniensi post
dampnationem eorum a rege collata. Et ibidem dominus
Robertus elemosinarum nomine[a] pro animabus dictorum
baronum fecit magnam distributionem pauperibus. Ex
hoc tamen parum promeruit, quia[b] non quid fiat sed
quo animo Deus attendit. Non potest dici elemosina
que fit[c] ex furto uel rapina. Nam, sicut dicitur alibi,
species furti ex bonis alterius inuito domino quicquam
largiri.

[a] elemosinarius nam MS
[b] quia] que MS
[c] sit MS
[1] 2 Sam. ii. 23, ii. 27
[2] Judges i. 6, 7
[3] i.e. Hugh Despenser, the father, created Earl of Winchester at the
Parliament of York, 1322.
[4] Henry le Tyeys (Teutonicus) was summoned to Parliament from
28 Ed. I, when he inherited his lands, to 14 Ed. II (Dugdale, *Baronage*, ii, 21).
At least three persons of this name in succession held the manor of Shirburn,
Oxon., with members in Cornwall and Wiltshire, of the honour of St Valery.
For a description of his death by hanging, in London, after Boroughbridge,
see *Chron. Ed. I & II* (R.S.) i, 103. The best view of the family lands is obtained

escape, for he afterwards perished by a similar wound.[1]
Thus at the beginning of the Book of Judges,[2] Judah
took the king of Bezel and made him captive, and
cut off his thumbs and his great toes. Then said the
captive king: 'God hath requited me, for I had taken
three score and ten kings in battle and all . . . .

[*Six leaves are lacking*]

time the Earl of Winchester,[3] with the king's leave,
went to the south country to inspect his manors, as
he had not seen them since they had been plundered
long ago. When I speak of the Earl of Winchester,
you are to understand that I mean Hugh Despenser
the elder.

So Robert le Ewer came to the Earl of Winchester's
manors, and carried off victuals and other necessaries
as he liked. He also visited the manors of Henry
Thyeys[4] and Warin de Insula, granted by the king
to the Earl of Winchester after their condemnation.
And there Sir Robert made a great distribution to
the poor in the name of Alms for the souls of the said
barons. From this he profited little, because God
has regard to the intention rather than the deed.
That cannot be called alms which comes from theft
or rapine. For, as is said elsewhere, it is a kind of theft
to distribute largesse from the goods of another without
the consent of the lord.

---

from *Cal. I.P.M.* VII. 23, 25 (A.D. 1327). His sister (or possibly his daughter)
Alice married Warin de Lisle of Kingston Lisle, who is better known.
Henry was sufficiently prominent to be condemned with the Mortimers and
Bohun (Conway Davies, *Baronial Opposition*, App. no. 44). He had been
appointed a conservator of the peace in the Isle of Wight in 1317 and was
later Constable there, but out of office by November 1320 (*C.P.R.*, 45).
In Warin de Lisle we have another Constable (in 1318-19 but not in April
1321), this time of Windsor (*C.P.R.* 303).

Audiens autem comes Wyntoniensis quod uenisset
Robertus eum comprehendere, intrauit castrum de
Wyndelsore, et fecit fieri excubias die et nocte, donec
congregasset uirtutem sufficientem ad excipiendum
Robertum et comitiuam suam. Venit etiam in auxilium
eius comes Cantie missus a latere regis. Sic ergo Robertus caruit proposito suo, et sui cotidie diuertebant ab eo.
Cumque uideret iam aliud subsidium nullum superesse,
ueniens clam apud Hamptone super mare, cogitauit
ibidem cum uxore sua transfretare. Sed omnibus incolis
facie notissimus, utpote apud illos diu conuersatus, latere
non potuit. Quodam die comprehensum in urbe
minister regis in carcerem detrusit. Productus uero
coram iustitiariis, interrogatus et accusatus in multis,
nichil respondit. Quem discretio iudicum ad peragen-
dam sententiam suam in carcerem retorsit. Pœna
siquidem, scienter obmutescentibus debita, talis per
regnum usitata. Sedebit incarceratus in area frigida et
nuda captiuus, unica sola et tenuissima ueste uelatus,
tanto pondere ferri quantum miserum corpus ferre
F.273 ualuerit oppressus. / Cibus erit illi panis deterrimus[a] et
modicus, et potus aque liquor turbidus et fœtidus. Die
qua commedit non potabit, nec die qua potauerit panem
gustabit. Communis humane nature uirtutem superaret
qui quintum uel sextum diem sub hac pœna transigeret.

Huiusmodi pœne per aliquot dies Robertus astrictus
tandem occubuit, et ita pro delictis[b] dignam ultionem
et anime salutiferam, si[c] tamen patienter ipsam tum
sustinuit, in fine reportauit. Ipse Robertus, in curia
regis olim educatus, in rebus bellicis cautus erat et
strenuus. Verumptamen de fauore curie confisus, et

[a] deterius MS
[b] pro delictis] per electis MS
[c] sibi MS

When the Earl of Winchester heard that Robert had come to arrest him, he took refuge in Windsor Castle, and set a watch night and day, until he should have collected a force sufficient to capture Robert and his retinue. The Earl of Kent, too, came from court to help him at the king's command. Thus Robert's plan failed, and his men deserted day by day. When he saw that no other help was available he came secretly to Southampton, thinking to cross from there with his wife. But as he was very well known by sight to all the inhabitants from long residence there, he could not hide himself. He was arrested one day in the town and a royal official cast him into prison. When he was brought before the justices, questioned and accused of many crimes, he did not answer. He was therefore thrust back into prison at the discretion of the judges to undergo his sentence. The customary punishment, indeed, for those mute of malice is carried out thus throughout the realm. The prisoner shall sit on the cold, bare floor, dressed only in the thinnest of shirts, and pressed with as great a weight of iron as his wretched body can bear. His food shall be a little rotten bread, and his drink cloudy and stinking water. The day on which he eats he shall not drink, and the day on which he has drunk he shall not taste bread. Only superhuman strength survives this punishment beyond the fifth or sixth day.

Afflicted with this treatment for some few days Robert at length died, thus receiving at last a punishment fitting for his crimes and healthy for his soul, provided he bore it with resignation. This Robert, who had been educated at court, was shrewd and active in military matters. Nevertheless, relying on his influence at court, and accustomed to lax morals

uariis moribus a iuuentute consuetus, ad predas et
homicidia semper erat precipuus. Ceterum quia tum
quendam bonum occidit, et uxorem eius superduxit,
quam etiam in adulterio prius posuerat, omne aliud
delictum longius excedit. Sic igitur Robertus cecidit ut
meruit, et comes Wyntoniensis indempnis euasit.

Aliud quoque non minus timendum accidit Wyntoniensi comiti periculum. Mauricius de Berkele, iam
fere per annum detentus,[1] tum moram traxit in castro
Walynfordie, ad quem solebat quidam armiger qui diu
steterat in obsequio ipsius frequenter intrare, et ob
priorem familiaritatem domino suo beneficium consola-
tionis impendere. Accidit autem quadam die ut armiger
ille cum tribus uel quatuor sociis intraret castrum, de
licentia custodis, propter solitum accessum in nullo suspectus. Eadem nocte rogauit Mauricius constabularium
ut cœnaret cum eo; insuper et ianitores et uigiles quotquot*a* erant in castro. Cœnantibus autem illis subito
surrexit armiger cum sociis suis, et petiit claues castri
sibi reddi, necnon et minas mortis intendebat cuilibet
repungnanti. /

F.274　Videns ergo constabularius quod non posset resistere,
tradidit claues sine dilatione. Tunc armiger ille ad
quandam priuatam portam accessit, et circiter xx*ti* socios
statim introduxit. Et hec quidem facta sunt sub tanto
silentio ut nec clamor nec murmur resonaret in castro.
Tandem puer quidam residens ad exteriorem portam,
postquam sentiit quod interior custodia insolito modo
tractabatur, latenter exiuit, adiensque [maiorem] uille*b*
castrum perditum et multos extraneos intrasse protinus
nuntiauit. Primum quidem nuntius a predicto armigero
cum litteris emissus testis accessit. Disposuerat enim

---

a quotquot] in quotquot MS
b audiensque velle MS
[1] February 1322 to January 1323

from youth, he was always ready for plunder and killing. But as he had killed a certain good man, and made off with his wife, with whom he had previously committed adultery, his crimes had overstepped all limits. In this fashion therefore he met his deserts, and the Earl of Winchester escaped unharmed.

Another danger no less fearful befell the Earl of Winchester. Maurice de Berkeley, in custody now for almost a year,[1] was at that time detained in Wallingford Castle, where a certain esquire who had long been in his service used often to visit him, and on account of their former intimacy was able to console him. But it happened one day that this esquire with three or four companions entered the castle, by leave of the guard, and because his visit was customary it was in no way suspicious. The same night Maurice invited the constable to dine with him, and all the doorkeepers and watchmen in the castle as well. As they were dining the esquire and his companions suddenly rose and demanded the keys of the castle, threatening with death anyone who resisted.

Seeing that he could not resist, the constable handed over the keys without delay. Then the esquire went to a certain private gate, and at once let in about twenty companions. This was done in such silence that not a sound was heard in the castle. At length a boy living at the outer gate, realising that affairs in the inner ward were not as they should be, secretly slipped out, went to [the mayor] of the town, and at once reported that the castle was lost, and that many strangers had entered. A certain messenger sent out by the esquire with letters came forth as a witness. For the esquire had planned to warn certain friends and to get his lord Maurice away at cockcrow together with the

armiger ille quosdam socios premunisse, et in gallicinio
dominum suum Mauricium et ceteros uinculatos*ª* pariter
eduxisse. Sed nuntius machinationis proditorie timens
periculum subire accessit ad maiorem uille. Populus
conuocatur, pulsantur campane, tonant cornua, et uox
horrida plebis extollitur.

Tunc qui erant infra castrum audientes populi
tumultum*ᵇ* suspicabantur consilium suum iam esse de-
tectum, et per consequens propositum eorum impeditum;
unde statuerunt custodes ad singulas [portas, et] excubias per totum murum ordinauerunt. Mane facto
diuulgata est res per totam patriam, accessitque uicecomes ad uillam, et hortabatur interiores ad castri deditionem. Illi uero asserebant*ᶜ* se regis auctoritate castrum
intrasse, nec cuiquam homini sine regis mandato reddere
uelle. Et hoc quidem responso usi sunt ad cautelam, ut
sic proditionem suam palliarent et nacta oportunitate
temporis a castro recederent.

Non credidit uicecomes responsum, quia non fecerunt
ei fidem de regis mandato. Immo statim accesserunt
robustiores totius patrie; et fecit fieri uigilias circa cas-
F.275 trum die ac nocte donec certificaretur super alle/gata
regis auctoritate. Aduenerunt in auxilium uicecomitis
comes Wyntonie et comes Cantie, quoniam tunc erant
in partibus illis; et statim disposuerunt*ᵈ* castrum inuadere et proditores ui et armis ad deditionem compellere.
Videntes autem interiores tot et tantos uiros ad obsidionem,*ᵉ* et captionem tandem euitari non posse, quantoque
diutius rebellarent, tanto grauiori pœne subiacerent,
portas aperiunt et liberum introitum cunctis promit-
tentes in quadam capella omnes conueniunt.

Tunc ingressi comites reperierunt Mauricium in

ª uinculatores MS   *ᵇ* populum tumultu MS   *ᶜ* asserebantur MS
ᵈ deposuerunt MS   *ᵉ* obsidicionem MS

other prisoners. But the messenger of this treacherous design went to the mayor of the town, fearing to run the risk. The townsmen were aroused, bells rung, horns sounded, and the harsh cries of the populace were heard.

Hearing the uproar of the people, the men in the castle guessed that their plan was discovered and consequently its execution thwarted. So they posted guards at all [the gates] and arranged watches all along the wall. By morning the news had spread throughout the countryside, and the sheriff came to the castle and exhorted those within to surrender. They replied that they had entered the castle by the king's authority, and that they would not yield it to any man without the king's mandate. They made this answer as a precaution, to palliate their treachery, so that given an opportunity they might leave the castle.

The sheriff did not believe this reply, because they had given him no proof of the king's mandate. The hardy country-folk came up immediately and the sheriff set a watch about the castle day and night until he had proof of the alleged royal authority. The Earl of Winchester and the Earl of Kent, who were then in those parts, came to the aid of the sheriff; and they at once arranged to attack the castle and compel the traitors to surrender by force of arms. Seeing the strength of the besieging force, and that they could not escape capture, and that the longer they rebelled the more severe would be their punishment, the men inside opened the gates and, promising free entry to all, gathered together in a certain chapel.

The earls then entered, finding Maurice in custody as usual, and the rest in the chapel. The immunity of the church was of no avail to them: they were at

T

solita custodia, reliquos autem in capella. Non profuit
eis immunitas ecclesie; nam protinus extracti truduntur
in castrum. Ille uero interrogatus cur proditores in
castrum regis aduocare presumpsit, nichil in preiudicium
domini regis machinatum constanter affirmauit, et
cognitorem omnium cordium et omnes homines exceptis
aduersariis suis testes adiecit. Tunc significauerunt
domino regi omnia acta cum responso Mauricii.
Rescripsit rex comiti Cantie . . . .
consensu Mauricii diligenter inquireret, et dictum armigerum ceterorum sig . . . . . suis

[Deest folium unum]

'sepius promouit; et, si per lapsum temporis populum
suum in unitate reduxerit, id quod prius profuit in
uanum redibit. Preterea diutina pax homines nostros
effœminatos reddet, et usus armorum suspensus inbellem
gentem nostram efficiet. Sed et hii qui nunc apti sunt
ad prelium inutiles fient, uergentes in senium; et hec
omnia nobis incommoda conferet tempus uacationis
producte. Super hiis igitur consulimus quod regi
F.276 Anglorum perpetua / concordia offeratur, et pax fiat,
alioquin de treugis initis non multum confidat. Et quia
rex Anglorum, sicut creditur, certamen est habiturus cum
Francis, eo citius speramus optinere quod petimus.'

Tunc misit Robertus le Brutz ad regem Anglie,
dicens[1]: 'Domine, placet Scotis in pacem perpetuam
treugas conuertere, et quid tibi placuerit, si bonum tibi
uidetur, uelitis rescribere. Multi enim nostris treugis
initis egre consenserant. Vnde timeo ne forsan pace
repulsa pacta seruabo, sed multorum grassantium rabiem
solus cohibere non potero. Nam et rex Getheus, qui

---

[1] See Tout, *Place of Edward II*, p. 135

once dragged out and crowded into the castle.   When Maurice was asked why he had presumed to call traitors to his aid in the king's castle, he stoutly maintained that he had plotted nothing to the prejudice of the lord king, and called to witness the searcher of all hearts and all men except his adversaries.   They then notified the king of what had been done and of Maurice's reply.   The king wrote back to the Earl of Kent . . . . . to enquire diligently with Maurice's consent, and to . . . . . the said esquire . . . . .

[One leaf is lacking]

(. . . *Saepius promovit*); and if in the course of time he reunites his people, what formerly was of profit will be worthless.   Further, a long peace will make our men effeminate, lack of practice in the use of arms will render them unwarlike.   Those who are now prepared for battle will become useless, bordering upon old age; all these disadvantages will be brought upon us by a long drawn-out rest.   In this, therefore, we advise that a perpetual agreement be offered to the King of England, and let it be peace, for if not let him have little faith in agreed truces.   And because the King of the English, as is thought, is on the point of fighting the French, we hope the more speedily to obtain what we seek.'

Then Robert Bruce sent to the King of England saying[1]: 'My Lord, the Scots wish to turn the truce into a perpetual peace, and if it seems good to you, may it please you to communicate your pleasure in the matter.   For many of my men have agreed to these truces with difficulty.   Whence I fear that if peace is refused I may be unable to keep my word, for I cannot

satis in Dauid sibi complacuit, eum tamen contra uota
satraparum sustinere non potuit.'[1]

Animaduertens rex Anglie quod artaret eum negotium Vasconie, quod et Scoti ex nimia causa proni essent
ad recidiuum concordie, rescripsit se uelle in pacem
perpetuam libenter consentire, placuitque de communi
consensu super tractanda apud Eboracum[2] partes conuenire. Quo cum uenissent, uidelicet rex Anglie ex
parte una et quidam magnates Scotorum ex altera,
petierunt Scoti Scotiam ab omni exactione regni Anglie
imperpetuum esse[a] immunem, et liberam petierunt iure
adquisitionis et dominii totam terram quam perambula-
uerant usque ad portas Eboraci. Erat et quedam
baronia in partibus Essexie quam Robertus de Brutz
propter rebellionem dudum demeruit; hanc petiit Robertus sibi restitui, etiam cum fructibus quos medio
tempore rex inde percepit. Petierunt etiam Scoti petram
illam regalem sibi restitui quam Edwardus rex senior
quondam de Scotia tulerat et apud Westmonasterium
collocauerat iuxta tumbam Sancti Edwardi.[3] Erat autem
lapis ille apud Scotos celebris memorie, eo quod super
F.277 hanc reges Scotie / solebant gubernacula regni cum
sceptro recipere. Scota filia Pharaonis hanc petram
secum a finibus Egipti eduxit, cum in partes Scotie
applicuit et terram subiugauit. Prophetauerat enim
Moises quod qui petram illam secum afferret amplas
terras suo dominio subiugaret. Vnde a Scota est dicta
Scotia que prius ab Albanacto uocabatur Albania. Ad

---

[a] esse] et MS
[1] 1 Sam. xxix
[2] The Scottish envoys had safe-conduct dated 3 November 1324 *Foed.*
ii. 578.
[3] On the Stone of Scone see the *Scottish Historical Review*, April 1950,
pp. 26, 33.

alone restrain the fury of a raging throng. For the King of Gath though much pleased by David, yet could not maintain him against the wishes of his satraps.[1]

The king of England realising that the matter of Gascony limited his scope of action, and that the Scots had every reason to welcome the restoration of peace, wrote back that he would willingly consent to a perpetual peace and it was agreed by common consent that the parties should meet at York[2] to treat of the matter. When they had come thither, that is the King of England on the one hand and certain Scottish magnates on the other, the Scots demanded that Scotland should be for ever free from every English exaction, and they demanded by right of conquest and lordship that the whole land that they had perambulated should be free as far as the gates of York. There was also a certain barony in Essex which Robert Bruce had long ago forfeited on account of his rebellion. Robert demanded that this should be restored to him, with the profits, moreover, that the king had received from it in the meantime. The Scots also demanded that the royal stone should be restored to them, which Edward I had long ago taken from Scotland and placed at Westminster by the tomb of St Edward.[3] This stone was of famous memory amongst the Scots, because upon it the kings of Scotland used to receive the symbols of authority and the sceptre. Scota, daughter of Pharaoh, brought this stone with her from the borders of Egypt when she landed in Scotland and subdued the land. For Moses had prophesied that whoever bore that stone with him should bring broad lands under the yoke of his lordship. Whence from Scota the land is called Scotland which was formerly called Albany from Albanactus. To better

hec in augmentum fœderis ac cumulum*ᵃ* pacis optulit
Robertus de Brutz filiam suam matrimonialiter copulari
filio regis. Postremo uoluerunt Scoti quod, presentibus
quorum interest coram domino papa, a rege Francie
confirmarentur uota procerum, ut fœdus pacis iam
initum*ᵇ* et tanta auctoritate uallatum nullum solueretur
in euum.

Auditis petitionibus Scotorum ait rex: 'Scoti uenerunt non ut nos pace allicerent sed ut occasiones dissen-
sionis magis quererent et sponte treugas infringerent.
Reuera preiudicialia nimis nobis exposcunt, unde et sine
effectu ad propria remeabunt. Quomodo enim sine
preiudicio corone nostre ius quod habemus in Scotia
possumus remittere, que ab adventu Britonum usque
aduentum Saxonum et deinceps usque ad tempus nostrum antecessoribus nostris semper dinoscitur fuisse
subiecta, que quamuis rebellando nostrum sepius declinaret imperium, ad iugum tamen debitum, licet
inuita, non ambigitur fuisse reducta? Ius in Marchia
uendicare non poterunt, cuius possessionem nunquam
habuerunt. Pedis enim positio priuato possessionem
tribuit, non extraneo.[1] Quod si ob perambulationem
Marchiam petant, consequens est ut et ipsi magnam
partem Scotie eadem ratione nobis concedant. Hereditatem quam Robertus de Brutz petit, pater meus ei ob /
F.278 manifestum delictum quondam abstulit, et non decet
filium irritare quod pater decreuit. Scimus etiam quod
pater meus deuicta Scotia petram illam regalem secum
tulit in signum uictorie: quod si restitueremus, uideremur
forsan ius sic acquisitum tanquam degeneres repudiare.

ᵃ ac cumulum] ad tumltu MS
ᵇ initum] in taᵘm MS; the text is uncertain
[1] cf. *Dig.* 41.2.1 and glosses

the treaty and seal the peace, Robert Bruce proposed that his daughter should be joined in marriage with the king's son. Finally the Scots wished that, those concerned being present before the lord pope, the wishes of the nobles should be confirmed by the king of France, that the treaty of peace now entered upon and strengthened by such authority, should never be broken.

When the king had heard the Scottish proposals he said: 'The Scots have come to us not to draw us into a peace but to seek opportunities for further discord and for unprovoked breaches of the truce. To grant these demands would be much to our loss, and they will return to their own country without satisfaction. For how without prejudice to our Crown can we surrender the right we have in Scotland, which from the coming of the Britons to the coming of the the Saxons and down to our own time, is known always to have been subject to our ancestors; which, although in rebellion it often spurned our authority, was, nevertheless, as no one doubts, reduced to its due state of servitude, though unwillingly? They cannot claim any right in the March, of which they never had possession. For the placing of the foot gives possession to the citizen but not to the foreigner.[1] But if they claim the March by perambulation, it follows by the same reasoning that they must grant us a large part of Scotland. Robert Bruce claims the inheritance which my father once took from him for manifest crime, and it is not fitting that the son should make void what his father decreed. For we know that my father, when Scotland had been conquered, took with him the famous royal stone as a sign of victory; and if we were to restore it we should seem basely to repudiate the right thus acquired. Nevertheless, we should make

Verumptamen super petra reddenda dissensio breuis, si
cetera non discreparent a limite rationis. Nuptias etiam
quas offert Robertus ad presens non admittimus, quoniam prout offeruntur nobis indecentes esse perpendimus.
Denique pacem quam Scoti coram domino papa et rege
Francie petunt confirmari, si contingeret eam debito
fine concludi, coram quolibet principe mundi uellemus
explicari. Sed, quia preiudicialia nimis nobis exposcunt,
infecto negotio ad propria remeabunt.'

Igitur responsum est Scotis formam oblatam regi non
placere, nec regem in tantum artatum esse ut tam
degenerem pacem cogatur inire. Conuentionem tamen
super treugis prius initam nichilominus censuit obser-
uandam, alioquin Scotis nunquam deinceps fidem ad-
hibendam. Nuntii uero Scotorum, accepto responso,
redeuntes retulerunt regi suo et hiis qui erant de consilio
responsa regis Anglie et conclusionem in fine. Inter quos
tandem deliberatum est et communiter consensum quod
predicte treuge cum Anglis inite in suo robore starent,
et religionem quam omnis natio et etas conseruat in
nullo macularent. Nam et Israel Gabaoni[ti]s seruauit
iusiurandum quamuis dolo in circumuentione fuisset
extortum.[1]

Dum durarent inducie[2] inter reges Anglorum et
Francorum discurrebant nuntii et mediatores, hinc inde
proponentes plures formas concordie; sed nulla placuit
regi Francie nisi satisfactio sibi pro terra Vasconie.
Videns igitur rex Anglie quod per huiusmodi nuntios /
F.279 nichil proficeret, disposuit mittere reginam si forsan ipsa

---

[1] Joshua ix
[2] Made by the Earl of Kent on 22 September 1324 with Charles of
Valois, to last till Easter (7 April)1325 (Ramsay, *op. cit.* 144).

little difficulty about returning the stone, if their other demands were not beyond all reason. The marriage which Robert offers we do not agree to at present, since we think that as offered it is unsuitable for us. Finally, the peace which the Scots seek to have confirmed in the presence of the Pope and the King of France, we should wish to recite before every prince in the world, if it should be brought to a due conclusion. But, as their demands are too damaging to us, they shall return home unsatisfied.'

Reply was therefore made to the Scots that the draft offered to the king did not please him, nor was the king so circumscribed that he could be forced to make such an ignoble peace. But he thought that the truce previously agreed upon should be observed, otherwise no credence could ever be given to the Scots. The Scottish ambassadors, having received the reply, returned and reported to their king and his counsellors the king of England's answers and final conclusion. After deliberation they agreed by common consent that the said truce made with the English should stand firm, and that they would in no wise dishonour that plighted faith which every nation and age preserves. For did not Israel keep her oath to the Gibeonites although it was extorted by treachery and guile?[1]

While the armistice lasted[2] between the Kings of the English and the French, ambassadors and mediators ran hither and thither proposing many forms of agreement. But the King of France would not agree to any that did not give him satisfaction for Gascony. The King of England saw that nothing was to be achieved through these ambassadors, and determined to send the queen, who might perhaps bring the matter to the

negotium ad effectum perduceret. Nam sicut inter duos reges erat sanguine media, ita efficacior uidebatur in pace procuranda.

Abiit[1] regina ualde gauisa, dupplici gaudio letificata; gaudens quippe natale solum et parentes uisitare, gaudens quorundam quos non diligebat comitiuam relinquere. Nimirum si Hugonem non diligat per quem auunculus eius periit, per quem famulis orbata et omnibus redditibus suis priuata remansit[2]; iccirco a multis reuersura non creditur, donec Hugo Despenser a latere regis penitus separaretur.

Veniens autem regina ad fratrem suum regem transmarinum, nichil plus aliis nuntiis optinuit, nisi quod rex frater eius amore ipsius usque ad gulam Augusti treugas prorogauit. Cernens itaque rex Anglie ex actis iam nichil aliud restare, nisi aut transfretare et regi Francie satisfacere, aut terram Wasconie indefensam perdere, transacto iam Paschate collegit exercitum copiosum, pedites uidelicet linea armat[ur]a incinctos, habentes arcus, secures aut gladios; singuli[a] arma singula in quibus se nouerant magis expertos. Est enim aliquis aptus ad hec, non ad illa; Saul ad gladium, Ionathas ad arcum, et Dauid in fundam. Iussitque eos rex ad mare procedere cum ductoribus suis, ibidemque residere donec aliud haberent in mandatis. Conuocauitque magnates regni sui Wyntoniam, disponere uolens communi consilio negotium expeditionis sue.[3]

Interim pedites petierunt uadia sua, sed non dabantur eis; quamobrem discurrebant per totam patriam spoliantes incolas uictualibus suis. Mirabantur omnes

---

[a] singulos MS
[1] 9 March 1325 (*Ann. Paul.* 308)
[2] On 18 September 1324 (Ramsay, *op. cit.* 145)
[3] The king was at Winchester 1-6 May, on which day the summons was issued for parliament on 25 June.

desired conclusion. For since she was related by blood to each king she might the more effectually procure peace.

The queen departed[1] very joyfully, happy with a twofold joy; pleased to visit her native land and her relatives, delighted to leave the company of some whom she did not like. Small wonder if she does not like Hugh, through whom her uncle perished, by whom she was deprived of her servants and all her rents[2]; consequently she will not (so many think) return until Hugh Despenser is wholly removed from the king's side.

When the queen came to her brother the king across the channel, she was no more successful than the other ambassadors, except that her brother out of affection for her prolonged the truce until the first of August. So the King of England seeing that there was nothing left to do, except to cross to France and satisfy the king, or to lose the defenceless land of Gascony, after Easter, collected a large army, to wit, of foot soldiers girded with linen armour, having bows, axes or swords; each bearing the arms in which he knew he was more skilled. For some are fitted for this and some for that: Saul to the sword, Jonathan to the bow, and David to the sling. And the king ordered them to proceed to the sea with their leaders, and to remain there until they received further orders. He also summoned the magnates of his kingdom to Winchester, wishing to arrange the business of his expedition by common counsel.[3]

Meanwhile the foot soldiers claimed their wages, but they did not receive them; wherefore they ranged the countryside, plundering the inhabitants for food.

quia non satisfaceret rex peditibus, cum rite uiuere non /
F.280 possent sine uadiis, et satis habundaret thesaurus regis.
Multi enim progenitores sui congregauerunt denarios,
ipse solus supergressus est uniuersos. Verumtamen imputatur Hugoni regis duritia sicut et alia mala que fiunt
in curia. Vnde et multi in necem eius coniurauerunt,
sed machinatione detecta quidam eorum capti sunt,
reliqui fugerunt.

Tunc iussit rex omnes pedites naues ascendere et in
fluctibus maris stationem facere, donec adueniret tempus
transfretandi in terram Vasconie; preposuitque eis comitem de Warenna, Iohannem de Sancto Iohanne, et alios
magnates terre, qui similiter ingressi sunt naues non
audentes resistere. Misit etiam rex litteras per singulos
comitatus mandans et precipiens omnes qui ab exercitu
ad partes suas sine licentia rediissent capi, et statim sine
interrogatione suspendi. Tantus siquidem rigor hodie
creuit in rege, ut nullus quantumcunque magnus et
consultus uoluntati regis audeat obuiare. Iccirco par-
liamenta, tractatus et consilia hiis diebus de nullo
decernunt. Nam proceres regni, minis et pœnis aliorum
interriti, uoluntatem regis liberis habenis ambulare per-
mittunt. Sic uoluntas hodie uincit rationem. Nam
quicquid regi placuerit, quamuis ratione careat, legis
habet uigorem.[1]

Sub ista tempestate, dum rex moraretur Wyntonie,
accusatus est Henricus de Lancastria comes de Leyces-
tria, quod foueret inimicum regis episcopum[a] Herfordie.[2]
Wyntoniensem et Lyncolniensem clementia regis in gratiam admisit; Herfordensis uero, quia ceteris asperior,
gratiam inuenire non potuit. Scripserat autem episcopus
Herfordie Henrico de Lancastria comiti Leicestrie sup-

[a] episcopum] spiritum MS
[1] *Instit.* I.2.6
[2] Adam de Orleton

All were astonished that the king did not satisfy the infantry, since they could not live properly without wages, and the king had plenty of treasure. Many of his forbears amassed money; he alone has exceeded them all. Howbeit, the king's meanness is laid at Hugh's door, like the other evils that afflict the court. Hence many conspired to kill him, but the plot was discovered, some were captured and the rest fled.

Then the king ordered all the infantry to board their ships and stand out to sea, until the time should come for crossing to Gascony; and he put in command the Earl Warenne, John de St John, and other great men of the land, who likewise went on board not daring to resist. The king also sent letters to every county commanding and ordering that all who had returned from the army to their homes without leave should be arrested, and hanged forthwith without trials. The harshness of the king has today increased so much that no one however great and wise dares to cross his will. Thus parliaments, colloquies, and councils decide nothing these days. For the nobles of the realm, terrified by threats and the penalties inflicted on others, let the king's will have free play. Thus today will conquers reason. For whatever pleases the king, though lacking in reason, has the force of law.[1]

About this time, while the king was staying at Winchester, Henry of Lancaster, Earl of Leicester, was accused of favouring the king's enemy the Bishop of Hereford.[2] The king's mercy had admitted to grace the Bishops of Winchester and Lincoln, but Hereford, sterner than the others, could find no favour. The Bishop of Hereford had written to Henry of Lancaster, Earl of Leicester, asking him to intercede with the king for him, that he might the more speedily

plicans quatinus apud regem pro eo uerba faceret, ut
eo citius gratiam regis ipsum promereri contingeret.
F.281 Et quidem Henricus, prout erat benignus et / compatiens
afflictis, huiusmodi uerba fertur rescripsisse:—

> Salutem in omnium Saluatore et tam inflictionum patientiam
> quam in agone fortiter dimicare. Pater, utinam que pateris sus-
> tineas patienter; omnis enim cordis aut corporis afflictio premio
> caret sine patientie adiuncto. Patientia reliquas uirtutes roborat
> et exornat, nam uidua est uirtus quam*a* patientia non firmat.
> Patientia uincit malitiam, et si qua uirtus adiungitur ipsam facit
> esse perfectam. Porro si legitime contendere*b* speras legitime certa,*c*
> oportune inoportune insta,¹ et fiducialiter perseuera. Nam et sacra
> scriptura testatur quod licet omnes uirtutes currant ad brauium,²
> sola perseuerantia coronatur. Spera in Deo et uiriliter age, quoniam,
> si pro Deo ascendisti ex aduerso, scito quod non deseret in tempore
> malo. Deus et Dominus dominantium, in cuius manu corda sunt
> regum, et qui procellam conuertit in auram,³ prosperum statum
> tibi restituat et regis mitiget iram.

Huiuscemodi uerbis consolatoriis usus est comes in
litteris suis. Delate sunt littere ad aures regis, quamobrem nitebatur rex arguere comitem proditionis. Adiecte
sunt et alie cause, quod uidelicet Henricus, ex gratia
regis iam comes Leycestrie, relictis armis propriis,
deferret arma fratris sui comitis Lancastrie; quod uisum
est regalibus regis iniuria, quasi dampnarentur pariter et
arma. Et quia [crucem] erexerat extra uillam Leicestrie
pro anima fratris sui comitis Lancastrie; quod uisum est
regalibus in scandalum regis redundare, quasi dampnato
corpore dampnaretur et titulus memorie.

Respondit comes ad litteras, non debere ascribi ad
proditionem uerba consolatoria in quibus nichil machinatum esset in principem. Ad arma respondit dicens se
non arma fratris sed patris potius acceptasse, que etiam

---

a quam] quod MS
b Hearne suggests coronari; *cf.* 2 Tim. ii. 5.
c circa MS
¹ 2 Tim. iv. 2   ² cf. 1 Cor. ix. 24   ³ Ps. cvii. 29 (Vulgate Ps. cvi. 29)

be received into favour. Henry, who was kind and
sympathetic to those in trouble, is said to have replied
in this wise:—

Greeting in the Saviour of all men, and patience in affliction
as well as strength to strive mightily. Father, may you bear with
patience what you suffer; for all affliction of heart or body lacks its
reward if patience is not present. Patience strengthens and decor-
ates the other virtues, for virtue is empty unfortified by patience.
Patience conquers malice, and subjoined to any virtue makes it
perfect. If you hope to strive lawfully, do so, be instant in season
and out of season,[1] and persist faithfully. For Holy Scripture bears
witness that though all virtues contend for the prize,[2] perseverance
alone is crowned. Hope in God and act manfully, since, if for God's
sake you have risen in opposition, know that He will not desert you
in the time of evil. May God the Lord of princes, in whose hand
are the hearts of kings, who changes the whirlwind into a breeze,[3]
restore thy prosperity and mitigate the king's wrath.

The Earl used some such consolatory words in his
letters. The letters were reported to the king, who
therefore tried to accuse the Earl of treason. Other
charges were made, too, namely that Henry, already
by the king's grace Earl of Leicester, had ceased to
bear his own arms and adopted those of his brother
the Earl of Lancaster; which seemed to the king's
party an insult to the king, as if the arms were condemned with the Earl; and that he had set up [a cross]
outside the town of Leicester for the soul of his brother
the Earl of Lancaster; and this was regarded by the
king's party as an offence to the king, as if the memory
of a man should be condemned when his body was
condemned.

As far as the letters went, the Earl replied that
consolatory words in which there was no design against
the prince should not be construed as treason. Concerning the arms he replied that he had not taken the
arms of his brother but rather of his father, which he

F.282 iure successionis dixit ad se pertinere, / maxime cum primogenitus frater eius obiisset sine prole. Allegabat et comes non in scandalum regis crucem erectam, sed ob deuotionem plebis pro anima fratris sui spiritualiter excitandam, et quidem pro fideli debet oratio bene fore licita, cum pro Iudeis et hereticis sancta frequenter oret ecclesia.

Hiis tandem pretermissis interrogauit rex prelatos et proceres qui tunc conuenerant, quidnam ipsi de transfretatione sua consulerent. Nolens autem Hugo Despenser filius, propter imminens periculum, quod aliquis transfretandi daret consilium, fertur coram aliquibus arroganter dixisse: 'Iam apparebit quis consulet domino regi ad inimicos suos transfretare; quoniam manifestus proditor est quicunque sit ille.' Auditis eius minis responderunt prelati cum proceribus ad consultationem domini regis dicentes: 'Domine, constat plures regni magnates absentes esse, unde non expedit nobis in tam arduo negotio sine paribus nostris respondere.'

Tunc decretum est prelatos et regni magnates uniuersos in crastino beati Iohannis Baptiste ad parliamentum Londoniis fore conuocandos. Sed et comes Leicestrie accepit mandata ad eundem diem uenire finaliter responsurus[a] obiectis.

In crastino Natiuitatis beati Iohannis Baptiste[1] conuenerunt Londoniis omnes prelati cum proceribus qui tunc erant infra regnum Anglie, consultique super regis transfretatione responderunt, saltem hii quibus ceteri non ualebant contradicere, oportere dominum regem omni modo transfretare, nec posse eos sine lesione conscientie et fidei in aliud consentire. Quid enim[b] si rex

---

[a] responsis MS
[b] enim] nunc MS
[1] 25 June 1325

said pertained to him by hereditary right, especially as his elder brother had died without issue. The earl also maintained that the cross had not been erected as a cause of offence to the king, but to excite the spiritual devotion of the populace for his brother's soul; and indeed prayer ought certainly to be allowed for the faithful, since Holy Church frequently prays for Jews and heretics.

At length this was postponed, and the king asked the bishops and nobles who had assembled, what they advised about his crossing to France. But Hugh Despenser the son, unwilling that anyone should advise the king to cross, on account of the imminent danger, is said to have remarked arrogantly to some: 'Now we shall see who will advise the king to cross over to his enemies; he is a manifest traitor whoever he may be.' On hearing these threats the bishops and nobles answered the king's enquiry saying: 'Lord, it is known that many magnates of the realm are absent, and it is not fitting for us to give answer in so weighty a matter without our peers.'

Then it was decided that all the bishops and magnates of the realm should be summoned to parliament at London for the morrow of the blessed John the Baptist. And the Earl of Leicester was ordered to come the same day to give a final answer to the charges against him.

On the morrow of the Nativity of the blessed John the Baptist[1] all the prelates and magnates who were then in England met in London, and being consulted about the king's crossing replied (or at least those whom the others did not dare to contradict) that by all means the lord king should go, and that without injury to their conscience and loyalty they could not agree to anything else. And if the king

U

F.283 non ierit? Rex Francie totam Vasconiam / statim occupabit, et rex noster alias, uel forsan filius eius cum ipsum regnare contigerit, proditionis et merito nos omnes accusabit.

Huiusmodi responso communiter prolato rex ad alios se conuertit, et, amoto Exoniensi episcopo[1] ab officio thesaurarii, archiepiscopum Eboracensem eidem substituit. Erat enim Exoniensis ultra modum cupidus, et durante officio suo uehementer diues effectus, unde uidebatur tam regi quam populo terre concussione[2] magis quam fideli commercio tanta copia uiro prouenisse. Iccirco amouit eum rex a potestate, ut, si contigisset eum aliquos lesisse, necesse haberet querelantibus respondere; et quidem bonum commune foret et consonum iuri, ut tanta potestate predicti annales fierent, ut qui tempore officii conueniri non possunt, saltem post annum iudicio starent, et non diutina uexatione subiectos opprimerent. Eboracensis iste, Willelmus nomine, olim curialis in omni commisso fidelis extitit, et, quamuis inter curiales diu conuersatus, mores tamen a conuictu non traxit, sed, obuiata Anglorum cupiditate, per Dei gratiam impollutus semper permansit. Sane est uberioris gratie, inter malos bene uiuere: sic Josep in Egipto, Clusi[3] cum Absolon, et Daniel innocenter uixit Babilone.

Audiens archipresul Cantuariensis quod rex Eboracensem gazis suis uellet preponere, respondit nequaquam sic fieri posse sine preiudicio Cantuariensis ecclesie; crucem suam deferri[a] faceret quocunque rex diuerteret

---

[a] differri MS
[1] Walter Stapeldon
[2] cf. *Dig.* for *concussio*
[3] 2 Kings 15, 32-37 (DV)

did not go? The king of France would at once seize the whole of Gascony, and at another time our king, or perchance his son when he comes to the throne, will accuse us all and rightly of treason.

When this answer had been given by all in common, the king turned to others, and having removed the Bishop of Exeter[1] from the office of Treasurer, he appointed the Archbishop of York in his place. For Exeter was unreasonably avaricious, and during his term of office had become remarkably rich, whence it seemed to king and people alike that he had made his wealth by extortion[2] rather than by honest dealing. Therefore the king removed him from power, in order that if he had harmed anyone he should have to answer to the plaintiffs; and indeed it would be to the common advantage and consonant with right, if offices of such great authority were made annual, that those who could not be summoned during their period of office should at least stand to judgment after a year, and not oppress those beneath them with long drawnout hardships. The Archbishop of York, William [Melton] by name, had formerly been a courtier faithful in everything committed to him, and although he had lived long at court, he had not been contaminated by this intercourse, but, escaping the greed of the English, by the grace of God remained always unpolluted. For it is a mark of more abundant grace to live well among the wicked. Thus Joseph lived innocently in Egypt, Clusi[3] with Absalom, and Daniel in Babylon.

When the Archbishop of Canterbury heard that the king proposed to set the Archbishop of York over his treasure, he replied that this could in no way be done without prejudice to the church of Canterbury; he would have his cross borne before him whithersoever

per totam Angliam 'quod quidem*ᵃ* ego,' inquit, 'sana conscientia sustinere non possem. Mota est enim illa inueterata dissensio super delationem crucis inter utramque ecclesiam, pro qua sanctus Thomas certauit usque ad mortem; a cuius diebus nullus archipresul Eboracensis per Cantuariensem / prouinciam hactenus crucem detulit, nisi forsan in stipite elationis, aliquorum magnatum auxilio suffultus, hoc presumpserit, uel nunc saltem in parliamentis, quod, ne per dissensionem priuatorum impediretur utilitas communis, hoc permittendum ratio persuasit.' Paruipendebat rex allegata ab archipresule, protestans se ob delationem crucis uel ob aliud cuiuscunque priuilegium necessarium ministrum nolle dimittere.

F.284

Comes Leicestrie in parliamento presens affuit, sed de sibi prius obiectis nichil audiuit, et forsan eo quod, ceteris illustrior, filio domini regis, patre*ᵇ* transfretante, regno preposito uidebatur necessarius. Nam licet Hugo Despenser, comes Wyntoniensis, cunctis prudentior et magis expertus tanto negotio foret preponendus, omnibus tamen incolis et ipsi filio regis habebatur exosus. Rex igitur iuxta consilium magnatum transfretare disposuit, et iussit necessaria preparari. Displicuit rex Hugoni Despenser, tam patri quam filio; sciebant enim quod abeunte rege nescirent locum quo possent uiuere tuti.

Circa idem tempus bone memorie Norwycensis[1] episcopus, pro negotiis regis ad transmarinas partes destinatus, in redeundo diem clausit extremum; statimque misit rex ad Norwicense capitulum uolens eos

ᵃ quod quidem] quia quod MS (as read by Hearne)
ᵇ fratre MS
[1] John Salmon, died 6 July

the king went throughout England, 'and this,' he said, 'I could not tolerate with a clear conscience. For this has been an age-long dispute between the two churches about the bearing of the cross, for which St Thomas strove until his death; and from that time to this no Archbishop of York has borne his cross in the province of Canterbury, unless perchance in the pride of insolence, propped up by the support of some magnates, he has presumed to do this, or perhaps in parliaments, as is only reasonable, lest the common good should be hindered by private quarrels.' The King took little notice of the Archbishop's arguments, protesting that he would not dismiss any necessary official on account of the bearing of the cross or any other privilege whatsoever.

The Earl of Leicester was present in parliament, but nothing was heard of the former charges against him, and perhaps because he was of better blood than the others, his presence was considered necessary to the lord king's son who would be in charge of the realm while his father was abroad. For though Hugh Despenser, Earl of Winchester, shrewder than all and more experienced, would have to be put in charge of such a business, yet he was hated by everyone and even by the king's son. The king therefore, according to the advice of the magnates prepared to cross and gave orders for the necessary preparations. This displeased the Despensers, father and son; for they realised that in the absence of the king they would not know where to live safely.

About the same time the Bishop of Norwich[1] of happy memory, who had been sent abroad on the king's business, died on the way home. The king

eligere Robertum de Baldok cancellarium suum. Monachi uero non audentes regi displicere direxerunt uota
sua in uirum uoluntatis regie. Erat autem tunc temporis
quidam clericus Willelmus Ermynne[1] dictus, uir prudens
et circumspectus et, precipue in hiis que tangunt can-
cellariam domini regis, efficax et expertus. Ipse unus
ex hiis transfretauerat cum regina. Optinuit ut et rex
Francie pariter et regina supplicarent domino pape pro
F.285 promotione sua. Dominus uero / papa nouit eum ex
nomine, eo quod iam pridem electus in episcopum
Karlionensis ecclesie cessit iuri suo ad mandatum
domini pape. Vnde tum propter bonum obedientie,
tum[a] propter preces regis Francie et sororis sue, con-
secrauit eum dominus papa in episcopum Norwicensis
ecclesie, et sic supplantatus est Robertus de Baldok en!
altera uice.

Veniens itaque rex ad mare, et quasi paratus nauem
ascendere,[2] nuntios regis Francie in ipso portu maris
obuios habuit, quelibet noua optata protinus accepit.
Nam rex Francie, multis precibus et arduis negotiis
regem Anglie tangentibus allegatis inductus, hoc indul-
sit, ut, si rex Anglie filium suum primogenitum trans-
mitte[re]t, idem filius ad ducatum Vasconie eisdem
conditionibus admitteretur, quibus et rex pater eius si
ueniret. Placuit regi et regis consilio conferre filio
Vasconiam,[3] et statim puer ad iussum patris nauigauit
in Franciam. Admisit eum benigne auunculus eius rex
Francie. Admisit et homagium ipsius pro terra Vasconie, sed non permisit ei possessionem nisi pro parte.

[a] tum] tamen MS
[1] For the events that follow see J. L. Grassi 'William Airmyn and the
Bishopric of Norwich' in *E.H.R.* (October 1955) lxx. 550-561.
[2] Preparations for the King's departure were kept up till late in
August. On the 24th Edward wrote that he was too ill to come (*Foed.* ii. 606).
[3] He was appointed Count of Ponthieu 2 September and Duke of
Aquitaine 10 September 1325 (*Foed.* ii. 607-8). He sailed on 12 September.

at once sent to the chapter of Norwich, wishing them
to elect Robert Baldock his chancellor, and the monks
not daring to displease the king gave their votes for
the royal candidate. There was at that time a certain
clerk, called William Ayermin,[1] a prudent and circumspect man, and especially in matters relating to the
royal chancery, efficient and experienced. He was
one of those who had gone abroad with the queen.
He contrived that the king of France and the queen
likewise should petition the lord pope for his promotion.
The lord pope indeed knew him by name, because
already as bishop-elect of the church of Carlisle he had
waived his right at the lord pope's mandate. Hence
as well on account of his obedience as of the prayers
of the king of France and his sister, the lord pope
consecrated him bishop of the church of Norwich,
and thus behold! Robert Baldock was supplanted
once more.

When the king reached the coast and was ready to
take ship,[2] messengers of the king of France met him
at the port. He forthwith accepted certain novel but acceptable proposals. For the King of France, influenced
by many petitions and the weighty matters in which
the King of England was said to be involved, allowed
him this, that if the King of England would send his
eldest son, the said son should be admitted to the duchy
of Gascony on the same conditions as the king his
father if he had come. The king and his council
agreed to grant Gascony to his son,[3] and by his father's
orders the boy at once sailed for France. His uncle,
the King of France, received him kindly. He also
accepted his homage for the land of Gascony, but
allowed him only partial possession of it. For the
King of France decided that the part which he had

Decreuit enim rex Francie partem quam ui occupauerat
non debere restitui, nisi satisfacto sibi pro sumptibus
quos fecerat occasione homagii retardati.
Exoniensis unus erat ex illis qui uenerant cum filio.
Curiales uero Francorum ipsum quasi alicuius sceleris
notatum respiciebant pre ceteris. Ipse uero nichil sibi
conscius uel ad uultus eorum caute premunitus, familiares suos ibidem relinquens qui presentiam suam fin-
gerent, clam fugam iniit, clam de nocte mutata ueste
usus duplomate ad mare deuenit, et quasi mercator uel
peregrinus nauem conscendens in Angliam rediit; et ita
F.286 si quid in eum machinatum exstitit, prudenter / euasit.
Igitur si periculosa fuit ei legatio sua, uideat ne uideatur
iterum in Francia.[1] Quatuor sunt quippe persone de
maioribus Anglie, Exoniensis episcopus nuper thesaurarius, Robertus de Baldoke nunc cancellarius, Hugo
Despenser pater et filius, qui si reperirentur infra regnum
Francie, non carerent utique mala mansione.[2] Asseritur
enim quod de consilio Exoniensis predia regine capta
erant in manu domini regis,[3] et ipsa destituta Francis
familiaribus suis. Robertus de Baldoke fautor erat in
nece[4] procerum. Nimirum si exosus habeatur parenti-
bus eorum, quorum licet multi sunt in Anglia, quidam
tamen eorum dominantur in Francia, et quidam ualentes
exulant, omnes autem et singuli tempus ultionis exspec-
tant. Sed quicquid in aliis arguitur, Hugoni Despenser
tam patri quam filio pre ceteris imputatur.

Inter alia, cum mitteret rex filium suum in Franciam, mandauit uxori sue quod sine dilatione rediret in

---

[1] He was murdered in London in September 1326
[2] *mala mansio:* 'a kind of punishment in which the captive was stretched
out and tied fast to a board'. *Dig.* 47, 10, 15; 16, 3, 7.
[3] *Foed.* ii. 569 (18 September 1324)
[4] *nex* = destruction, a legal usage (*Dig.*)

seized by force ought not to be restored, until he had
been satisfied for the expenses that he had incurred
by reason of the delayed homage.

The Bishop of Exeter was one of those who had
come with the boy. The French court officials regarded
him in particular as if he were guilty of some crime.
But he having a clear conscience or cautiously warned
by their attitude, leaving his household to pretend
that he was there, secretly took flight, changed his
clothes, and travelling post-haste came secretly to
the coast by night, and taking ship as a merchant or
pilgrim returned to England; so if anything had
been plotted against him he prudently escaped. Therefore if his mission was dangerous to him, let him take
care not to be seen again in France.[1] There are indeed
four great personages in England, the Bishop of Exeter
lately Treasurer, Robert Baldock now Chancellor,
the Despensers father and son, who if they are found
within the kingdom of France will assuredly not lack
bad quarters.[2] For it is asserted that it was by the
Bishop of Exeter's advice that the queen's lands were
taken into the lord king's hands,[3] and she herself
deprived of her French servants. Robert Baldock
brought about the ruin[4] of great men. It is not surprising that he is hated by their kinsmen, of whom,
though there are many in England, some are in power
in France, some thrive in exile, but one and all await
the day of vengeance. Whatever may be thought of
the others, the Despensers father and son are held
guilty beyond the rest.

Amongst other things, when the king sent his son
to France, he ordered his wife to return to England
without delay. When this command had been laid
by the messengers before the King of France and the

Angliam. Quo quidem mandato tam regi Francie quam
ipsi regine per nuntios exposito, respondit regina, 'Ego,'
inquit, 'sentiens, quod matrimonium sit uiri*a* et mulieris
coniunctio, indiuiduam uite consuetudinem retinens,
mediumque esse qui inter maritum meum et me huiusmodi uinculum nititur diuidere; protestor me nolle
redire donec auferatur medius ille, sed, exuta ueste
nuptiali, uiduitatis et luctus uestes assumam donec de
huiusmodi Phariseo uiderim ultionem.' Sed et rex
Francie ne uideretur eam detinere respondit: 'Regina,'
inquit, 'libere uenit, libere redeat si uoluerit. Sin autem
maluerit in hiis partibus remanere, soror mea est, nolo
eam expellere.' Reuersi sunt nuntii et narrauerunt hec
omnia regi. /

F.287   Tunc rex, conuocatis apud Westmonasterium prelatis
et proceribus terre,[1] sic cœpit prius acta breui sermone
referre. 'Nostis,' inquit, 'omnes dissensionem et causas,
inter regem Francie et nos pro terra Wasconie dudum
exortas, et quomodo satis prouide, ut tunc uisum erat,
pro formanda concordia regina transfretauit, habuitque
in mandatis facta legatione sua statim rediisse. Quod
et ipsa repromisit bona uoluntate. Nulli quoque in
recessu suo uidebatur offensa. Licentiata enim omnes
salutauit, et abiit iocosa. Nunc autem nescio quis
animum eius immutauit; nescio quis adinuentionibus*b*
ipsam instruxit. Noui enim quod ex proprio capite
nullam confinxit offensam, tametsi*c* dicit Hugonem
Despenser aduersarium et inimicum esse.' Subiungit et
hoc: 'Mirum unde contra Hugonem rancorem con-
ceperit, que cum recederet nulli alii me excepto tam se
iocundam exhibuit. Quamobrem Hugo tristis effectus

---

a sit uiri] sicut uir MS   *b* adinuentionibus] in aduentionibus MS
c tametsi] tamen se MS
[1] Parliament sat 18 November to 5 December (*Parl. Writs*, II.i.334,
346).

queen herself, she replied, 'I feel that marriage is a joining together of man and woman, maintaining the undivided habit of life, and that someone has come between my husband and myself trying to break this bond; I protest that I will not return until this intruder is removed, but, discarding my marriage garment, shall assume the robes of widowhood and mourning until I am avenged of this Pharisee.' The King of France not wishing to seem to detain her said, 'The queen has come of her own will, and may freely return if she so wishes. But if she prefers to remain in these parts, she is my sister, and I refuse to expel her.' The messengers returned and reported all this to the king.

Then the king having summoned the prelates and magnates of the land to Westminster,[1] began to rehearse what had happened in a short speech. 'You know', he said, 'all the long-standing disputes and processes between the King of France and us over the land of Gascony, and how providently, as it then seemed, the queen crossed to France to make peace, being told that when her mission was accomplished she should at once return. And this she promised with a good will. And on her departure she did not seem to anyone to be offended. As she took her leave she saluted all and went away joyfully. But now someone has changed her attitude. Someone has primed her with inventions. For I know that she has not fabricated any affront out of her own head. Yet she says that Hugh Despenser is her adversary and hostile to her.' And he added: 'It is surprising that she has conceived this dislike of Hugh, for when she departed, towards no one was she more agreeable, myself excepted. For this reason Hugh is much cast down; but he is nevertheless prepared to show his innocence in any

est ualde; uerumtamen innocentiam suam paratus est quomodolibet ostendere. Vnde constanter credo reginam in huiusmodi errorem ad suggestionem alicuius inductam esse, et reuera malignus et inimicus est homo quicunque sit ille. Nunc igitur sapienter consulite, ut quam doctrina malorum in uersutiam instruit et instigat, uestra prudens et blanda correptio ad debitam unitatem inuitet*a* et reducat.' Tunc de consilio regis ordinatum est quod omnes episcopi regine scriberent, et singulas litteras sub eodem tenore uerborum eidem destinarent, quibus eam tanquam filiam carissimam ad uirum suum redire mouerent, rancorem sine causa conceptum dimittere, et Hugonem Despenser pariter excusarent. Singularum uero litterarum communis et unus tenor talis erat:— /

F.288   Carissima et prepotens domina mea, de nouis et responsis tuis ad dominum nostrum regem a te nuper transmissis, turbatur tota patria; et ex eo quod in odium Hugonis Despenser differs reditum tuum, multa mala presagiunt omnes in futurum. Porro Hugo Despenser coram omnibus innocentiam suam solempniter ostendit, et se regine nunquam nocuisse, sed omne commodum eius pro posse procurasse, et hoc semper inposterum se facturum fore corporali sacramento firmauit. Addidit quoque se non posse credere huiusmodi minas ex solo capite tuo unquam prodiisse, sed aliunde forsan procuratas esse, maxime cum ante recessum tuum et in ipso recessu hillarem sibi faciem ostenderis, et litteras amicabiles postea ei transmiseris, quas in pleno parliamento in argumentum fidei protulit coram multis. Quamobrem, carissima, rogo te tanquam dominam; moneo te tanquam filiam, quatinus ad dominum nostrum regem, uirum tuum, redeas, rancorem dimittas, et que pro bono pacis abieras*b* pro bona pace redire non differas.*c* Timent enim habitatores terre nostre, eo quod redire negasti, multa mala contingere. Timent alienigenarum adventum et depredationem bonorum suorum; nec reputant ex debita affectione prouenire, odio unius hominis, populum tam tibi deuotum uelle destruere. Quod autem scripsistis, ea que frater tuus rex Francie et alii amici tui eiusdem

a inuitet] mitem MS
b abieras] adhibeas MS
c differas] disperas MS

way whatsoever. Hence I firmly believe that the queen has been led into this error at the suggestion of someone, and he is in truth wicked and hostile whoever he may be. Now therefore deliberate wisely, that she whom the teaching of evil men incites to guile, may be led back to the due path of unity by your prudent and kindly reproof.' Then it was ordained by the king's council that all the bishops should write to the queen, and that they should each address her in the same words, by which they might persuade her as their dearest daughter to return to her husband, putting aside her baseless ill-feeling, and at the same time they would excuse Hugh Despenser. The text common to all these letters was as follows:—

Most dear and potent lady, the whole country is disturbed by your news and the answers which you have lately sent to our lord king; and because you delay your return out of hatred for Hugh Despenser everyone predicts that much evil will follow. Indeed Hugh Despenser has solemnly demonstrated his innocence before all, and that he has never harmed the queen, but done everything in his power to help her; and that he will always in future do this, he has confirmed by his corporeal oath. He added moreover that he could not believe that these threats ever proceeded from your head alone, but that they came from some other source, especially as before your departure and during it you showed yourself gracious to him, and afterwards sent him friendly letters, which he produced in full parliament before many people as evidence of his loyalty. Wherefore, dearest lady, I beseech you as my lady, I warn you as a daughter, to return to our lord king, your husband, putting aside all rancour. You who have gone away for the sake of peace, do not for the sake of peace delay to return. For all the inhabitants of our land fear that many evils will result from your refusal to return. They fear the arrival of foreigners and that their goods will be plundered; they do not think that this comes from due affection, that you should wish to destroy a people so devoted to you through hatred of one man. But as for what you have written, that what your brother the king of France and your other friends of that country intend to do on your behalf, will turn out not to the prejudice of the lord king or any one else, but to the destruction

patrie pro uoto suo facere intendunt, non in preiudicium domini regis nec alicuius alterius, sed in exterminium solius Hugonis redundabunt:—Carissima et potentissima domina, noli tali negotio initium prebere, cuius progressus dampnum irrecuperabile uerisimiliter posset afferre. Presagit enim populus Anglicanus ex huiusmodi minis aduentum alienorum, et dicit, si Franci ueniant terram utique spoliabunt. Impossibile quin tam insontes quam sontes communiter dampna sustineant, et que non rapuerunt innoxii tunc exsoluent. Heu quam sperabamus habuisse et patronam, si sic eueniant, continget nos, proh dolor! sentire nouercam. Heu! querula uoce clerus et populus frequenter ingeminat, timentes ne odio unius hominis se et sua penitus exterminari contingat. Quocirca, domina regina, F.289 utere sano consilio, et ad maritum / tuum redire non differas. Nam desideratus aduentus tuus malitias hominum refrenabit et occasiones mali sedabit uniuersas.

Sed mater et filius huiusmodi litteris non obstantibus ad Angliam redire noluerunt.[1]

---

[1] cf. *Foed.* ii. 615 (1 December 1325)

of Hugh alone:— Dearest, and most powerful lady, refuse to give an opening to such a business, as its furthering can in all probability bring irreparable loss. The English people predicts from these threats the coming of foreigners, and says, if the French come they will plunder the land. It is impossible that the innocent should not suffer equally with the guilty, and what the innocent do not snatch away they shall lose. Alas! if things turn out thus, it may happen that we shall regard as a stepmother her whom we had hoped to have as a patron. Alas! Clergy and people with complaining voice reiterate their fear that they and theirs will be utterly destroyed through the hatred felt for one man. Wherefore, my lady queen, accept wise counsel, and do not delay your return. For your longed-for arrival will restrain the malice of men and restrict all opportunities for evil.

But notwithstanding this letter mother and son refused to return to England.[1]

INDEX

Printed in Great Britain by
Thomas Nelson and Sons Ltd, Edinburgh